Practical Game AI Programming

Create game AI and implement cutting edge AI algorithms from scratch

Micael DaGraça

BIRMINGHAM - MUMBAI

Practical Game AI Programming

First published: June 2017

Production reference: 1280617

Published by Packt Publishing Ltd.
Livery Place
35 Livery Street
Birmingham
B3 2PB, UK.

ISBN 978-1-78712-281-9

www.packtpub.com

Credits

Author
Micael DaGraça

Reviewer
Davide Aversa

Commissioning Editor
Amarabhab Banerjee

Acquisition Editor
Shweta Pant

Content Development Editor
Aditi Gour

Technical Editors
Leena Patil
Akansha Bathija

Copy Editor
Safis Editing

Project Coordinator
Ritika Manoj

Proofreader
Safis Editing

Indexer
Tejal Daruwale Soni

Graphics
Jason Monterio

Production Coordinator
Shraddha Falebhai

About the Author

Micael DaGraça is a game designer and an AR developer living in Porto, Portugal. He has worked for multiple game studios, contributing to the creation of different indie games and interactive apps.

Micael grew up playing video games, and that passion never went away. So, later on in his life, he decided to learn how to create games. Without any previous knowledge in coding or 3D animation, he slowly started to create simple games, learning each time more with those experiences. When the games started to work and the gameplay became enjoyable, he started to make plans to publish a game in collaboration with an old friend. Micael was responsible for the technical aspect of the game, making sure that the game worked as planned, while his friend created all the artwork for the game. Finally, the game was published, and it received some positive feedback from other indie game developers. Since the game generated some revenue, the dream of becoming a game designer turned into reality.

Today, Micael works for other studios, helping others to develop their game ideas, and has also integrated into a company that focuses on the creation of games and interactive apps for health and well-being purposes. Even though he doesn't have the time to keep working on personal projects, he has a few frozen game projects that are still under development with the help of his friend.

"I would like to thank to my parents for the unconditional support throughout the years, because without them my life as a game designer would not have been possible; a warm thank you to my sister, Alexandrina, for all of your help when I needed it the most and for sharing your office with me so I could start working as a game designer. A thank you to my old friend Vicente for the eternal rivalry, forcing me to always push my limits, making me a better professional. I also would like to thank my girlfriend, Marta, for her smile, which always make me happy, and for taking care of everything so that I could focus on my work. And finally, I would like to dedicate this book to my grandpa, who inspired me to be the person that I am today."

About the Reviewer

Davide Aversa completed his masters in robotics and artificial intelligence and his Ph.D. in computer science at La Sapienza University of Rome where he has been involved in research applied to pathfinding and decision making for digital games characters and computational creativity.

www.PacktPub.com

For support files and downloads related to your book, please visit www.PacktPub.com.

Did you know that Packt offers eBook versions of every book published, with PDF and ePub files available? You can upgrade to the eBook version at www.PacktPub.com and as a print book customer, you are entitled to a discount on the eBook copy. Get in touch with us at service@packtpub.com for more details.

At www.PacktPub.com, you can also read a collection of free technical articles, sign up for a range of free newsletters and receive exclusive discounts and offers on Packt books and eBooks.

https://www.packtpub.com/mapt

Get the most in-demand software skills with Mapt. Mapt gives you full access to all Packt books and video courses, as well as industry-leading tools to help you plan your personal development and advance your career.

Why subscribe?

- Fully searchable across every book published by Packt
- Copy and paste, print, and bookmark content
- On demand and accessible via a web browser

Customer Feedback

Thanks for purchasing this Packt book. At Packt, quality is at the heart of our editorial process. To help us improve, please leave us an honest review on this book's Amazon page at `www.amazon.com/dp/1787122816`.

If you'd like to join our team of regular reviewers, you can e-mail us at `customerreviews@packtpub.com`. We award our regular reviewers with free eBooks and videos in exchange for their valuable feedback. Help us be relentless in improving our products!

Table of Contents

Preface

Developing games is a passion for some, and I believe that this is because we are able to create a world that is completely imagined by us; this is like being a god, and the AI characters that we place there are the habitants of that world that we have just created. We are free to imagine how they will behave, we can create a society according to our imagination, we are able to create a sweet and kind character, but also we can create the most devilish character that ever existed--the possibilities are endless, and that is why we will always have new game ideas coming out. No matter what game genre we decide to develop, the world and their characters will be the essence of our vision; this is what will make our game unique, and ideally we should be able to create everything that we have in mind, just as we imagine. This book was conceived with that in mind, that all of us should be able to create the ideas that we have and that we shouldn't limit our imagination, so this book will cover the foundations of creating an artificial character, and after reading it, we should be able to explore all the topics that you have learned, creating AI characters that fit perfectly with what we have imagined.

What this book covers

Chapter 1, *Different Problems Require Different Solutions*, is a brief introduction to the video game industry and game AI.

Chapter 2, *Possibility and Probability Maps*, focuses on how to create and use probability and possibility maps for AI characters.

Chapter 3, *Production Systems*, describes how to create a set of rules necessary for the character AI to achieve their goals.

Chapter 4, *Environment and AI*, focuses on the interaction between the characters in the game and their environment.

Chapter 5, *Animation Behaviors*, shows best practices to implement animations in our game.

Chapter 6, *Navigation Behavior and Pathfinding*, focuses on how to calculate the best options for the AI to move in real time.

Chapter 7, *Advanced Pathfinding*, focuses on the use of theta algorithms to find short and realistic-looking paths.

Chapter 8, *Crowd Interactions*, focuses on how the AI should behave when there are a lot of characters on the same scene.

Chapter 9, *AI Planning and Collision Avoidance*, discusses the anticipation of the AI, knowing in advance what they will do when arriving at a position or facing a problem.

Chapter 10, *Awareness*, focuses on working with awareness systems to create stealth genre mechanics.

What you need for this book

It is recommended that you have install a game engine that uses C# (Unity3D has a free version, and it was used for the examples covered on the book).

Who this book is for

This book is intended for developers who have already created their first games in C# and seek to expand their capabilities with AI, creating crowds, enemies, or allies that can behave autonomously.

Conventions

In this book, you will find a number of text styles that distinguish between different kinds of information. Here are some examples of these styles and an explanation of their meaning.

Code words in text, database table names, folder names, filenames, file extensions, pathnames, dummy URLs, user input, and Twitter handles are shown as follows: "The variables that we'll be using for now are Health, statePassive, stateAggressive, and stateDefensive."

A block of code is set as follows:

```
if (playerPosition == "triggerM")
{
 transform.LookAt(playerSoldier); // Face the direction of the player
 transform.position = Vector3.MoveTowards(transform.position,
 buildingPosition.position, walkBack);
 backwardsFire();
}
```

New terms and **important words** are shown in bold. Words that you see on the screen, for example, in menus or dialog boxes, appear in the text like this: "In Unity we click under the **Layers** button to expand more options, and then we click where it says **Edit Layers....**"

Warnings or important notes appear in a box like this.

Tips and tricks appear like this.

Reader feedback

Feedback from our readers is always welcome. Let us know what you think about this book-what you liked or disliked. Reader feedback is important for us as it helps us develop titles that you will really get the most out of. To send us general feedback, simply e-mail feedback@packtpub.com, and mention the book's title in the subject of your message. If there is a topic that you have expertise in and you are interested in either writing or contributing to a book, see our author guide at www.packtpub.com/authors.

Customer support

Now that you are the proud owner of a Packt book, we have a number of things to help you to get the most from your purchase.

Downloading the example code

You can download the example code files for this book from your account at http://www.packtpub.com. If you purchased this book elsewhere, you can visit http://www.packtpub.com/support and register to have the files e-mailed directly to you. You can download the code files by following these steps:

1. Log in or register to our website using your e-mail address and password.
2. Hover the mouse pointer on the **SUPPORT** tab at the top.
3. Click on **Code Downloads & Errata**.
4. Enter the name of the book in the **Search** box.
5. Select the book for which you're looking to download the code files.

6. Choose from the drop-down menu where you purchased this book from.
7. Click on **Code Download**.

Once the file is downloaded, please make sure that you unzip or extract the folder using the latest version of:

- WinRAR / 7-Zip for Windows
- Zipeg / iZip / UnRarX for Mac
- 7-Zip / PeaZip for Linux

The code bundle for the book is also hosted on GitHub at `https://github.com/PacktPubl ishing/Practical-Game-AI-Programming`. We also have other code bundles from our rich catalog of books and videos available at `https://github.com/PacktPublishing/`. Check them out!

Downloading the color images of this book

We also provide you with a PDF file that has color images of the screenshots/diagrams used in this book. The color images will help you better understand the changes in the output. You can download this file from `https://www.packtpub.com/sites/default/files/down loads/PracticalGameAIProgramming_ColorImages.pdf`.

Errata

Although we have taken every care to ensure the accuracy of our content, mistakes do happen. If you find a mistake in one of our books-maybe a mistake in the text or the code-we would be grateful if you could report this to us. By doing so, you can save other readers from frustration and help us improve subsequent versions of this book. If you find any errata, please report them by visiting `http://www.packtpub.com/submit-errata`, selecting your book, clicking on the **Errata Submission Form** link, and entering the details of your errata. Once your errata are verified, your submission will be accepted and the errata will be uploaded to our website or added to any list of existing errata under the Errata section of that title. To view the previously submitted errata, go to `https://www.packtpub.com/book s/content/support`and enter the name of the book in the search field. The required information will appear under the **Errata** section.

Piracy

Piracy of copyrighted material on the Internet is an ongoing problem across all media. At Packt, we take the protection of our copyright and licenses very seriously. If you come across any illegal copies of our works in any form on the Internet, please provide us with the location address or website name immediately so that we can pursue a remedy. Please contact us at copyright@packtpub.com with a link to the suspected pirated material. We appreciate your help in protecting our authors and our ability to bring you valuable content.

Questions

If you have a problem with any aspect of this book, you can contact us at questions@packtpub.com, and we will do our best to address the problem.

1

Different Problems Require
Different Solutions

A brief history of and solutions to game AI

To better understand how to overcome the problems that game developers are currently facing, we need to dig a little bit into the history of video game development and take a look at the problems and their solutions that were so important at the time. Some of them were so avant-garde that they actually changed the entire history of video game design itself, and we still use the same methods today to create unique and enjoyable games.

One of the first relevant marks that is always worth mentioning when talking about game AI is computer chess programmed to compete against humans. It was the perfect game to start experimenting with artificial intelligence, because chess usually requires a lot of thought and planning ahead, something that a computer couldn't do at the time because it was necessary to have human features in order to successfully play and win the game. So, the first step was to make it able for the computer to process the game rules and think for itself in order to make a good judgement of the next move that the computer should do to achieve the final goal, that is, winning by checkmating. The problem is that chess has many possibilities; so, even if the computer had a perfect strategy to beat the game, it was necessary to recalculate that strategy, adapting it, changing, or even creating a new one every time something went wrong with the first strategy.

Humans can play differently every time; this makes it a huge task for the programmers to input all the possible data into the computer in order to win the game. So, writing all the possibilities that could exist wasn't a viable solution, and because of that, the programmers needed to think again about the problem. Then, one day, they finally came out with a better solution, that is, to make the computer decide for itself every turn, choosing the most plausible option for each turn; that way, the computer could adapt to any possibility in the game. Yet, this involved another problem–the computer would only think the short-term moves, and not create any plans to defeat the human in the future moves; so, it was easy to play against it, but at least we started to have something going on. It was decades later that someone defined the word **Artificial Intelligence (AI)** by solving the first problem that many researchers had by trying to create a computer that was capable of defeating a human player. Arthur Samuel is the person responsible for creating a computer that could learn for itself and memorize all the possible combinations. That way, there wasn't necessarily any human intervention and the computer could actually think on its own, and that was a huge step that is still impressive even by today's standards.

Enemy AI in video games

Now, let's move to the video game industry and analyze how the first enemies and game obstacles were programmed; was it that different from what we are doing now? Let's find out.

Single-player games with AI enemies started to appear in the 1970s, and soon, some games started to elevate the quality and expectations of what defines a video game AI. Some of those examples were released for arcade machines, such as *Speed Race* from *Taito* (a racing video game), or *Qwak* (a duck hunting game using a light gun), and *Pursuit* (an aircraft fighter) both from Atari. Other notable examples are the text-based games released for the first personal computers, such as *Hunt the Wumpus* and *Star Trek, which* also had enemies. What made those games so enjoyable was precisely that the AI enemies that didn't reacted like any other before because they had random elements mixed with the traditional stored patterns, making them unpredictable, and hence providing a unique experience every time you played the game. However, that was only possible due to the incorporation of microprocessors that expanded the capabilities of a programmer at that time. Space Invaders brought the movement patterns and Galaxian improved and added more variety, making the AI even more complex. PAC-MAN later on brought movement patterns to the maze genre.

The influence that the AI design in PAC-MAN had is just as significant as the influence of the game itself. This classic arcade game makes the player believe that the enemies in the game are chasing him, but not in a crude manner. The ghosts are chasing the player (or evading the player) in a different way as if they have an individual personality. This gives people the illusion that they are actually playing against four or five individual ghosts rather than copies of the same computer enemy.

After that, Karate Champ introduced the first AI fighting character and *Dragon Quest* introduced the tactical system for the RPG genre; over the years, the list of games that explored artificial intelligence and used it to create unique game concepts kept expanding, and all of that came from a single question, how can we make a computer capable of beating a human in a game?

All the games mentioned above are of a different genre, and they are unique in their style, but all of them used the same method for the AI called **finite-state machine** (**FSM**). Here, the programmer inputs all the behaviors necessary for the computer to challenge the player, just like the computer that first played chess. The programmer defined exactly how the computer should behave on different occasions in order to move, avoid, attack, or perform any other behavior to challenge the player, and that method is used even in the latest big budget games of

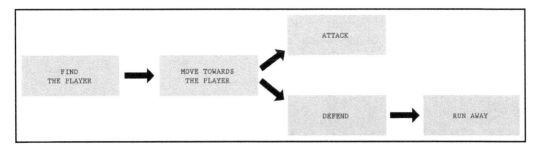

From simple to smart and human-like AI

Programmers face many challenges while developing an AI character, but one of the greatest challenges is adapting the AI movement and behavior in relation to what the player is currently doing, or will do in future actions. The difficulty exists because the AI is programmed with predetermined states, using probability or possibility maps in order to adapt their movement and behavior according to the player. This technique can become very complex if the programmer extends the possibilities of the AI decisions, just like the chess machine that has all the possible situations that may occur in the game.

It's a huge task for the programmer because it's necessary to determine what the player can do and how the AI will react to each action of the player, and that takes a lot of CPU power. To overcome that challenge, programmers started to mix possibility maps with probabilities and perform other techniques that let the AI decide for itself on how it should react according to the player's actions. These factors are important to be considered while developing an AI that elevates the game quality as we are about to discover.

Games kept evolving and players got even more exigent, not only with the visual quality but also with the capabilities of the AI enemies and the allied characters. To deliver new games that took into consideration the player expectations, programmers started to write even more states for each character, creating new possibilities and more engaging enemies, implementing important allied characters, which meant more things for the player to do, and creating a lot more features that helped redefine different genres and created new ones. Of course, this was also possible because technology kept improving, allowing developers to explore even more artificial intelligence in video games. A great example of this that is worth mentioning is Metal Gear Solid, the game that brought a new genre to the video game industry by implementing stealth elements, instead of the popular straightforward shooting. However, those elements couldn't be fully explored as Hideo Kojima intended because of the hardware limitations at the time. Jumping forward from the third to the fifth generation of consoles, Konami and Hideo Kojima presented the same title, but this time with a lot more interactions, possibilities, and behaviors from the AI elements of the game, making it so successful and important in video game history that it's easy to see its influence in a large number of games that came after *Metal Gear Solid*:

Metal Gear Solid - Sony Playstation 1

Visual and audio awareness

The game in the preceding screenshot implemented visual and audio awareness for the enemy AI, a feature that later on we'll explore in detail in this book. This feature established the genre that we know today as a stealth game. So, the game uses Path Finding and a FSM, features that were already known from the beginning of the video game industry; But, in order to create something new, they also created new features, such as interaction with the environment, navigation behavior, visual/audio awareness, and AI interaction; a lot of things that didn't existed at the time but that are widely used today in different game genres, such as sports, racing, fighting, or FPS games, were also introduced:

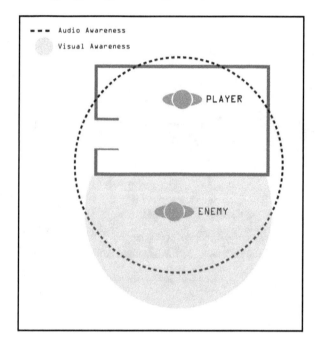

After that huge step for game design, developers still faced other problems, or should I say, these new possibilities brought even more problems, because they were not perfect. The AI still didn't react as a real person, and many other elements was necessary to be implemented, not only in stealth games, but in all other genres, and one in particular-needed to improve their AI to make the game feel realistic.

We are talking about sports games, especially those that tried to simulate real-world team behaviors, such as basketball or football. interaction with the player is not the only thing that we need to care about; we left chess long time ago, where it was 1 versus 1. Now, we want more, and watching other games get realistic AI behaviors, sport fanatics started to ask for the same features in their

favorite games; after all, those games was based on real-world events, and for that reason, the AI should react as realistically as possible.

At this point, developers and game designers started to take into consideration AI interaction with itself, and that just like the enemies from PAC-MAN, the player should get the impression that each character in the game thinks for itself and reacts differently to the others. If we analyze it closely, the AI that is present in a sports game is structured like an FPS or RTS game, using different animation states, general movements, interactions, individual decisions, and finally tactics and collective decisions. So, it shouldn't be a surprise that sports games could reach the same level of realism as the other genres that had already greatly evolved in terms of AI development. However, there are few problems that only sports games had at the time: how to make so many characters on the same screen react differently but at the same time work together to achieve the same objective. With this problem in mind, developers started to improve the individual behaviors of each character, not only for the AI that was playing against the player but also for the AI that was playing alongside the player. Once again, Finite State Machines made up a crucial part of Artificial Intelligence, but the special touch that helped to create a realistic approach in the sports genre was the anticipation and awareness used in stealth games. The computer needed to calculate what the player was doing, where the ball was going, and coordinate all of that, as well as give a false impression of a team mindset toward the same plan. Combining the new features used in the new genre of stealth games with a vast number of characters on the same screen, it was possible to innovate the sports genre by creating a sports simulation type of game, which has gained so much popularity over the years. This helps us to understand that we can use almost the same methods for any type of game, even if it looks completely different; the core principles that we saw in the computer that played chess is still valuable to the sports game released 30 years later.

Let's move on to our last example, which also has great value in terms of how an AI character should behave to make it more realistic: the game is F.E.A.R., developed by Monolith Productions. What made this game so special in terms of Artificial Intelligence was the dialog between the enemy characters. While it wasn't an improvement from a technical point of view, it was definitely something that helped to showcase all of the development work that was put into the characters' AI, and this is so crucial because if the AI doesn't say it, it didn't happen. This is an important factor to take into consideration while creating a realistic AI character, giving the illusion that it's real; that means the false impression that the computer reacts like humans, and humans interact, so the AI should do the same. Not only did the dialog help to create a human-like atmosphere, it also helped to exhale all of the development put on the character that otherwise the player wouldn't notice was there. When the AI detects the player for the first time, it shouts that it found the player; when the AI loses sight of the player, it expresses that. When the squad of AI's are trying to find the player or ambush him, they speak about that, leaving the player imagining that the enemy is really capable of thinking and planning against him. Why is this so important? Because if we only had numbers and mathematical equations for the characters, they will react that way, without any human features, just math, and to make it look more human, it's necessary to input mistakes, errors, and dialog into the character AI, just to distract the player from the fact that he's playing against a machine.

The history of video game artificial intelligence is still far from perfect, and it's possible that it will take us decades to improve just a little bit more from what we achieved between the early 1950s and this present day, so don't be afraid of exploring what you are about to learn, combine, change, or delete some of the things to find different results, because great games did it in the past and they had a lot of success with it.

Summary

In this chapter, you learned about the impact of AI on the video game history, how everything started from a simple idea to have a computer to compete against humans in traditional games, and how that naturally evolved into the world of video games. You also learned about the challenges and difficulties that were present since the day one, and how coincidentally, programmers kept facing and still face the same problems. In the next chapter, we'll start from that precise point, the most used technique and the technique that caused a lot of debate and evolution that was present on past games as well on present and futures ones.

2
Possibility and Probability Maps

In this chapter, we'll be talking about possibility and probability maps, understanding how and where they are used. We'll also be learning the best practices for creating an AI that reacts to the player and that also chooses the best options, as we look to create a character that can make decisions as a human would.

As we saw previously, video games used to rely heavily on predetermining the behavior of what the AI could do in different scenarios that were either created by the game itself or by the player's actions. This method has been present since day one and is still being used today, making it an extremely valuable method for creating quality AI characters. Before explaining, in detail, what each of the maps do, and before demonstrating how to create them in order to develop good AI behavior, it's always good to have a general idea of what possibility and probability maps are and where or when they are applied.

As gamers, we tend to enjoy the product as a whole, experiencing every part of the game with enthusiasm and dedication, forgetting about the technical aspects of the game. For that reason, we sometimes forget that even simple things that happen while we play were already destined to occur that way, and that there is a lot of thought and planning behind that moment. Everything happens for a reason, as we often hear, and this can also be applied to video games. From the moment you clicked the start button to begin the game to the last awesome combo that you performed to defeat the final boss of the game, everything was planned to happen and it was necessary for a programmer to input all of those possibilities within the game. If you clicked the A button and your character jumped, that happened because it was determined to be that way. The same thing is valid for AI enemies or allies on the game; when they do something to defeat or help you, it was necessary for that behavior to be programmed, and to do that we use states.

Game states

To understand how to create possibility or probability maps we need to first acknowledge the principle aspect necessary to create them, which is called game states, or simply states. We call game states to the actions that are predetermined throughout different occasions in the game, and those actions can be applied to both the player or to the enemy character. Some examples can be simple behavior, such as run, jump, or attack, and those states can be expanded a little more, for example when the character is in the air and cannot attack or if the character has low magical energy and cannot perform a magic attack. In these cases, the character goes from one state to another or can't perform one if it's doing another.

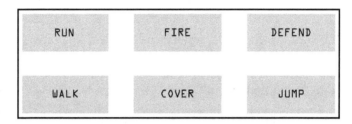

Possibility maps

Now let's take a deeper look at the possibility maps that we encountered in the examples in the first chapter, from the chess machine to the Metal Gear Solid video game. As we can see, it's a technique that is still being used today, and it is almost impossible to create a game AI without it.

As the name suggests, possibility maps allow the programmer to define the possibilities available to the player or the AI character within the game. Everything that is possible inside the game needs to be planned and coded, but what happens when you allow the character to do a lot of things–can they do them all at the same time? If played during different stages of the game, can they react in the same way at all of the stages? To allow, and restrain, the possible actions, we also need to think about the possible scenarios that can occur in the game, and when you put all of that together it's called a possibility map.

How to use possibility maps

Let's take a look at a simple example of a common FPS game, and for that we'll be using the states demonstrated in the preceding image.

Imagine that we are the enemy character of the game and our goal is to shoot and kill the player using only the states walk, run, cover, jump, fire, and defend. We need to take into consideration that the player will do his best to kill us, and therefore a lot of possible scenarios may arrive. Let's start with the basics–we are walking from one point to another while protecting our space and as the player goes near that space, our goal changes from protecting our space to the definitive goal, that is, killing the player. What should we do next? Fire? Run towards the player and fire from close range? Cover and wait until the player is nearby? What if the player saw us first and is preparing to fire at us? A lot of things could happen, and a lot of things can be done with just a few states. So, let's map every possible situation and plan how we should act or react in each individual situation. Examples that I would choose for my game are as follows:

- Walk slowly to a cover position, wait for the player, and shoot him
- Run for cover and then fire from that position
- Defend (moving away from the bullets) while running to a cover position
- Fire against the player, running towards him, and keep firing

Depending on the type of game that we want to create, we can use the same states to shape it into a different genre. We also need to take into consideration the personality of the character that we are programming. If it's a robot, it probably won't be afraid to keep firing against the player, even if the chances of getting destroyed are 99%. On the other hand, if it's an inexperienced soldier, it might feel reluctant to get shot and will run for cover instantly. The list goes on and on just by changing the personality of the character.

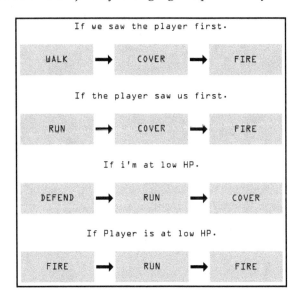

Preparing a possibility map (FPS)

At this point, we are able to understand what a possibility map is and how it can be used to create an AI character that behaves accordingly to different situations in the game. Now that we understand how to use a possibility map, let's create a practical example where we programmed our AI character to successfully defeat the player. For this example, I'll be using two models, one represents the AI enemy that we are programming and the other one represents the player.

We'll create a common example, where the AI is protecting the entrance of a building that the player needs to enter in order to deactivate a bomb and complete the level. Let's imagine that we already have the player fully programmed and that we now need to focus on our AI enemy, as shown in the following screenshot:

Before writing any line of code we need to think about the possible situations that can occur and how our AI will react to them. First, we'll be simplifying the situation by breaking down our stages into a simple 2D visualization that will be used as a reference to determinate distances and other relevant parameters.

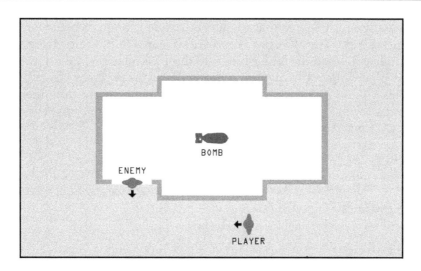

After simplifying the situation, we are ready to start planning the possibilities. The player is allowed to move around the building. Note that there's only one entrance, and that entrance is protected by our enemy AI. The arrows represents the direction that the characters are facing, and this will be an important aspect to our planning.

Creating a possibility map (FPS)

We'll learn how to create an awareness behavior for the AI character later, so for now we will just be using simple Boolean variables to determine if the player is near our position and what direction it is facing. Taking that into consideration, let's break our image into trigger zones to define when our enemy AI should react.

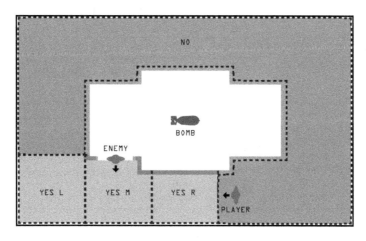

The **YES** zones represents the area that triggers our AI to change its behavior from the passive to offensive state. The **NO** zones represent the area that doesn't have an impact on our AI behavior. I've divided the **YES** zones into three because we want our AI character to react differently according to the player's position. If the player comes from the right side (**YES R**), the enemy has a wall that can be used for cover; if it comes from the left side (**YES L**), we can't use that wall anymore, and once the player is in the middle (**YES M**), the AI can only move backwards inside of the building.

Let's prepare our script for the enemy AI. In this example, we will use the C# language, but you can adapt the script to any programming language that you prefer, as the principles remains the same. The variables that we'll be using for now are `Health`, `statePassive`, `stateAggressive`, and `stateDefensive`:

```
public class Enemy : MonoBehaviour {
private int Health = 100;
private bool statePassive;
private bool stateAggressive;
private bool stateDefensive;
// Use this for initialisation
void Start () {
}
// Update is called once per frame
void Update () {
}
}
```

Now that we know the basic information required for the AI, we need to think about when those states will be used and how the AI will choose between the three available options. For this, we'll use a possibility map. We already know the areas that trigger our character, and we have already chosen the three behavior states, so it's time to plan the transitions and reactions according to the player's position and behavior.

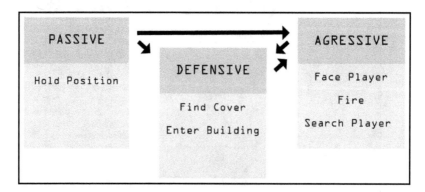

Our enemy AI can go from **PASSIVE** to **DEFENSIVE** or **AGGRESSIVE**, from **AGGRESSIVE** to **DEFENSIVE**, and from **DEFENSIVE** to **AGGRESSIVE**, but once our AI knows that the player is around, it will never go back to the passive behavior.

Defining the states

Let's define what triggers each state and how the AI should choose the correct state in different scenarios. The PASSIVE state will be the default state, and the game will start in that position until the player comes across our character. The DEFENSIVE state will be used in two different situations—if the player comes from the right side and if he has already confronted the player and has low HP. Finally, the AGGRESSIVE state will be activated if the player comes from the left side or has already arrived at the middle area:

```
public class Enemy : MonoBehaviour {
private int Health = 100;
private bool statePassive;
private bool stateAggressive;
private bool stateDefensive;
private bool triggerL;
private bool triggerR;
private bool triggerM;
// Use this for initialisation
void Start () {
 statePassive = true;
}
// Update is called once per frame
void Update () {
 // The AI will remain passive until an interaction with the player occurs
 if(Health == 100 && triggerL == false && triggerR == false && triggerM
 == false)
 {
  statePassive = true;
  stateAggressive = false;
  stateDefensive = false;
 }
 // The AI will shift to the defensive mode if player comes from the
 right side or if the AI is below 20 HP
 if(Health<= 100 && triggerR == true || Health<= 20)
 {
  statePassive = false;
  stateAggressive = false;
  stateDefensive = true;
 }
 // The AI will shift to the aggressive mode if player comes from the
 left side or it's on the middle and AI is above 20HP
```

```
if(Health> 20 && triggerL == true || Health> 20 && triggerM == true)
{
 statePassive = false;
 stateAggressive = true;
 stateDefensive = false;
 }
 }
}
```

We added the trigger variables `triggerL`, `trigger`, and `triggerM` and also defined when the AI should change from one behavior state to another. At this point, our enemy already knows what to do in different situations that may occur during gameplay according to the player's position.

Now we just need to determine what will happen on each state, because that is what differentiates a DEFENSIVE state from an AGGRESSIVE one. For this specific enemy, where his main function is to protect the entrance of the building, we want him to stay put at all times and to never run after the player. This is because the AI doesn't know that it is just one person and can't take the risk of going after just one soldier if there's a possibility of being greeted by several. This will help to give a little realism to the actions of the enemy. We'll also use the defensive behavior state for the moment where the enemy feels that it is losing the battle and is about to die, or when it has the advantage of using the building to protect itself while the player doesn't. Finally, the aggressive state will be used when the AI sees a clear advantage to kill or if it doesn't have any other options.

DEFENSIVE state

So, let's start with the situation where the player comes from the right side and our enemy has already spotted him. We want our AI to take advantage of the wall that protects him, making it difficult for the player as well as demonstrating a human-like intention, rather than simply opening fire. The enemy will move towards the wall and stay there firing on the corner until the player arrives to that position.

The enemy will change from the PASSIVE state into the DEFENSIVE state, instead of OFFENSIVE, only because doing that gives him a slightly better advantage over the player. Being defensive on the first encounter shows some personality to the AI, which is very important when making the behavior of the computer character believable. In future chapters we'll learn how to use the environment to help define our AI character in depth:

```
Void Defensive () {
if(playerPosition == "triggerR")
{
// Check if player is currently
located on the triggerR position
transform.LookAt(playerSoldier);
// Face the direction of the player
if(cover == false)
 {
   transform.position = Vector3.MoveTowards(transform.position,
   wallPosition.position, walk);
 }
if(cover == true)
 {
   coverFire();}
 }
 }
```

We added the core for the `Defensive` state that we want to implement on our enemy AI when the player is coming from the right side. We also added new variables, such as `speed`, `cover`, `playerSoldier`, and `coverFire`. First, we need to check if the player is currently positioned in the `triggerR` zone; if the result is positive, the character should move towards the cover position. Once the enemy AI is at the cover position, he can start firing against the player (`coverFire`). Now let's input the following situation–if the player is still alive, our enemy needs to move to another situation, otherwise it will be cornered, which isn't a good scenario for the character we are creating. Let's add that situation to our script.

We want our character to walk back and get inside the building, while always facing the player and firing at the same time. We could use another tactic, or decide to be more aggressive and confront the player directly, but for now let's stick to a simple strategy. We can add more complex behavior later:

```
if (playerPosition == "triggerM")
{
 transform.LookAt(playerSoldier); // Face the direction of the player
 transform.position = Vector3.MoveTowards(transform.position,
 buildingPosition.position, walkBack);
 backwardsFire();    }
```

In this part of the code we added a situation where the player comes from the right side and is still alive going to the middle, so we needed to change the previous behavior to a new one. Our AI character goes from the cover position to a newer position that is inside the building, firing at the player the whole time. At this point, the enemy will keep getting back until one of the two characters die–either the player or the AI character. We close the situation where the player comes from the right side. Now that we have completed this part, we need to complete the scenario and add the last situation, which is where the player goes around the building and comes from the left side. Our AI will need to adapt to these circumstances and behave differently, so let's work on that part and complete the example.

AGGRESSIVE state

Before we started programming, we defined how many states we would need for this enemy AI, and we chose three different states: PASSIVE, DEFENSIVE, and AGGRESSIVE. Now that we already have the two behavior states in place (passive and defensive), there is just one more needed to complete our enemy AI, that is, to protect the building.

We previously decided that the character would only directly confront the player if he couldn't use the wall as cover, and that moment is where the player comes from the left and the enemy is surprised with its presence.

Once again, we need to first check if the player triggered the left area, as that will activate our enemy AI from the PASSIVE state into the AGGRESSIVE state we intended. Then, we need to define what he should do in that case. Let's start writing it in our script:

```
Void Aggressive () {
if(playerPosition == "triggerL" || playerPosition == "triggerM")
{
 transform.LookAt(playerSoldier); // Face the direction of the player
 frontFire();
}
else {
 transform.position = Vector3.MoveTowards(transform.position,
 triggerLPosition.position, walk);
}
}
```

This time we added our two possible situations when attacking a player that comes from the left; the first is if the player comes from the left and continues towards the enemy, or remains in the same position. The second situation that could occur is if the player soon retreats as soon as he sees the enemy, and in that scenario we have chosen to make the enemy search for the player, going towards the `triggerL` position where initially the player appeared.

This is the completed script, written using the possibility map example that we've been working on in this chapter. Let's take a look at the full script:

```
Private int Health = 100;
Private bool statePassive;
Private bool stateAggressive;
Private bool stateDefensive;
Private bool triggerL;
Private bool triggerR;
Private bool triggerM;
public Transform wallPosition;
public Transform buildingPosition;
public Transform triggerLPosition;
private bool cover;
private float speed;
private float speedBack;
private float walk;
private float walkBack;
public Transform playerSoldier;
staticstring playerPosition;
```

In the previous block of code, we can see all of the variables that have been used in our script so far. The rest of the script is as follows:

```
// Use this for initialization
Void Start () {
statePassive = true;
}
// Update is called once per frame
Void Update () {
// The AI will remain passive until an interaction with the player occurs
if(Health == 100 && triggerL == false && triggerR == false && triggerM ==
false)
{
 statePassive = true;
 stateAggressive = false;
 stateDefensive = false;
}
// The AI will shift to the defensive mode if player comes from the right
side or if the AI is below 20 HP
if(Health<= 100 && triggerR == true || Health<= 20){
 statePassive = false;
 stateAggressive = false;
 stateDefensive = true;
}
// The AI will shift to the aggressive mode if player comes from the left
side or it's on the middle and AI is above 20HP
if(Health> 20 && triggerL == true || Health> 20 && triggerM == true){
 statePassive = false;
 stateAggressive = true;
 stateDefensive = false;
}
walk = speed * Time.deltaTime;
 = speedBack * Time.deltaTime;
}
Void Defensive () {
    if (playerPosition == "triggerR")
    {
    // Check if player is currently located on the triggerR position
    transform.LookAt(playerSoldier); // Face the direction of the
    player
    if(cover == false)
     {
       transform.position = Vector3.MoveTowards(transform.position,
       wallPosition.position, walk);
     }
    if(cover == true)
    {
     coverFire();
```

```
        }
      }
    if(playerPosition == "triggerM")
      {
        transform.LookAt(playerSoldier); // Face the direction of the
        player
        transform.position = Vector3.MoveTowards(transform.position,
        buildingPosition.position, walkBack);
        backwardsFire();
      }
    }
Void Aggressive () {
if (playerPosition == "triggerL" || playerPosition == "triggerM")
 {
   transform.LookAt(playerSoldier); // Face the direction of the player
   frontFire();
 }
else {
   transform.position = Vector3.MoveTowards(transform.position,
   triggerLPosition.position, walk);
 }
}
Void coverFire () {
// Here we can write the necessary code that makes the enemy firing while
in cover position.}
Void backwardsFire () {
// Here we can write the necessary code that makes the enemy firing while
going back.}
voidfrontFire() {
}
```

Possibility map conclusion

We have finally completed our first possibility map example. The principles that were shared in this chapter can be used in a wide range of game genres. In fact, almost any game that you plan to create in the future can greatly benefit from a possibility map. As we saw, this technique is used to plan every situation that the player can create, and how the character AI should behave according to that. By planning this carefully we can avoid a lot of issues in gameplay, as well as a lack of diversity regarding the character AI behavior. Another interesting point that is worth mentioning is to try to create a different Possibility Map for different characters of the game, as not all humans react equally. A computer AI should follow that same rule.

Probability maps

A probability map is a more complex and detailed version of a possibility map because it relies on probabilities in order to change the behavior of the character, rather than a simple on or off trigger. Its similarity with the possibility map is that it's also required for planning ahead the possible states for our character. This time, however, we add to it a percentage, using which the AI will calculate what behavior he will be using. Imagine the next example using the situation that we previously created for the possibility map—our enemy AI could be more aggressive in the daytime than at night. For that, we create a statement that explains to our enemy that if it's night time, there is a lesser chance of seeing the player character, and for that reason it will choose a more defensive approach instead of an aggressive one. Or, simply, we could define that our enemy calculates the probability of killing the player simply based on the distance between the two characters. If the player gets closer to the enemy, the probability of the AI getting back and surviving are lesser than if he keeps firing against the player, so we can add that equation into the AI.

Let's take a look at our human behavior, the choices we make; usually, we make our decision by taking into consideration past events and what we've done before. When we feel hungry and we decide to go out for dinner, can our friend guess which restaurant we have chosen? Our friend may have calculated the probability of our choice and given their answer by taking into consideration the higher percentage chance. That's exactly what we need to do to our AI friend; we need to assign some probabilities to his choices, such as what's the probability of the AI character falling asleep while protecting the building during the day and during the night? What's the probability of the enemy running if he has low hp? If we apply probability to our AI character, it helps to create that unpredictable behavior that humans have and makes the game more engaging and natural.

How to use probability maps

In this example, we'll continue using the same scenario that we created before, where our AI guard is protecting a building that contains an atomic that the player needs to deactivate. The only entrance to the building is protected by our AI character.

Let's imagine that we are the guard and we have orders to stay there for 16 hours straight–we would probably need to eat, drink, and move a little bit to be able to stay active and alert the whole time. We will therefore add that to our character, making it more unpredictable for the player. If the AI decides to eat or drink, he will be inside the building, and if he decides to walk a little bit he will be patrolling from the `triggerL` to `triggerR` position. Most of the time, he will be just standing on his guard position.

Time	Guard	Eat/Drink	Walk
Morning	0.87	0.1	0.03
Afternoon	0.48	0.32	0.2
Night	0.35	0.40	0.25

This is a probability map, and here we define the percentage of each state that our character exists in. It means that every time the player sees the enemy AI, the enemy can be doing one of those things. This will differ greatly when you take into consideration the time of day at which the player decided to appear. If the player arrives in the morning, it has an **0.87** chance of finding the enemy in a guard position in front of the building, a **0.10** chance of finding him eating or drinking inside the building, and finally a **0.03** chance of finding him walking outside from one point to another. If the player arrives in the afternoon, it has a **0.48** chance of finding the enemy in a guard position in front of the building, a **0.32** chance of finding him eating or drinking inside the building, and finally a **0.2** chance of finding him walking around from one point to another. At night, the player has a **0.35** chance of finding the enemy in the guard position, a **0.40** chance of finding him eating or drinking inside the building, and a **0.25** chance of finding the enemy walking around.

This will help to create that unpredictable aspect to our character by not making it as obvious that he will be in the same position every time you play the level. We can also update this probability every five minutes or so, in case the player stays still, waiting for our enemy to change position. This technique is used in a lot of games, but especially in stealth games, where observation is key. This is because the player has the opportunity to stay in a safe position and observe the enemy behavior, similar to heist movies, where actors wait for the guards to change shifts before getting inside the bank. Because of this popular behavior that we're used to seeing in movies, players like to feel that same sensation in games, and so probability maps have changed the way how we play.

An example of how probability can be used in a script is as follows. For this, I've used the `Passive` state and added the probability that we previously decided to use:

```
Void Passive () {
rndNumber = Random.Range(0,100);
If(morningTime == true &&  13)
{
// We have 87% of chance
goGuard();
}
if(morningTime == true && rndNumber =< 13 && rndNumber< 3)
{
// We have 10% of chance
goDrink();
}
if(morningTime == true && rndNumber<= 3)
{
// We have 3% of chance
goWalk();
}
if(afternoonTime == true && rndNumber> 52)
{
// We have 48% of chance
goGuard();
}
if(afternoonTime == true && rndNumber =< 34 && rndNumber< 2)
{
// We have 32% of chance
goDrink();
}
if(afternoonTime == true && rndNumber<= 2)
{
// We have 2% of chance
goWalk();
}
if(nightTime == true && rndNumber> 65)
```

```
{
// We have 35% of chance
goGuard();
}
if(nightTime == true && rndNumber =< 65 && rndNumber< 25)
{
// We have 40% of chance
goDrink();
}
if(nightTime == true && rndNumber<= 25)
{
// We have 25% of chance
goWalk();
}
}
```

To calculate the percentage, we first need to create a random number from 0 to 100, and then we create a statement that will use that number to check to which statement it belongs. On the first statement, for example, we have an 87% chance of the AI staying in the guard position, so if the random number is higher than 13, it fits within this category and the character is made to stay in the guard position. A number higher than 3 and equal or less than 13, gives us a 10% of chance, and a number equal or less than 3 gives us a 3% chance.

Where to go from here

Now that we understand how to use a probability and possibility map, a pertinent question that we might question ourselves is, what can we do with this? Well we saw how important is to use a possibility map to define the behaviors of a character and how the probability helps to make those behaviors unpredictable, but we can do a lot more with what we learned depending on the type of game that we are creating or the type of AI that we want. Remember that flaws makes part of what we are as humans and we are surrounded by probabilities, even if it's just *0,000001%* the probability of happening the unexpected exists that's why no one is perfect, so it's a fun fact to remember when creating an AI character, giving them some probability of human stuff happening, or simply making good or bad decisions, that builds a personality to the computer character that you are creating.

Another special thing that we can do with probability maps, is giving the AI the opportunity to learn from himself, making him smarter every time the player decides to play the game. Both the player and the enemy AI will learn, making the challenge always updated according to the hours spent on the game. If the player has the tendency to use the same weapon or coming from the same direction, the computer should update that information and use it on future events. If the player confronted the computer *100* times and *60%* of those times he used a grenade, the AI should have that in mind and react according to that probability. That will push the player to think in other strategies, also not being so obvious exploring other ways of defeating the enemy.

Summary

This chapter has described possibility and probability maps and we have learned how to let the AI take decisions for itself according to the player actions. Possibility and probability maps is the foundation of an AI character and now we can explore this technique to create new and unique artificial intelligence for our games. In the next chapter, we'll learn how the AI should behave according to the different options that it has on that moment instead of using a possibility map. We want the character to analyze the situation and think about what to do, taking in consideration many factors, such as health, distance, weapon, bullets, and any other relevant factors.

3
Production System

In this chapter, we'll be talking about different ways to perfect our AI character and how to adapt the same techniques to work on different types of game that we want to create. We'll also be discussing the following topics:

- Automated finite-state machines (AFSMs)
- Calculating chance
- Utility-based functions
- Dynamic gaming AI balance

After exploring possibility and probability maps, we need to understand how to use them in conjunction with other techniques and strategies to create a well-balanced and human-like AI character. Possibility maps or even probability maps can be used alone to create enjoyable and challenging games; in fact, many video games only relied on maps, and kept with the same approach in order to create their AI enemies, and they became very successful doing it that way. A perfect example would be a generic platform game, such as *Super Mario Bros* from Nintendo. They don't need to create a complex AI system in order to make enemies challenging and that is why for decades they kept using the same formula for enemies, because it works perfectly for the genre. So it's also important to remember that, depending on the game that we are creating, some techniques could work better than others and it's up to us to decide to use, and when to use it. Now, the same should be applied to the character that we are creating–it should know what to do and when to do it at every single second of the game.

Let's continue with the *Super Mario Bros* example and analyze what some common enemies do:

The enemy in the screenshot is called Goomba. As soon as he appears in the game, you will notice that he moves from right to left, and only if he hits something (excluding the player) does he change his direction and move from left to right. If he's on a higher platform, he keeps moving from right to left until he falls and on the lower platform he keeps moving from right to left. This enemy never tries to defeat the player and it's very predictable. So we can determine that he only has one goal, that is, moving, and can be placed anywhere on the stage as he will behave in exactly the same way in terms of position that he is in. Now let's MOVE TO our next enemy:

In this second example, the enemy is called Hammer Bro and he has a different function from the previous one. This AI can move left or right, always facing the player, and he throws a hammer in the direction of the player. So his main objective in the game is to defeat the player. Exactly the same as the previous enemy, this one can also be placed anywhere in the game and will behave according to his goal. Now, imagine that we picked up the enemy AI that we developed in the previous chapter and we placed him in a different position or stage of the game. He wouldn't react because we haven't supplied directions on what he should do if placed on a different position. Depending on the game that we are creating, we need to develop an AI character that will react as we intended. Sometimes he will be fixed in a single position but most of the time it will be required for the same AI to react the same way in different positions in the game. Imagine if the creators of *Super Mario Bros* had to redefine their AI character every time they inserted it in the game; it would take a lot of time and work. So let's learn how to use FSMs to make our character adaptable to every situation of the game.

Automated finite-state machines (AFSMs)

As we observed in the *Super Mario Bros* example, enemies know how to react no matter what position they are placed in. Obviously, it is not required for them to perform complex tasks or plan ahead what they will do, but it served perfectly as an example, especially when compared with other video games with different genres. For example, we can see the same principles being used on Halo with the Grunts (the small enemies). They simply move from one side to another and if they find the player they start shooting at him. It's the same principle, where they simply added a personality to their character that would run away every time they lost the combat against the player. For that, they used a statement where, every time the character is below a certain number of HP, they start running away. FSMs are what we used to create our possibility and probability maps; this is also what the character should do in different situations he is facing at the moment. Now let's create **automated finite-state machines** (**AFSMs**), where the character will choose the best option according to the factors that he will be able to calculate (position, player HP, current weapon, and so on). This method is extremely useful if we plan to use the same character on different stages or in games that involve an open world.

When planning AFSMs, it's a good start if we can break actions into two or three main columns; in one side of the column we put the main information, such as orientation, speed, or goals, and in the other columns we put actions that can be performed over the first column actions, such as moving, shooting, charging, finding cover, hiding, using the object, and so on. Doing that, we can ensure that our character can react according to our first column independently of the position in which he is currently placed. Imagine that the goal assigned to the AI is to guard the position that we defined. That goal is the primary objective so it will be placed on the first column. Now imagine that the character starts the game far away from the position that he should be guarding. At that point, he will be using the second column actions to fulfill the first column objectives. What we should put in the second column to make that possible depends heavily on the type of game that we want to create. So let's create an example and chose the best options for it.

We'll continue using the FPS genre as the main stage for our example, but the same principles can be used on almost any video game. That is why we've chosen *Super Mario Bros* as a reference, to show that no matter the type of game that we want to create, AI development tends to follow the same process of creation:

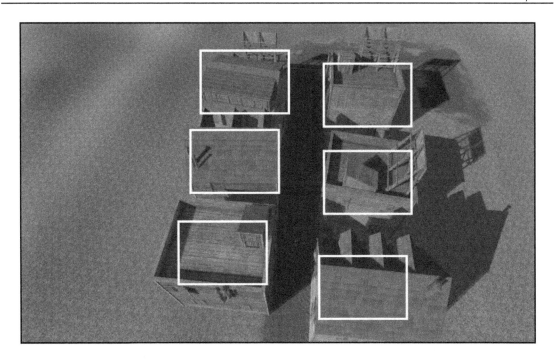

So, in our example, the map will have six buildings and neither the player nor the enemy can get inside them but they are allowed to move anywhere else. The main goal of this game is to defeat the opponent as many times as possible in a limited time; bullets and health points will appear occasionally in the game. Now let's develop an AI that can react the same way on any map. For that, we need to assign the main goal to the character and let him know about the possibilities available in order to fulfill that goal and also ensure that he is doing something every second of the game.

On a basic form, we have two main goals for this AI character: **DEFEAT PLAYER** and **SURVIVE**. We need to make sure that we are able to kill the player when we have the chance and to survive when we don't. For now, let's simplify this formula and define goals by taking into consideration the current HP of our character. If he's above 20% of his total HP, the main goal will be defeating the player and, on the other hand, if he's below 20% of his HP, the main goal switches to surviving:

>20HP DEFEAT PLAYER		
<20HP SURVIVE		

Once we have defined this, we can MOVE TO the second column and write the secondary goals that our AI will choose in order to complete the first column goals. So for this example, we will give our character three secondary goals: **FIND PLAYER**, **FIND COVER**, and **FIND POINTS**. By using these three objectives, our AI will be able to fulfill the main goals, will always have something to do, and will not wait for the player to do something, as follows:

>20HP DEFEAT PLAYER	FIND PLAYER	
	FIND COVER	
<20HP SURVIVE	FIND POINTS	

Now that, we have already defined the secondary objectives, we'll write down all the possible actions in the game, such as **MOVE TO, FIRE, USING OBJECT**, and **CROUCH** as follows. Once again, all of the things that a player or enemy AI is able to do in the game are defined while we think about the game design and all of that should be in this column. This is also an important strategy to analyze whether all the actions available to the characters of the game are relevant or not to the main or secondary goals. This will save us time in the future because there's no point in programming a complex action if that doesn't contribute to the success of the main goal, as with, *Super Mario Bros*, where they have chosen not to assign complex actions to their enemies because it wasn't necessary for the type of game that they were creating. For this example, the character has the possibility to move freely, fire the weapon, use objects (reload weapon or use health points) and crouch:

>20HP DEFEAT PLAYER	FIND PLAYER	MOVE TO
	FIND COVER	FIRE
<20HP SURVIVE		USE OBJECT
	FIND POINTS	CROUCH

Now, we have the three columns filled with all of the information needed for our AI to choose the best options according to his current situation. As we'll see in a moment, this is a different method from what we used in the previous chapter, because back then we used the map to give him instructions about what he should do and we assigned him orders according to that position only. In this example, we want our character to decide the best option for himself no matter the map or position that he is placed on. This will move us to the next level of developing an AI character because if we take a look at human behavior, we rarely make a decision according to a single criterion.

The same process will be applied to our current enemy: they will choose the best option according to different criteria and we'll make sure that they choose the best option based on their decision. For example, it is more urgent being at 1% health than being down to only 1% of ammunition or even completing the main goal of the game.

Once we have our three columns ready, we can move on to the next step and link every action in the third column to the second, and all of the behaviors in the second to the first column goals. While doing this, we need to think about what the AI should be doing if he wants to find the player, find cover position, or find points. Also, we need to define when he should be looking for points, cover position, or the player. To find the player, we need to use the MOVE TO action, so our character will be walking around until he finds the player and ultimately fires at him. Then is, finding cover; once again, we'll be using the MOVE TO action, so our character will walk until he is near to a wall that can serve as a cover position, then we can choose whether he is crouching or not depending on what he wants to achieve. Finally, to find points, we'll be using MOVE TO and after that, we'll make the AI decide whether he will be using points or not (USE OBJECT). Now, let's think about what behavior or behaviors he should choose when he is trying to defeat the player and when he is trying to survive. In order to defeat the player, our AI character needs to find him, so we'll use the FIND PLAYER behavior for this goal; also, we'll let him choose the FIND COVER behavior if he has already found the player and they are close to a wall. For the SURVIVE goal, we'll be choosing FIND COVER, in case he's being attacked by the player, and FIND POINTS, to regain more HP points.

Calculating chances

Now that we have everything set, we are ready to input all of this information into our code. We'll be using Booleans to define the main goals and then we'll create statements that will make the character AI choose between all of the other options. We already defined the primary statement that will switch our goal from defeating the player to simply surviving, but now we'll be adding more details to our AI behavior because of this question; What happens if the enemy has enough HP to confront the player but doesn't have enough bullets? What if he has enough bullets but his previous attempts to shoot the target have failed? The character will need to prioritize his choices and for each choice that they will be making, they need to compare it to the other alternatives and choose the one that has more chance of success in that goal.

Let's start with the chances of hitting the player: imagine that our AI already fired ten bullets and only four have hit the player. We can say that he has a 40% chance of hitting the player the next time he shoots. Now imagine that he only has two bullets in his gun; what should he do? Fire against the player with a not so favorable chance of being successful and then remain defenceless? Or run right away toward the point position where he can reload his weapon? To help in deciding this, the character will also be calculating the chance of being hit by the player; if the player has less chance of hitting the character, our AI will take the risk and fire against the player, otherwise it will try to reload its weapon. We'll start adding this information into our code. You can see an example of how it should look as follows:

```
Private int currentHealth = 100;
Private int currentBullets = 0;
private int firedBullets = 0;
private int hitBullets = 0;
private int pFireBullets = 0;
private int pHitBullets = 0;
private int chanceFire = 0;
private int chanceHit = 0;
public GameObject Bullet;
private bool findPlayer;
private bool findCover;
private bool findPoints;
```

These are the variables that we'll be using for now. `firedBullets` represents how many bullets the character has already fired in the entire game; `hitBullets` represents how many of those bullets hit the target; `pFireBullets` and `pHitBullets` are the same but take player bullets into consideration. We can move on to the calculation of the chances of hitting the target or being hit. `chanceFire` will represent the percentage of bullets that hit the target and `chanceHit` the percentage of getting hit:

```
void Update ()
{
 chanceFire = ((hitBullets / firedBullets) * 100) = 0;
 chanceHit = ((pHitBullets / pFiredBullets) * 100) = 0;
 if(currentHealth > 20 && currentBullets > 5)
 {
  Fire();
 }
 if(currentHealth > 20 && currentBullets < 5 && chanceFire < 80)
 {
  MoveToPoint();
 }
 if(currentHealth > 20 && currentBullets < 5 &&chanceFire>80)
 {
  Fire();
```

```
    }
    if(currentHealth > 20 && currentBullets > 5 && chanceFire < 30&&
    chanceHit > 30)
    {
     MoveToCover();
    }
    if(currentHealth < 20 && currentBullets > 0 && chanceFire > 90 &&
    chanceHit < 50)
    {
     Fire();
    }
  }
```

We have used the chances of hitting or being hit to determine what the AI should do in certain given situations. If he has more than 20 health points and has more than five bullets in his gun, he is free to shoot against the player until one of those two conditions doesn't match. Once when he only has five bullets, is it time to think about the next move, so in this example, if he has less than an 80% chance of being successful and hitting the player, he will decide not to shoot and will move towards the point position where he can reload his weapon. If he has more than an 80% chance, that means that he is being successful and he is free to try his luck. If, in the middle of the combat, the AI has less than a 30% chance of hitting the player and the player has more than a 30% chance, the character should immediately look for cover. Finally, if the AI character has less than 20% of his total health but he has a 90% chance of hitting the player and less than a 50% chance of being hit, he will choose to fire.

If we wanted to be even more precise about the percentages, we could add a time variable into this equation, where the AI will take into consideration the last two minutes or so instead of the whole time, or compare both percentages and analyze whether he has been more or less successful in the last two minutes in comparison with the rest of the game:

```
    if(recentPercentage > wholePercentage)
```

By calculating chances, we give our AI enough methods to calculate his next step, where he can freely decide which goal has more importance at that specific moment and choose his action according to that. Doing this will also give the AI the ability to choose between two or more options that are available to him. We start developing a more intelligent character, that can think for itself, and we can define personalities by simply changing the percentage values to make him take more risks or carefully choose his possibilities.

Utility-based functions

Now that we know how to calculate chance and use AFSMs, it's time to explore them a little more and make our characters look smart. This time, we'll use an AI character that is set to behave autonomously in a simulation game such as *The Sims*. This is a perfect environment to test artificial intelligence because it mimics real-life needs and choices.

In the video game *The Sims*, the player has the opportunity to control a human-like character and the main goal of the game is to make sure that the character is always in good situations and that their personal and professional life is always on a positive note. Meanwhile, time goes by, just like in real life, and the character gets older until he finally dies at the end. The player is responsible for the life of that being but if the player doesn't give any orders to the character, he will react autonomously to fulfill his needs. It was revolutionary the way that an AI character could behave in a video game; people could relate to that virtual character and look at him just as an independent living being. The secret is that we already know what is necessary to create a character that can behave exactly like characters in *The Sims*.

Without further ado, let's jump to our next example:

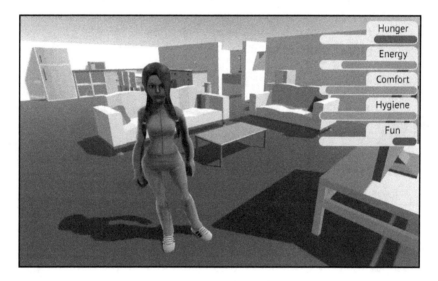

Let's give a name to the character in this example and call her Sophie. She is a virtual human being. She has a home with everything necessary to live: sofa, shower, television, bed, oven, and so on. Just like a human being, she has human-like necessities such as hunger, energy, comfort, hygiene, and fun. As time passes, she needs to fulfill her necessities in order to stay healthy. Now that we have the problem, let's work on the solution and make Sophie completely autonomous and able to decide for herself what she needs to do:

We can simplify and divide the objectives into two columns: on the left side, we put the main objectives of the game and on the right side, the actions the character perform. For example, if she is hungry, she needs to move towards the kitchen and interact with the fridge. This is exactly the same principle that we used to create the automated finite-state machines in the FPS example. But this time we'll explore this concept even further.

Let's think for a minute about the hunger feeling. Let's say that when we eat breakfast, we fulfill our hunger need and we don't feel hungry anymore. At this point, we can say that our hunger necessity is at 100%, right? Imagine that a few minutes have passed by and now we are at 98%; why we don't go right on to fulfill the 2% that is missing? We can say that feeling hungry is a state where we are no longer full and not necessarily that we are empty and because of that we switch our priorities towards other necessities. So it's important to remember that when developing an autonomous AI character: he needs to have that thought in mind and not go to eat soon as he loses 1% of food. That would not look like human behavior; we tend to balance everything, otherwise we would sleep five minutes and work five, not so healthy or productive perhaps because it's not enough to fall asleep and isn't enough to start working. So, we sleep a fair number of hours to compensate for the other time that we are awake, and we eat a fair number of food to remain fulfilled for a few hours. We can make judgment decisions and decide that we are a little bit hungry but we need to finish the work first. Also, we make comparative judgments, for example, I'm hungry but I'm tired even more. It is important to understand our behavior when creating a virtual human being like Sophie because otherwise it will act like a robot.

To help Sophie determine what is more important at any specific moment, we'll be using percentages and then she will be able to compare and decide what she wants to do. Before complicating it too much, let's start writing the basic information in our code:

```
Private float Hunger = 0f;
Private float Energy = 0f;
Private float Comfort = 0f;
Private float Hygiene = 0f;
Private float Fun = 0f;
private float Overall = 0f;
public Transform Fridge;
public Transform Oven;
public Transform Sofa;
public Transform Bed;
public Transform TV;
public Transform Shower;
public Transform WC;
void Start ()
{
    Hunger = 100f;
    Energy = 100f;
    Comfort = 100f;
    Hygiene = 100f;
    Fun = 100f;
}
void Update ()
{
  Overall = ((Hunger + Energy + Comfort + Hygiene + Fun)/5);
    Hunger -= Time.deltaTime / 9;
    Energy -= Time.deltaTime / 20;
    Comfort -= Time.deltaTime / 15;
    Hygiene -= Time.deltaTime / 11;
    Fun -= Time.deltaTime / 12;
}
```

We wrote down the basic variables relating to the necessities of the character that we are creating. As time goes by, those values will decrease, with different attributed values depending on necessity. Also we have an `Overall` variable that serves to calculate the overall situation of the character and could perfectly represent the mood of our virtual human being. That will be an important factor and will help Sophie to decide what is the best option for her.

Now let's individualize each necessity and create a decision tree for all of them. To do so, we need to plan the process of decision-making that Sophie will think through before choosing any action. Let's start with the hunger necessity:

```
             DO I HAVE FOOD?

AM I HUNGRY?    CHECK FRIDGE        EAT

                    COOK
```

If Sophie feels hungry and she decides that is a priority, these would be the steps that she will follow. First she feels hungry and then asks herself if she has enough food; to answer that, she moves towards the fridge and checks whether she has. If the answer is yes, she moves on, cooks, and finally eats. In the event any of the segments can't be accomplished, the process will be interrupted and she will move on to a different priority. Let's say that she only has food in her fridge if she goes to work and for every day of work she receives, for example, two days of food. So going to work will become a priority very soon if she wants to keep healthy and alive:

```
Private float Hunger = 0f;
Private float Energy = 0f;
Private float Comfort = 0f;
Private float Hygiene = 0f;
Private float Fun = 0f;
private float Overall = 0f;
public Transform Fridge;
public Transform Oven;
public Transform Sofa;
public Transform Bed;
public Transform TV;
public Transform Shower;
public Transform WC;
private int foodQuantity;
public float WalkSpeed;
public static bool atFridge;
void Start ()
{
    Hunger = 100f;
    Energy = 100f;
    Comfort = 100f;
    Hygiene = 100f;
    Fun = 100f;
}
void Update ()
{
```

```
    Overall = ((Hunger + Energy + Comfort + Hygiene + Fun)/5);
    Hunger -= Time.deltaTime / 9;
    Energy -= Time.deltaTime / 20;
    Comfort -= Time.deltaTime / 15;
    Hygiene -= Time.deltaTime / 11;
    Fun -= Time.deltaTime / 12;
}
void Hungry ()
{
    transform.LookAt(Fridge); // Face the direction of the Fridge
    transform.position vector3.MoveTowards(transform.position.
    Fridge.position, walkSpeed);
    //checks if already triggered the fridge position
    if(atFridge == true)
    {
     //interact with fridge
     if(foodQuantity > 1)
     {
      Cook();
     }
     else()
     {
      // calculate next priority
     }
  }
  }
```

In the preceding code we have an example of how the decision tree can be represented in our code. We'll continue writing what she will be doing for every necessity, and once we have that done, we can determine how she will prioritize and decide which necessity needs to be taken care of first:

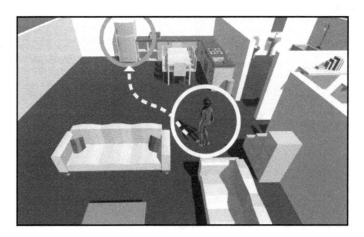

The next one on the list is energy:

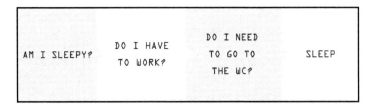

If Sophie feels sleepy and she decides that is a priority, these will be the steps that she follows. First, she feels sleepy and then asks herself if she has to work. If she has free time then she will make a final judgment and decide whether she needs to go to the bathroom before sleeping. Once every state is approved, she can finally complete her goal and go to sleep. We can see an example of how it could be represented in the following code:

```
void Sleepy ()
{
    if(hoursToWork > 3&&Energy < Hygiene)
{
        transform.LookAt(Bed); // Face the direction of the Bed
        transform.position = vector3.MoveTowards(transform.position.Bed.
        position, walkSpeed);
          //checks if already triggered the bed position
          if(atBed == true)
          {
          //interact with the bed
          }

    }
if(hoursToWork > 3 && Energy > Hygiene)
{
    useWC(); //Go to the bathroom
}
  if(hoursToWork < 3)
{
    //choose another thing to do
}
}
```

Let's assume that, for every hour that Sophie sleeps, she gains +10 points of **Energy** but loses 10 points of **Hygiene**. She'll need to confirm first that she won't need to use the bathroom in the middle of her sleep and for that we compare the number of **Energy** points that she needs with the number of **Hygiene** points:

Let's move on to the **Comfort** necessity. This one is a little bit special because we can assign two objectives at the same time while gaining **Comfort** points. For example, she will be capable of deciding whether she wants to eat sitting on a chair or not. The same can be applied when she is watching TV. This is an important example that can be applied in many games, where a character decides to do two things at the same time when he has the opportunity and understands that it is important to do so. In the example that follows, we'll be taking that into consideration:

AM I UNCOMFORTABLE?	AM I DOING OTHER THINGS?	CAN I SEAT NOW?	SEAT

If Sophie feels uncomfortable, she will check first whether at that moment she is doing something. This question can only have two answers: yes or no. If the answer is yes, she'll need to think whether it is possible for her to keep on doing it seated. Otherwise, she'll finish what she is doing at that moment and then will start asking the same question. If possible or available, she'll finally sit and get comfortable. We can check an example of how it should look in the following code:

```
private bool isEating;
private bool isWatchingTV;
private bool Busy;
...
void Uncomfortable ()
{
    if(isEating == true || isWatchingTV == true)
    {
            transform.LookAt(Sofa); // Face the direction of the Sofa
            transform.position = vector3.MoveTowards(transform.position.
            Sofa.position, walkSpeed);
            //checks if already triggered the bed position
            if(atSofa == true)
            {
            //interact with the sofa
            }
        }
    else
    {
      if(Comfort < Overall&& Busy == false)
    {
        transform.LookAt(Sofa); // Face the direction of the
        Sofa
        transform.position =
        vector3.MoveTowards(transform.position.Sofa.position, walkSpeed);
                //checks if already triggered the bed position

                if(atSofa == true)
                {
                //interact with the sofa
                }
        }
    if(Busy == true && isEating == false && isWatchingTV == false)
        {
         //Keep doing what she is doing at that moment
        }
    }
}
```

We added three more variables: `isEating`, `isWatchingTV`, and `Busy`. This will help her decide the best option, taking into consideration those three values. In the event that she feels uncomfortable but is eating or watching TV, she can perform both of the actions together. Otherwise, she needs to compare the rest of the necessities and judge whether it's more important to sit instead of doing other things. In the event that she is doing something at that moment and it's not possible for her to sit - let's say, for example, that she is taking a shower or working - she'll ignore the fact that she feels uncomfortable and, as soon as Sophie has the opportunity, she'll sit and gain **Comfort** points:

There remain two more necessities to finish this example and soon we will have an AI character that could live by itself without the need for someone to control and decide what is best for her. We are developing an AI system that works on a simulation game but this same method can also be used on different genres of game. Imagine a real-time strategy game where the workers make autonomous decisions and, instead of being idle waiting for orders, immediately go to work on what they think is more important at that moment and, as soon as other priorities arrive, switch to another occupation.

Let's move on to the next objective, Hygiene. Just for the sake of simplicity, we will use this necessity as everything related to the bathroom:

DO I NEED A SHOWER?	AM I DOING OTHER THINGS?	TAKE SHOWER

The hygiene necessity is simpler than the previous ones; it's just a question of whether she is available or not to take a shower. The extra factor that we'll be using on this one is that, no matter the circumstances, going to the bathroom is the most important one and she will immediately pause what she is doing and go straight towards the bathroom.

The only things that she could possibly do while taking a shower are brushing her teeth or any other sub-segment of the hygiene criterion. But for now, let's stick with as few options as possible to test the AI; once we have the basic functions working properly, we then can start adding more actions. For prototype purposes, that is also a good methodology to follow: by first having the basic functions working, we can move on and gradually add more details. Now let's take a look at an example of how the `Hygiene` function would look:

```
void useBathroom ()
{
if(Hygiene<10)
{
        transform.LookAt(Bathroom); // Face the direction of the
        Bathroom
        transform.position = vector3.MoveTowards(transform.position.
        Bathroom.position, walkSpeed);
        //checks if already triggered the bed position
if(atBathroom == true)

{

    //choose randomly what to do in the bathroom

}

}

}
```

Let's jump right away into the next and last necessity, Fun. This one will have the opportunity to be the most flexible of them all, because we can eat and watch TV at the same time, we can sit and watch TV at the same time, and we can eat sitting down while watching TV. We give the option to our AI to be able to do three distinct things at the same time. At first glance, allowing our character to boost her points in three different necessities looks ideal, but we'll be discussing that later on. For now, let's just focus on the Fun factor and plan the steps that she'll be using to determine whether she needs to, and can, watch TV:

If Sophie feels bored, she'll start asking herself whether she can watch TV. First, if she is available, she's free to watch TV and, in the default state, she watches TV seated. But if she is busy at that time, she needs to ask herself whether she can watch TV at the same time that she is doing whatever she's doing (in this example, that represents eating, sitting, or both at the same time). Once again, for the sake of simplicity, let's assume that she doesn't need to reach the television in order to turn it on. We can see an example of how that could be represented in our code as follows:

```
private bool isSeat;
private bool televisionOn;
void Bored ()
{
if(Fun<Overall&& Busy == false)
{
    televisionOn = true; // turns on the television
        transform.LookAt(TV); // Face the direction of the television
        transform.position = vector3.MoveTowards(transform.position.
        Sofa.position, walkSpeed);
        //checks if already triggered the bed position
        if(atSofa == true)
        {
         //interact with the sofa
        }
  }
if(Fun < Overall && Busy == true)
{
    f(isEating == true) {
        televisionOn = true; // turns on the television
            transform.LookAt(TV); // Face the direction of the
        television
```

```
        }
  if(isSeat == true)
    {
            televisionOn = true; // turns on the television
            transform.LookAt(TV); // Face the direction of the television

    }
  if(isSeat == true && isEating == true)
  {
            televisionOn = true; // turns on the television
            transform.LookAt(TV); // Face the direction of the television
            }
  }
  else()
  {
      //continue doing what she is doing
  }
  }
```

Finally, we conclude the necessity behaviors using different approaches for each one. Doing this, we can ensure that she will know what to do in different situations of the game and will always be looking to do something. There are some flaws in the AI design that we'll need to perfect; for example, she can't decide to continue watching TV even if she is hungry or tired. To make that possible, we would need to simply add a probability map and use the Overall variable to define whether she is happy or not; let's say that, in the event that she's above 50% for happiness, she can decide to watch TV even if she feels tired. All of those restrictions can now be assigned to the code and we can continuously add more details to the behavior of our character. But, for now, we will just focus on two more details: AI balance and dynamic problem-solving.

Dynamic game AI balancing

Another interesting and very useful topic to learn about AI development is game difficulty. If we play against a human player, the difficulty of the game will solely depend on the experience of the player that is playing against us. If they are very skillful with that specific video game, obviously they will have a greater advantage against a player who is just starting the game. Usually, video-games tend to increase the difficulty step by step, so the player can adapt to it and doesn't get frustrated too soon or simply bored because the game doesn't offer a challenge. Dynamic game difficulty balancing is used to solve this problem, by creating an interesting experience for each gamer. To balance the AI character using this method, we take into consideration some dynamic game elements that can be adjusted according to player experience; those attributes can be the following:

- Speed
- Health
- Magic
- Power

Usually, we use these attributes to define the difficulty of the AI character, adjusting them to the difficulty desired. Another way to balance the difficulty is by adjusting the quantity of weapons and enemies that the player faces during the game. When adjusting the difficulty, we also need to be careful to not create an enemy that behaves like a rubber band; for example, if the AI car is behind the player, it gets significantly faster in order to keep challenging the player. When the player is behind the opponent car, that car will decrease its speed and this method, if not moderated, can become uninteresting.

In a generic fighting game, developers usually define AI combat like this: if the player is reachable, the AI uses kicks or punches; if not, he goes towards the player. Then the difficulty is adjusted by using percentages and time gaps between attacks.

In an FPS shooter, for example, the game AI is adjusted by taking into consideration the player performance while in the development stage, where the programmers input all the AI stat values and tactics that match the overall performance of the human players. For example, if the shoot rate of the player is about 70%, the AI characters will use that value to stay relatively close to a human performance.

Crash Bandicoot used *Dynamic Game Difficulty Balancing* not directly in the behavior of the AI characters themselves, but rather in the animation speed, making it slower if the player was having difficulty passing the level. This difficulty adjustment takes place according to the players number of deaths. This is a smart and simple way to adjust the difficulty of the AI character, by considering the number of times that the player died trying to beat the game.

Resident Evil 4, released in 2005 by Capcom, based the difficulty adjustment on the same principle but employed a more complex system. The adjustment took into consideration player performance and, without notice, the player was rated by the game from one to ten, where one meant that they were not very successful in the game and ten that they were very skillful. Taking those rates into consideration, enemies would behave differently, being more or less aggressive and taking more or less damage. The rating was constantly updated and many things were taken into consideration to determine how good the player was, such as how many bullets he needed to kill a zombie, how many hits he took, and so on.

Left 4 Dead also took into consideration how well the player was doing, but instead of only increasing the difficulty of the enemies' AI, they decided to change where the enemies would appear, creating a different challenge every time the player decided to play the same level. If the player just started the game, the enemies would appear in easier places; if the player had already passed that level, the enemies would appear in more difficult positions.

To summarize the choices that game developers are making while adjusting the difficulty of character AI, we need to mention that the difficulty not always is meant to be adjusted or to increase or decrease taking into consideration player performance. One great example is simulation games, where it's crucial to meet real-life difficulties and not make them more difficult or easier, otherwise it won't feel like a simulation. Other examples could be games such as Ghosts'n Goblins or, more recently, Dark Souls, where developers explicitly chose to make the game hard from start to finish without changing the AI behavior regarding the difficulty.

Summary

In this chapter, we discovered how to create AI characters that make their own decisions no matter where we place them by using AFSMs. Then we learned how to calculate chance and how to use it in conjunction with the previous techniques to create a character that could calculate a better option for his next step. Using all of the the set techniques, we moved on to how to use utility-based functions to create a human-like character that can behave autonomously. Finally, we talked about different ways of adjusting the values that we input in our characters to make them balanced compared to player performance. In the next chapter, we'll be talking in depth about environment and AI, taking into consideration different genres of video game and different types of AI, how the AI should use the available space on the map to create a challenge for the player, how to interact with the environment, how to use the environment in its favor, and a lot more.

4
Environment and AI

When creating AI for video games, one of the most important aspects is its placement. As we discovered previously, the position of the AI character can completely change his behavior and future decisions. In this chapter, we'll be exploring how the environment of the game can influence our AI and how he should be using it properly, in-depth. This will cover a wide range of game genres with different map structures such as open world, arcade, and racing.

As a player, we like to have a vivid world to explore, with many things to do, and interact with. As a game developer or game designer, that generally means a lot of work because everything that the player is able to interact with has to be carefully planned and executed the right way, to avoid bugs or any other unfortunate distractions from the gameplay. The same goes for the AI characters that we are creating. If we allow the character to interact with the environment, that requires a lot of work, thought, planning, and coding to make it work properly. The number of options available for the player or AI usually equals the number of issues that can occur, so we need to give special attention to the environment while creating our games.

Not every game necessarily has a map or terrain, but perhaps the position where the action is happening at the time still has importance for the gameplay, and the AI should have that in mind. Also, sometimes, the environment or positioning has a subtle impact on the characters of the game that we don't notice while playing the game but, most of the time, those subtle changes contribute to a good and enjoyable experience. That is why the interaction with the environment is an important aspect while creating a video game because it is responsible for giving life to the characters and, without it, they would remain simple 3D or 2D models.

On the other hand, we can't forget the opposite, interaction with the environment by the characters of the game. If our life could be represented in a video game, the impact that we have on the environment should be one of the aspects involved in the game. For example, if we throw a cigarette into a forest, it has a high probability of burning some leaves and causing a fire, leaving all the animals that inhabit that forest with ailments, and the consequences just keep growing. So, it's also interesting to look at how the environment should react according to what is happening in the game. During the game design process, we have the opportunity to choose if that interaction is relevant to the gameplay or if it's only there for visual purposes, but, either way, it certainly contributes to a rich environment that everybody loves. In this chapter, we'll have the opportunity to explore all of the options above in depth and we'll start exploring the basic interactions that don't change the gameplay. We'll finish the chapter with advanced interactions that have a deep impact on the game experience.

Visual interactions

Visual interactions are the basic ones that don't influence the gameplay directly but help to polish our video game and characters, making them part of the environment that we are creating, contributing significantly to the immersion of the player in the game. There are many examples of this subject and we can find them in almost any type of game. This shows us the importance of the environment being part of the game and not merely existing to help fill the screen. It's getting more usual to see these types of interaction in games and players expect them. If there's an object in the game, it should do something, important or not. This makes the environment that we are creating more vibrant and alive, which is definitely a good thing.

We can find one of the first examples of environment interaction in the original *Castlevania*, released in 1986 for the Nintendo Entertainment System. Right from the start, the player can use the whip to destroy the candles and fire pits that originally made up part of the background.

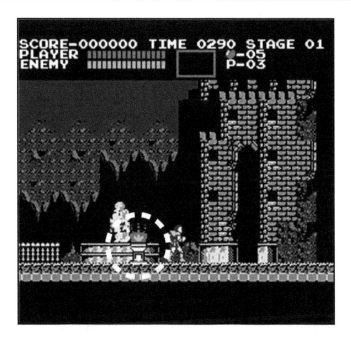

This game and a few others released at the time, opened many doors and possibilities in terms of the perception that we have in relation to the background or environment that surround the characters of the game. Obviously, because of the hardware limitations of this generation of consoles, it was much harder to create simple things that we see as common by today's standards. But every generation of consoles kept bringing more capabilities and creators like us kept using that in our favor to create amazing games.

So, our first example of a visual interaction is the object in the background that can be destroyed without interfering directly with the gameplay. This type of interaction can be seen in multiple games and is as simple as coding an object to animate when it's attacked. Then, we can decide if the object drops some points or collectibles just to reward the player for exploring the game. We'll now move on to our next example, the assets in the game that are animated or which move when the characters pass through them. It's the same principle as the destroyable object but this time, a subtler interaction that requires the character to move near the position where the asset is positioned. This can be applied to different things inside the game, from the grass moving, to dust or water, birds that fly away, or people that perform a funny gesture; there are endless possibilities. When we analyze these interactions, we can easily determine that they don't necessarily have an artificial intelligence behind them, where most of the time, it is just a Boolean function that activates according to some predetermined action. But they make up part of the environment and, for that reason, they needs to be taken into consideration when we want a good integration between environment and AI.

Basic environment interactions

As we saw previously, the environment became part of the video game experience and that sparked many new concepts and ideas for future game titles. The next step was to integrate those slight changes into the gameplay and use them to shape the way characters behave inside the game. This definitely had a positive contribution to video game history, where everything inside the scene started to gain life and the player became aware of those rich surroundings. Using the environment to achieve goals inside the game started to be part of the gameplay experience.

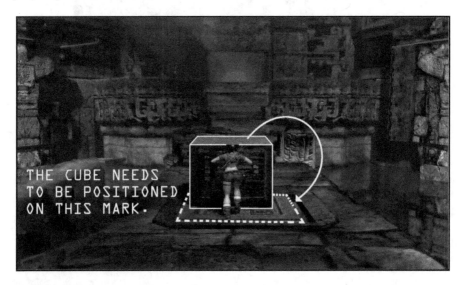

To demonstrate one example of an environment object that directly influences the gameplay, we have the Tomb Raider franchise that showcases this perfectly. In this example, our character, Lara Croft, needs to push the cube until it is positioned on top of the marked area. This will change the environment and unlock a new path that allows the player to move forward in the level. We can find this type of challenge in a number of games where it's necessary to trigger a specific position in the map in order to make something happen in another part, and this can be used to accomplish a specific objective in the game. Usually we need to change the environment as it is, in order to progress on that level. So, when we plan the map or stage, we take those interactions into consideration and then we create all the rules that belong to each interaction. For example:

```
if(cube.transform.position == mark.transform.position)
{
    openDoor = true;
}
```

Now let's imagine for a minute that Lara Croft had an allied character whose main task was to help her put that box in place? And that's exactly one type of interaction that we will be looking at in this chapter, where the AI character understands how the environment works and how to use it.

Moving environment objects

Let's jump right into that scenario and try to recreate the situation where we have an AI character that is able to help our player achieve his goal. For this example, let's assume that our player is trapped in a position where he cannot access the interactive object that releases him from that situation. The character that we'll be creating needs to be able to find the cube and push it toward the desired position.

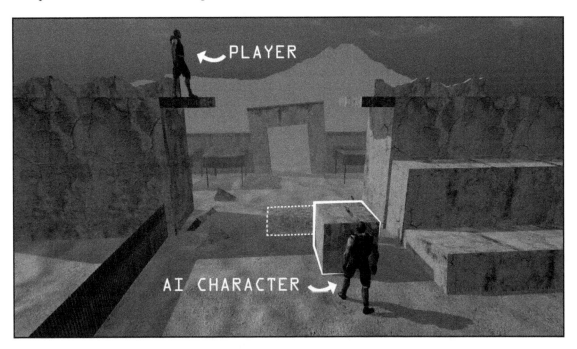

So now that we have all the characters and objects set in our environment example, let's plan how the AI character should behave in this situation. First, he needs to see that the player is near so he can start searching and move the cube to the right position. Let's assume that if the cube is on that mark, a new block will rise from the sand allowing the player to proceed in the level. The AI character can push the cube in four different directions, left, right, front, and back, making sure it aligns perfectly with the position mark.

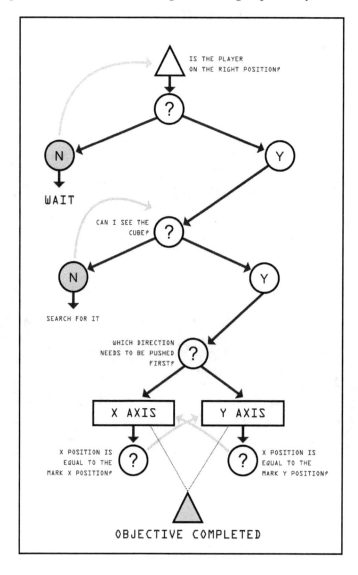

The AI character needs to question and validate every action demonstrated in the behavior tree previously. The first and most important thing in order to proceed with the objective is the character needs to be sure that the player is positioned on his mark. If the player has not arrived yet, our character needs to wait and hold position. If the player has arrived already, the AI character proceeds and asks himself if he is near the cube object or not. If not, our character needs to go toward the cube, and once that action is validated, he will ask the same question again. Once the answer is yes and the character is near the cube, he needs to calculate in which direction the cube needs to be pushed first. Then he will be pushing towards the **Y AXIS** or **X AXIS** until the cube is aligned with the MARK POSITION and the objective gets completed.

```
public GameObject playerMesh;
public Transform playerMark;
public Transform cubeMark;
public Transform currentPlayerPosition;
public Transform currentCubePosition;

public float proximityValueX;
public float proximityValueY;
public float nearValue;

private bool playerOnMark;


void Start () {

}
void Update () {

// Calculates the current position of the player
currentPlayerPosition.transform.position = playerMesh.transform.position;

// Calculates the distance between the player and the player mark of the X
axis
proximityValueX = playerMark.transform.position.x -
currentPlayerPosition.transform.position.x;

// Calculates the distance between the player and the player mark of the Y
axis
proximityValueYplayerMark.transform.position.y -
currentPlayerPosition.transform.position.y;

// Calculates if the player is near of his MARK POSITION
if((proximityValueX + proximityValueY) < nearValue)
{
    playerOnMark = true;
```

```
      }
   }
```

We start adding the information into our code that allows the character to validate if the player is near his marked position. For this, we create all the variables necessary to calculate the distances of the player and the position that he needs to be in. `playerMesh` refers to the 3D model of the player where we'll extract his position and use it as `currentPlayerPosition`. To know if he is near his mark, we need a variable that represents the MARK POSITION and in this example, we created the `playerMark` variable where we can write down the position in which we want our player to be. Then we added three variables that allow us to know if the player is near. `proximityValueX` will calculate the distance between the player and the mark on the X axis. `proximityValueY` will calculate the distance between the player and the mark on the Y axis. Then we have the `nearValue` where we can define how far the player can be from the MARK POSITION so that our AI character can start working on the objective. Once the player is near his mark, the `playerOnMark` Boolean changes to true.

 To calculate the distance between the player and his mark, we used this: Distance between the player and his mark is the same as (mark.position - player.position).

Now, to discover if the AI character is near the cube, we will be doing the same equation, calculating the distance between the AI and the cube. Also, we completed the code, as follows, with the positions of both marks (player and cube mark):

```
public GameObject playerMesh;
public Transform playerMark;
public Transform cubeMark;
public Transform currentPlayerPosition;
public Transform currentCubePosition;

public float proximityValueX;
public float proximityValueY;
public float nearValue;

public float cubeProximityX;
public float cubeProximityY;
public float nearCube;

private bool playerOnMark;
private bool cubeIsNear;

void Start () {
```

```
    Vector3 playerMark = new Vector3(81.2f, 32.6f, -31.3f);
    Vector3 cubeMark = new Vector3(81.9f, -8.3f, -2.94f);
    nearValue = 0.5f;
    nearCube = 0.5f;
}

void Update () {

// Calculates the current position of the player
currentPlayerPosition.transform.position = playerMesh.transform.position;

// Calculates the distance between the player and the player mark of the X
axis
proximityValueX = playerMark.transform.position.x -
currentPlayerPosition.transform.position.x;

// Calculates the distance between the player and the player mark of the Y
axis
proximityValueY = playerMark.transform.position.y -
currentPlayerPosition.transform.position.y;

// Calculates if the player is near of his MARK POSITION
if((proximityValueX + proximityValueY) < nearValue)
{
    playerOnMark = true;
}

cubeProximityX = currentCubePosition.transform.position.x -
this.transform.position.x;
cubeProximityY = currentCubePosition.transform.position.y -
this.transform.position.y;

if((cubeProximityX + cubeProximityY) < nearCube)
{
    cubeIsNear = true;
}

else
{
    cubeIsNear = false;
}
}
```

Now, our AI character knows if he is near the cube or not, this will answer the question and determine if he can proceed to the next branch that we have planned. But what happens when our character is not near the cube? He will need to walk toward the cube. So, we'll add that into our code:

```
public GameObject playerMesh;
public Transform playerMark;
public Transform cubeMark;
public Transform cubeMesh;
public Transform currentPlayerPosition;
public Transform currentCubePosition;

public float proximityValueX;
public float proximityValueY;
public float nearValue;

public float cubeProximityX;
public float cubeProximityY;
public float nearCube;

private bool playerOnMark;
private bool cubeIsNear;

public float speed;
public bool Finding;


void Start () {

  Vector3 playerMark = new Vector3(81.2f, 32.6f, -31.3f);
  Vector3 cubeMark = new Vector3(81.9f, -8.3f, -2.94f);
  nearValue = 0.5f;
  nearCube = 0.5f;
  speed = 1.3f;
}

void Update () {

// Calculates the current position of the player
currentPlayerPosition.transform.position = playerMesh.transform.position;

// Calculates the distance between the player and the player mark of the X
axis
 proximityValueX = playerMark.transform.position.x -
currentPlayerPosition.transform.position.x;

// Calculates the distance between the player and the player mark of the Y
axis
```

```
proximityValueY = playerMark.transform.position.y -
currentPlayerPosition.transform.position.y;

// Calculates if the player is near of his MARK POSITION
if((proximityValueX + proximityValueY) < nearValue)
{
    playerOnMark = true;
}

cubeProximityX = currentCubePosition.transform.position.x -
this.transform.position.x;
cubeProximityY = currentCubePosition.transform.position.y -
this.transform.position.y;

if((cubeProximityX + cubeProximityY) < nearCube)
{
    cubeIsNear = true;
}

else
{
    cubeIsNear = false;
}

if(playerOnMark == true && cubeIsNear == false && Finding == false)
{
    PositionChanging();
}

if(playerOnMark == true && cubeIsNear == true)
{
    Finding = false;
}

}

void PositionChanging () {

Finding = true;
Vector3 positionA = this.transform.position;
Vector3 positionB = cubeMesh.transform.position;
this.transform.position = Vector3.Lerp(positionA, positionB,
Time.deltaTime * speed);
}
```

So far, our AI character is able to calculate the distance between himself and the cube; if they are too far apart, he will go toward the cube. Once this quest is completed, he can move on to the next phase and start pushing the cube. The last thing that he needs to calculate is how far the cube is from the mark position and he then decides which side needs to be pushed first by taking into consideration how far it is from each side.

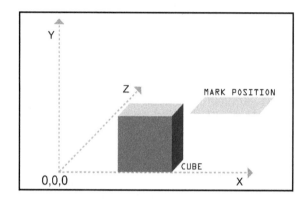

The cube can only be pushed on the **X** axis or **Z** axis and the rotation isn't relevant for now as the button is activated once the cube is on top of it. Taking that into consideration, our character AI needs to calculate how far the cube is from the **X MARK POSITION** and **Z MARK POSITION**. Then he will compare the two different axis values and choose which one is farther away from the desired position and start pushing from that one. The character will push in that direction until the cube is aligned with the marked position and then switch to the other side, and push it until it's completely on top of the **MARK POSITION**:

```
public GameObject playerMesh;
public Transform playerMark;
public Transform cubeMark;
public Transform cubeMesh;
public Transform currentPlayerPosition;
public Transform currentCubePosition;

public float proximityValueX;
public float proximityValueY;
public float nearValue;

public float cubeProximityX;
public float cubeProximityY;
public float nearCube;

public float cubeMarkProximityX;
public float cubeMarkProximityZ;
```

```
private bool playerOnMark;
private bool cubeIsNear;

public float speed;
public bool Finding;


void Start () {

        Vector3 playerMark = new Vector3(81.2f, 32.6f, -31.3f);
        Vector3 cubeMark = new Vector3(81.9f, -8.3f, -2.94f);
        nearValue = 0.5f;
        nearCube = 0.5f;
        speed = 1.3f;
}


void Update () {

// Calculates the current position of the player
currentPlayerPosition.transform.position = playerMesh.transform.position;

// Calculates the distance between the player and the player mark of the X
axis
 proximityValueX = playerMark.transform.position.x -
currentPlayerPosition.transform.position.x;

// Calculates the distance between the player and the player mark of the Y
axis
 proximityValueY = playerMark.transform.position.y -
currentPlayerPosition.transform.position.y;

// Calculates if the player is near of his MARK POSITION
 if((proximityValueX + proximityValueY) < nearValue)
 {
    playerOnMark = true;
 }

 cubeProximityX = currentCubePosition.transform.position.x -
this.transform.position.x;
 cubeProximityY = currentCubePosition.transform.position.y -
this.transform.position.y;

 if((cubeProximityX + cubeProximityY) < nearCube)
 {
    cubeIsNear = true;
 }

 else
```

```
{
    cubeIsNear = false;
}

if(playerOnMark == true && cubeIsNear == false && Finding == false)
{
    PositionChanging();
}

if(playerOnMark == true && cubeIsNear == true)
{
    Finding = false;
}

cubeMarkProximityX = cubeMark.transform.position.x -
currentCubePosition.transform.position.x;
cubeMarkProximityZ = cubeMark.transform.position.z -
currentCubePosition.transform.position.z;

if(cubeMarkProximityX > cubeMarkProximityZ)
{
    PushX();
}

if(cubeMarkProximityX < cubeMarkProximityZ)
{
    PushZ();
}

}

void PositionChanging () {

Finding = true;
Vector3 positionA = this.transform.position;
Vector3 positionB = cubeMesh.transform.position;
this.transform.position = Vector3.Lerp(positionA, positionB,
Time.deltaTime * speed);


}
```

With the final actions added to our code, our AI character should be able to conclude its objective and find and push the cube to the desired position, so the player can proceed and finish the level. In this example, we focused on how to calculate distances between objects of the scene and characters. This will help create similar types of interactions where it's necessary to put an object in the game in a certain position.

The example demonstrates an allied AI character that helps the player, but the same principles could be applied if we wanted the opposite effect (being an enemy) where the character would need to find the cube as fast as possible to stop the player.

Obstructive environment objects

As we saw previously, we can use or move objects in the game to fulfill an objective, but what happens if the character has an object obstructing his way? The object could be placed by the player or simply designed to be in that position of the map and either way, the AI character should be able to determine what to do in that situation.

We can observe this behavior, for example, in a strategy game called *Age of Empires II* developed by Ensemble Studios. Every time the characters of the game can't access the enemy territory because of their surrounded fortified walls, the AI characters focus and start destroying a portion of the wall so they can get in. This type of interaction is very smart and important as well, because otherwise they would just be going around the wall searching for an entry and that wouldn't look intelligent. Because the fortified wall is created by the player, it can be placed anywhere, with any shape or form and for that reason, it is necessary to think about that when developing an AI opponent.

This example is also relevant because, in the planning phase, when we are creating behavior trees, we need to think about what happens if something gets in the way of the character and he can't accomplish his objectives. That will be explored in depth in a future chapter of the book, but for now, we'll simplify this situation and analyze how the AI character should behave if an environment object is interfering with his objective.

In our example, the AI character needs to enter the house but when he arrives near, realizes that it is surrounded by wooden fences and he can't pass through. At that point, we want the character to choose a target and start attacking until that portion of the fence is destroyed so he can find a way to enter the house.

For this example, we'll need to calculate which fence our character needs to attack, taking into consideration the distance and the current health state of the fence. The fence with low HP should have a higher priority to be attacked first compared to a fence that is at full HP, so we'll be including that in our calculation.

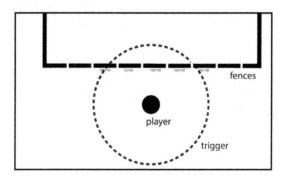

We want to define a circumference around the character where the closest fences give their information to the AI so he can decide which one is the easiest to destroy. This can be done with different methods, either by using collision detection on the fences that get triggered by the player, or having them calculate the distance between fences/objects and the player; we define a distance value where the player perceives the condition of the fence. For this example, we'll be calculating the distance and use it to alert the character about the HP of the fences.

Let's start by creating the code that will be implemented on the `fence` object; all of them will have the same script as follows:

```
public float HP;
public float distanceValue;
private Transform characterPosition;
private GameObject characterMesh;

private float proximityValueX;
private float proximityValueY;
private float nearValue;

// Use this for initialization
void Start () {

HP = 100f;
distanceValue = 1.5f;

// Find the Character Mesh
characterMesh = GameObject.Find("AICharacter");
}

// Update is called once per frame
void Update () {

// Obtain the Character Mesh Position
characterPosition = characterMesh.transform;

//Calculate the distance between this object and the AI Character
proximityValueX = characterPosition.transform.position.x -
this.transform.position.x;
proximityValueY = characterPosition.transform.position.y -
this.transform.position.y;

nearValue = proximityValueX + proximityValueY;
}
```

In this script, we added the basic information about the HP and distances that we'll be using to connect with the AI character. This time, we are adding the script that calculates the distances into the `environment` object instead of the character; this gives more dynamism to the object and allows us to create more things with it. As an example, if the characters of the game are the ones responsible for creating the fences, they will have different states, such as currently building, completed, and damaged; then the character will receive that information and use it to his advantage.

Let's move forward and define our AI character to interact with the `environment` object. His primary objective is to access the house, but when he arrives near, he realizes that he cannot get inside because it's surrounded by the wood fences. After analyzing the situation, we want our character to destroy a fence so he can finally accomplish his objective and get into the house.

In the character script, we'll be adding a `static` function, where the fences can input their information about their current health; this will help the AI character choose a better fence to destroy.

```
public static float fenceHP;
public static float lowerFenceHP;
public static float fencesAnalyzed;
public static GameObject bestFence;

private Transform House;

private float timeWasted;
public float speed;


void Start () {

        fenceHP = 100f;
        lowerFenceHP = fenceHP;
        fencesAnalyzed = 0;
        speed = 0.8;

        Vector3 House = new Vector3(300.2f, 83.3f, -13.3f);

}

void Update () {

        timeWasted += Time.deltaTime;

        if(fenceHP > lowerFenceHP)
```

```
        {
            lowerFenceHP = fenceHP;
        }

        if(timeWasted > 30f)
        {
            GoToFence();
        }
}

void GoToFence() {

        Vector3 positionA = this.transform.position;
        Vector3 positionB = bestFence.transform.position;
        this.transform.position = Vector3.Lerp(positionA, positionB,
Time.deltaTime * speed);
}
```

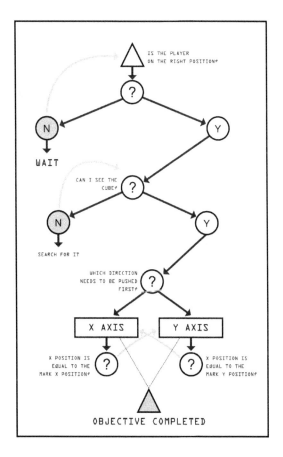

We already added the basic information into our character. `fenceHP` will be the static variable where every fence triggered by the character gives their information about the current HP. Then the AI character analyzes the collected information and compares it with the lowest HP fence that is represented as `lowerFenceHP`. The character has a `timeWasted` variable that represents the number of seconds that he has already spent looking for a good fence to attack. `fencesAnalyzed` will be used to know if there's already a fence in the code, and if not, it will have added the first fence that he finds; in the case of the fences having the same HP value, the character will attack them first. Now let's update our fence code, so they can access the character script and input some useful information.

```
public float HP;
public float distanceValue;
private Transform characterPosition;
private GameObject characterMesh;

private float proximityValueX;
private float proximityValueY;
private float nearValue;
void Start () {

        HP = 100f;
        distanceValue = 1.5f;

        // Find the Character Mesh
        characterMesh = GameObject.Find("AICharacter");
}

void Update () {

        // Obtain the Character Mesh Position
        characterPosition = characterMesh.transform;

        //Calculate the distance between this object and the AI Character
        proximityValueX = characterPosition.transform.position.x -
this.transform.position.x;
        proximityValueY = characterPosition.transform.position.y -
this.transform.position.y;

        nearValue = proximityValueX + proximityValueY;

        if(nearValue <= distanceValue){
            if(AICharacter.fencesAnalyzed == 0){
                AICharacter.fencesAnalyzed = 1;
                AICharacter.bestFence = this.gameObject;
            }

            AICharacter.fenceHP = HP;
```

```
        if(HP < AICharacter.lowerFenceHP){
            AICharacter.bestFence = this.gameObject;
        }
    }
}
```

We finally conclude this example, where the fence compares their current HP with the data that the character has (`lowerFenceHP`) and if their HP is lower than the lowest value that the character has, that fence will be considered the `bestFence`.

This example demonstrates how to adapt the AI character to different dynamic objects of the game; the same principle can be expanded and used to interact with almost any object. It's also relevant and useful to use the objects to interact with the character as well, linking information between the two.

Breaking down the environment by area

When we create a map, often we have two or more different areas that could be used to change the gameplay, areas that could contain water, quicksand, flying zones, caves, and much more. If we wish to create an AI character that can be used in any level of our game, and anywhere, we need to take this into consideration and make the AI aware of the different zones of the map. Usually that means that we need to input more information into the character's behavior, including how to react according to the position in which he is currently placed, or a situation where he can choose where to go.

Should he avoid some areas? Should he prefer others? This type of information is relevant because it makes the character aware of the surroundings, choosing or adapting and taking into consideration his position. Not planning this correctly can lead to some unnatural decisions; for example, in *Elder Scrolls V: Skyrim* developed by Bethesda Softworks studio, we can watch some AI characters of the game simply turning back when they do not have information about how they should behave in some parts of the map, especially on mountains or rivers.

Depending on the zones that our character finds, he might react differently or update his behavior tree to adapt to his environment. We have previously created a soldier that changed the way he would react according to his health, aim success, and player health, and now we are exploring the environment so the character can use it to better define what to do. We could also use this to update one of our previous examples, the real-life simulation. If the Sofie character goes to one specific section of the house, she could use that information to update her priorities and replenish all the necessities that are attached to that portion of the house. Let's say that she was in the kitchen; once she is there, after preparing the breakfast, she takes the opportunity to take out the garbage. As we see, the environment that surrounds our characters can redefine their priorities or completely change their behaviors.

This is a little similar to what Jean-Jacques Rousseau said about humanity: "*We are good by nature, but corrupted by society.*" As humans, we are a representation of the environment that surrounds us, and for that reason, artificial intelligence should follow the same principle.

Let's pick a previous character that we have already created and update his code to work on a different scenario. The chosen one for this example is the soldier and we want to change his behavior according to three different zones, beach, river, and forest. So, we'll create three public static Boolean functions with the names `Beach`, `Forest` and `River`; then we define the zones on the map that will turn them on or off.

```
public static bool Beach;
public static bool River;
public static bool Forest;
```

Because in this example, just one of them can be true at a time, we'll add a simple line of code that disables the other options once one of them gets activated.

```
if(Beach == true)
{
Forest = false;
River = false;
}

if(Forest == true){
Beach = false;
 River = false;
}

if(River == true){
Forest = false;
 Beach = false;
}
```

Once we have that done, we can start defining the different behaviors for each zone. For example, in the beach zone, the characters don't have a place to get cover, so that option needs to be taken away and updated with a new one. The river zone can be used to get across to the other side, so the character can hide from the player and attack from that position. To conclude, we can define the character to be more careful and use the trees to get cover. Depending on the zones, we can change the values to better adapt to the environment, or create new functions that would allow us to use some specific characteristics of that zone.

```
if (Forest == true)
 {// The AI will remain passive until an interaction with the player occurs
 if (Health == 100 && triggerL == false && triggerR == false && triggerM ==
 false)
```

```
    {
    statePassive = true;
    stateAggressive = false;
    stateDefensive = false;
    }

    // The AI will shift to the defensive mode if player comes from the right
    side or if the AI is below 20 HP
    if (Health <= 100 && triggerR == true || Health <= 20)
    {
    statePassive = false;
    stateAggressive = false;
    stateDefensive = true;
    }

    // The AI will shift to the aggressive mode if player comes from the left
    side or it's on the middle and AI is above 20HP
    if (Health > 20 && triggerL == true || Health > 20 && triggerM == true)
    {
    statePassive = false;
    stateAggressive = true;
    stateDefensive = false;
    }

    walk = speed * Time.deltaTime;
    walk = speedBack * Time.deltaTime;
    }
```

This segment will be explored in depth later on when talking about AI Planning and Decision Making, as well as Tactics and Awareness.

Advanced environment interactions

As the video game industry and the technology associated with it kept evolving, new gameplay ideas appeared, and rapidly, interaction between the characters of the game and the environment became even more interesting, especially when using physics. This means that the outcome of the environment could be completely random, where it was required for the AI characters to constantly adapt to different situations. One honorable mention on this subject is the video game *Worms* developed by Team17, where the map can be fully destroyed and the AI characters of the game are able to adapt and maintain smart decisions.

The objective of this game is to destroy the opponent team by killing all their worms, the last man standing wins. From the start, the characters can find some extra health points or ammunition on the map and from time to time, it drops more points from the sky. So, there are two main objectives for the character, namely survive and kill. To survive, he needs to keep a decent amount of HP and away from the enemy, the other part is to choose the best character to shoot and take as much health as possible from him. Meanwhile, the map gets destroyed by the bombs and all of the fire power used by the characters, making it a challenge for artificial intelligence.

Adapting to unstable terrain

Let's decompose this example and create a character that could be used in this game. We'll start by looking at the map. At the bottom, there's water that automatically kills the worms. Then, we have the terrain where the worms can walk, or destroy if needed. Finally, there's the absence of terrain, specifically, the empty space that cannot be walked on. Then we have the characters (worms) they are placed in random positions at the beginning of the game and they can walk, jump, and shoot.

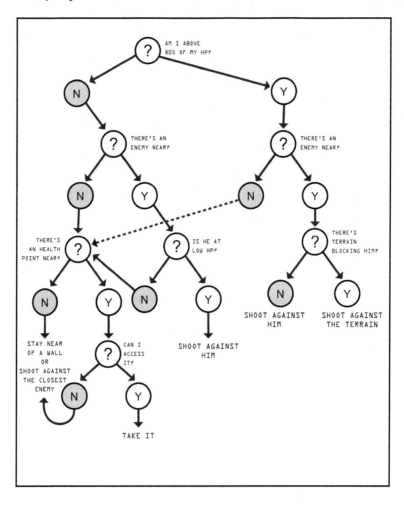

The characters of the game should be able to constantly adapt to the instability of the terrain, so we need to use that and make it part of the behavior tree. As demonstrated in the diagram above, the character will need to understand the position where he is currently placed, as well as the opponent's position, health, and items.

Because the terrain can be blocking them, the AI character has a chance of being in a situation where he cannot attack or obtain an item. So, we give him options on what to do in those situations and many others that he might find, but the most important is to define what happens if he cannot successfully accomplish any of them. Because the terrain can be shaped into different forms, during gameplay there will be times that it is near impossible to do anything, and that is why we need to provide options on what to do in those situations.

For example, in this situation where the worm doesn't have enough free space to move, a close item to pick up, or an enemy that can be properly attacked, what should he do? It's necessary to make information about the surroundings available to our character so he can make a good judgment for that situation. In this scenario, we have defined our character to shoot anyway, against the closest enemy, or to stay close to a wall. Because he is too close to the explosion that would occur from attacking the closest enemy, he should decide to stay in a corner and wait there until the next turn.

Using raycast to evaluate decisions

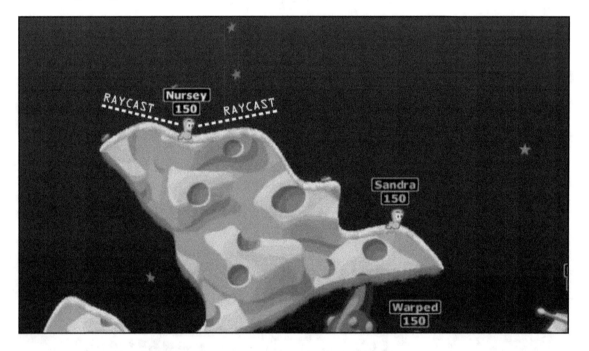

Ideally, at the start of the turn, the character has two raycasts, one for his left side and another for the right side. This will check if there's a wall obstructing one of those directions. This can be used to determine what side the character should be moving toward if he wants to protect himself from being attacked. Then, we would use another **raycast** in the aim direction, to see if there's something blocking the way when the character is preparing to shoot. If there's something in the middle, the character should be calculating the distance between the two to determine if it's still safe to shoot.

So, each character should have a shared list of all of the worms that are currently in the game; that way they can compare the distance between them all and choose which of them are closest and shoot them. Additionally, we add the two raycasts to check if there's something blocking the sides, and we have the basic information to make the character adapt to the constant modifications of the terrain.

```
public int HP;
public int Ammunition;

public static List<GameObject> wormList = new List<GameObject>();
//creates a list with all the worms
public static int wormCount; //Amount of worms in the game
public int ID; //It's used to differentiate the worms

private float proximityValueX;
private float proximityValueY;
private float nearValue;
public float distanceValue; //how far the enemy should be

private bool canAttack;

void Awake ()
{
        wormList.Add(gameObject); //add this worm to the list
        wormCount++; //adds plus 1 to the amount of worms in the game
}

void Start ()
{
        HP = 100;
        distanceValue = 30f;
}

void Update ()
 {
        proximityValueX = wormList[1].transform.position.x -
this.transform.position.x;
        proximityValueY = wormList[1].transform.position.y -
this.transform.position.y;
        nearValue = proximityValueX + proximityValueY;

        if(nearValue <= distanceValue)
        {
            canAttack = true;
        }

        else
```

```
        {
            canAttack = false;
        }

        Vector3 raycastRight =
transform.TransformDirection(Vector3.forward);

        if (Physics.Raycast(transform.position, raycastRight, 10))
            print("There is something blocking the Right side!");

        Vector3 raycastLEft =
transform.TransformDirection(Vector3.forward);

        if (Physics.Raycast(transform.position, raycastRight, -10))
            print("There is something blocking the Left side!");
    }
```

Summary

In this chapter, we explored different ways to interact with the environment. The techniques demonstrated in this chapter can be expanded to a wide range of game genres and used to accomplish basic to advanced interactions between the AI characters and the environment. Now we understand how to create interactive and dynamic objects that can be used by the AI characters, it will make the game a new and different experience every time we play. In addition, have lightly touched on some related topics that will be covered in depth in the next chapters, such as the interaction with other AI characters of the game and decision making.

In our next chapter, we'll be talking about animation behavior. Animations make up part of the visual perception that the player has of the artificially intelligent characters that we create, and it's very important to use that to demonstrate how realistic our AI behaves. We will be discussing animation graphs, gameplay and animation, animation behaviors, and animation architecture.

5
Animation Behaviors

When we think about AI, usually we imagine smart robots, mechanical objects that perfectly perform a vast array of actions, and the same thought happens with video game AI. We tend to think about opponents or allies that act, react, think, or do a lot of things with smart decisions, and that's correct, but one more important aspect is usually left behind, the animations. In order to create believable and realistic AI characters, the animation is one of the most important aspects. Animations define the visual interaction, that is, what it looks like when the character is doing something. It's very important to have the animations working as well as the functional mechanics in order for the character to be believable. In this chapter, we'll be looking at some useful techniques and solutions to use, re-use, and create animations that smoothly fit the characters' behaviors. The way we create and use animations are the same for the player as for the AI characters, but we'll be focusing on how to integrate animations with the techniques that we have already learned about to create AI.

2D animation versus 3D animation

Video game animation can be put into two genres, 2D and 3D animation. Both have distinct features, and we need to take that into consideration and use them to our advantage when developing a game. Let's take a look at some of the main differences between the two.

2D animation - sprites

As soon as consoles and computers allowed developers to integrate animation into the video games that they were making, games became much richer, relying on good-looking visuals to express the movement and actions of the characters. It also opened many doors to create new game genres or update older genres, making them more appealing, and since then, almost every game has started to implement animations.

The process of 2D animation used on video games is similar to what Disney use to use create their movies. They would draw and paint every frame of the movie, and every second would have around 12 frames. Games couldn't use real-life drawings at the time, but they could use coordinates to paint every bit of the game to make it look like a person or an animal if they wanted. The rest of the process is about the same. They needed to use that in order to create every frame of the animation, but because it was a hard and long process, they had a lot less detail and complexity. Now that they have all the frames needed to animate a character, it is necessary to program the machine to read the frames in a specific order, only using the ones that belong to the action that the character is doing.

In the preceding figure, we can see an example of the 8-bit era that shows every animation of the *Super Mario Bros* character called Mario. As we can see, there is the run animation, jump, swim, die, stop, and crouch, some of which are just a single frame. Smooth transitions didn't appear right away, and the animations were combined into the gameplay. So, if we wanted to include more animations in the game, it would be necessary to create more frames. The same goes for the complexity of the animation; if we wanted the animation to include more detail, it would be necessary to create more frames and transitional frames. This makes the process of creating animations very long, but with the evolution of hardware capabilities, this process has started to take less time to implement, and the results are famous.

One example of the 2D animation capabilities on video games is *Prince of Persia*, released in 1989 (the following sprite sheet shows the character's animations in *Prince of Persia*). By using real-world references of a person doing the movements of the game, the quality, detail, and smooth transitions were stupendous, raising the bar even higher for the next generation of games. So at this time, game developers started to worry about transitions, smooth animations, and how to create a lot of actions without it being necessary to add more frames to the sprite sheet:

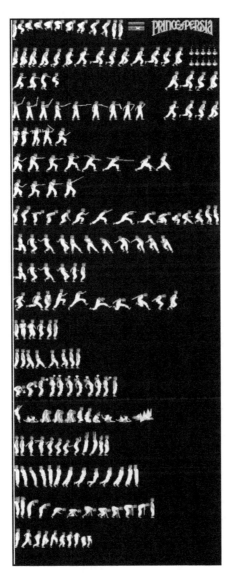

Today, we still use the same process on 2D games, we have a sprite sheet with all the animations that we want, then we code to animate them at the same time the character is performing an action. Working with sprite sheets is not as flexible as working with 3D animations that use bone structures, but there are some useful tips that we can use to create smooth transitions and separate the code animation from the gameplay code.

3D animation - bone structure

Using 3D models and 3D animations to create games is a very popular choice at the moment, and one of the main reasons is related to the time that it takes to create them. We only need to create the 3D model once, and then we can implement a bone structure to animate it as we want. We can also use the same bone structure and skin it to another 3D model and it will get the same animations as the previous one. Using 3D animations is obviously convenient for larger projects, saving hours of hard work and allowing us to update the character without the need to create it all over again. This is due to the bone structure of the character, which helps us improve the quality of the animations, saving time and resources. Because of this, we can decide to animate just one specific area and leave the rest of the body completely still or doing some other animation. It is very useful to smoothly change from one animation to another, or to have two animations playing at the same time:

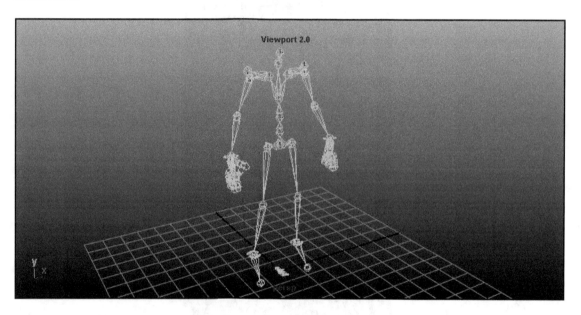

The main differences

Sprite sheets versus bones structure are the two main differences between the two types of animation that will change the way we integrate the animations with the gameplay. Using sprites, we stick to how many images we have available and we cannot change the way they look in the code, whereas with the bone structure, we can define which portion of the character we want to animate and we can use physics to shape the animation according to the situation.

Recently, there are some new options that allow us to implement a similar technique as bone structure in the 2D models, but it's still a very limited option compared to what we can do in 3D.

Animation state machines

We have already talked about behavior states, where we define the possible actions of a character and how to link them. Animation state machines is a very similar process, but instead of defining the actions, we define the animations of a character. While developing the character and creating the behavior states, we could assign the animations in the action code, defining at which point the character starts to run, and once that happens, the walk animation stops and the run animation starts playing. This way of integrating the animations with the gameplay code looks like an easier approach to do it, but it's not the best way and it gets complicated if we want to update the code later on.

The solution to this problem is to create a separate state machine just for the animations. This will allow us to have better control of the animations without worrying about changing our character's code. It is a good method to use between programmer and animator as well, because the animator can add more animations to the animation state machine without interfering with the code:

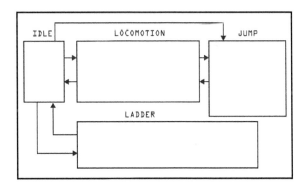

In the preceding diagram, we can see a simple example of a behavior state machine, where the character can stay still, move, jump, and use a ladder. Once we have this part completed, we can start designing and implementing an animation state machine to work according to the behavior state machine principles:

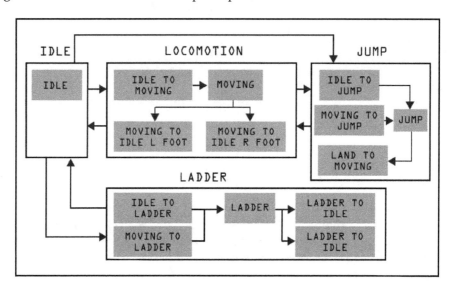

As we can see, there are more animation states than behavior states, which is why the best method to integrate the animations into our characters is to separate the gameplay from the animation. When developing our game, we use statements and values, so the only difference between walk and run is the number that defines how fast our character is moving. That is why we need to use the animation states to convert this information into visual output, where the character is animated according to the gameplay states. Using this method does not necessarily mean that we cannot use the animations to interfere with the gameplay, because we can also do it by simply reporting that information back to our gameplay code and changing the gameplay if we want to.

This can be used both for 2D and 3D animations. The process is exactly the same, and can be used with the most popular game engines, such as CryENGINE, Unity, and Unreal Development Kit. To make it work, we need to import all of the animations into our game and then we assign the animations into the animation state section:

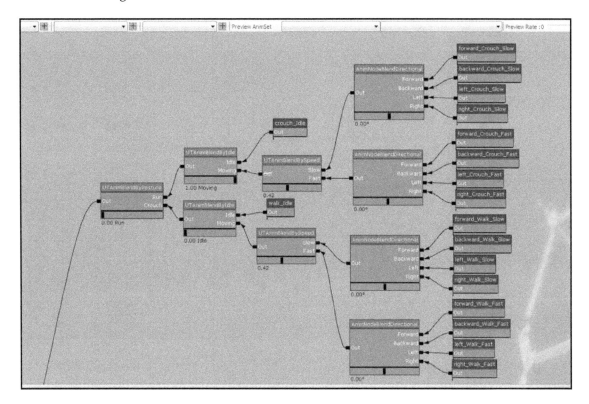

Now that, we have imported the animations into the animation state section, we need to configure when the animations will be played according to the values that we used in our code. The values or statements that we can use are integers, floats, Booleans, and triggers. With these, we can define when each animation will be played. When linking the animations, we'll be using the values to determine when to change from one animation state to another:

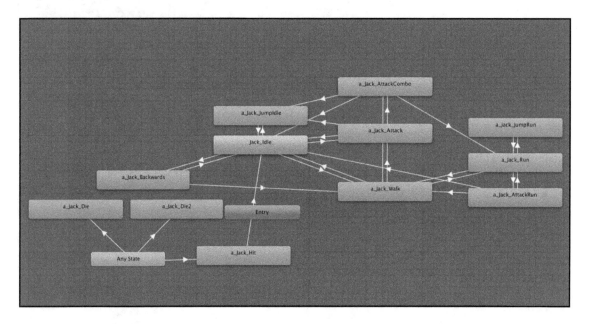

This is where we define the difference between walking and running. If the movement speed of our character reaches a certain value, it will start playing the run animation, and once that value decreases it will play the walk animation again.

We can have as many animations states as we want, regardless of the gameplay states. Let's take a look at the locomotion example. We can define that if the character is moving really slowly, it would animate like he is sneaking; a little bit faster and it starts walking; even faster and the characters starts running; and ultimately, if the movement speed is really high, he can grow a pair of wings to give the impression that he is flying. As we can see, it is more convenient to separate the animations from the gameplay, because that way we can change the animations, remove them, or add new ones, without modifying our code.

Now let's move on to the example. Using all the topics that we have explored in the previous chapters, we'll configure our character to animate according to the gameplay behavior and the environment. We start by importing the model and all the animations into our game. Then we create a new animation state machine; in this case it's called **animator**. After that, we just need to assign that animation state machine to our character:

The model that we import into the game ideally should be in a neutral pose, such as the T-pose (demonstrated on the preceding screenshot). Then we import the animations and add them into the **Animator Controller**.

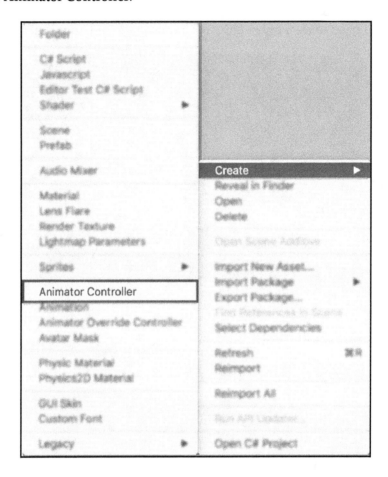

Now, if we click on the **character** and open the animation state machine that we created, it will be empty. That is normal, because we need to manually add the animations that we want to use:

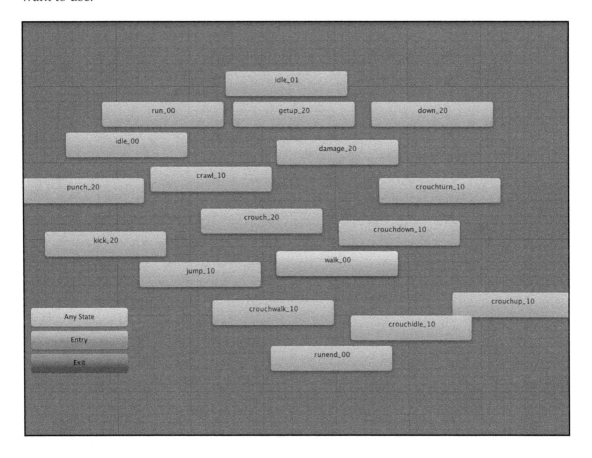

Once we have done this, we'll need to organize everything to make it easy to link the animations:

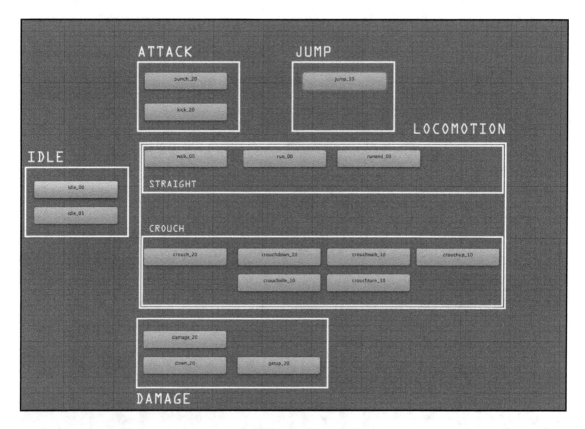

So, we have separated the different animations taking in consideration gameplay states such as **IDLE**, **ATTACK**, **JUMP**, **LOCOMOTION**, and **DAMAGE**, as shown in preceding diagram. We have two distinct animations for the **IDLE** state and another two for **ATTACK**. We want them to play in a random order, and separate from the gameplay code, so we can add as many animations we want there to add more diversity. Inside of the locomotion state, we have two separate groups, walking **STRAIGHT** and **CROUCH**. We have chosen to include both groups in the locomotion state because they will animate according to the position of the movement joystick.

Now, we can start linking the animations, and at this point we can forget about how the animations will be activated and focus only on the play order:

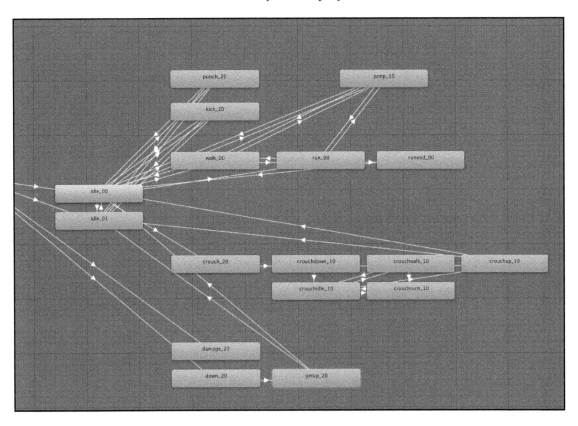

Once we have all the animations linked in the desired order, we can start defining how they will be played. At this point, we need to take a look at the character code and use the variables to change the animations. In our code, we have variables that accesses the animation state machine. In this case, they are the `Animator`, `Health` and `Stamina` integer values, `movementSpeed`, `rotationSpeed`, `maxSpeed`, `jumpHeight`, `jumpSpeed` and `currentSpeed` as float values, and finally a Boolean variable to check whether the player is alive:

```
public Animator characterAnimator;
public.int Health;
public int Stamina;
public float movementSpeed;
public float rotationSpeed;
public float maxSpeed;
public float jumpHeight;
```

```
public float jumpSpeed;

private float currentSpeed;
private bool Dead;

void Start () {

}

void Update () {

    // USING XBOX CONTROLLER
    transform.Rotate(0,Time.deltaTime * (rotationSpeed *
    Input.GetAxis ("xboxlefth")), 0);

    if(Input.GetAxis ("xboxleft") > 0){
        transform.position += transform.forward * Time.deltaTime *
        currentSpeed;
        currentSpeed = Time.deltaTime * (Input.GetAxis
        ("xboxleft") * movementSpeed);
    }

    else{
        transform.position += transform.forward * Time.deltaTime *
        currentSpeed;
        currentSpeed = Time.deltaTime * (Input.GetAxis
        ("xboxleft") * movementSpeed/3);
    }

    if(Input.GetKeyDown("joystick button 18") && Dead == false)
    {

    }

    if(Input.GetKeyUp("joystick button 18") && Dead == false)
    {

    }

    if(Input.GetKeyDown("joystick button 16") && Dead == false)
    {

    }

    if(Input.GetKeyUp("joystick button 16") && Dead == false)
    {

    }
```

```
        if(Health <= 0){
            Dead = true;
        }
    }
```

Let's start passing these values into the animation state machine. The movement and the `currentSpeed` value of the character are controlled by the left analog joystick, so if we push the joystick just a little bit, the character should play the walk animation. If we push it all the way it should play the run animation.

In the `Animator` section, we can choose between four parameters, and for the locomotion of the character we have chosen **Float**. We now need to link this value with the `currentSpeed` variable that we have in our code. We will assign this at the beginning of the `Update` function:

```
public Animator characterAnimator;
public int Health;
public int Stamina;
public float movementSpeed;
public float rotationSpeed;
public float maxSpeed;
public float jumpHeight;
public float jumpSpeed;

private float currentSpeed;
private bool Dead;

void Start () {

}

void Update () {

    // Sets the movement speed of the animator, to change from
    idle to walk and walk to run
    characterAnimator.SetFloat("currentSpeed",currentSpeed);

    // USING XBOX CONTROLLER
    transform.Rotate(0,Time.deltaTime * (rotationSpeed *
```

```
        Input.GetAxis ("xboxlefth")), 0);

        if(Input.GetAxis ("xboxleft") > 0){
            transform.position += transform.forward * Time.deltaTime *
            currentSpeed;
            currentSpeed = Time.deltaTime * (Input.GetAxis
            ("xboxleft") * movementSpeed);
        }

        else{
            transform.position += transform.forward * Time.deltaTime *
            currentSpeed;
            currentSpeed = Time.deltaTime * (Input.GetAxis
            ("xboxleft") * movementSpeed/3);
        }

        if(Input.GetKeyDown("joystick button 18") && Dead == false)
        {

        }

        if(Input.GetKeyUp("joystick button 18") && Dead == false)
        {

        }

        if(Input.GetKeyDown("joystick button 16") && Dead == false)
        {

        }

        if(Input.GetKeyUp("joystick button 16") && Dead == false)
        {

        }

        if(Health <= 0){
            Dead = true;
        }
    }
```

We've already connected the two parameters. This way, the animation state machine can use the same value of the currentSpeed found in the code. We gave it exactly the same name in the Animator section that we have in the code. It's not necessary, but it makes it easier to understand which values they represent.

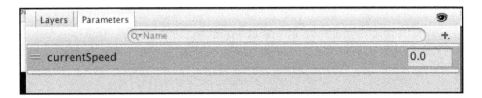

So at this point, we can start defining the values of the links that connect the locomotion animations of the character. In this case, we can click on the link and a new window will open so we can add the values that will change the animations from one state to another:

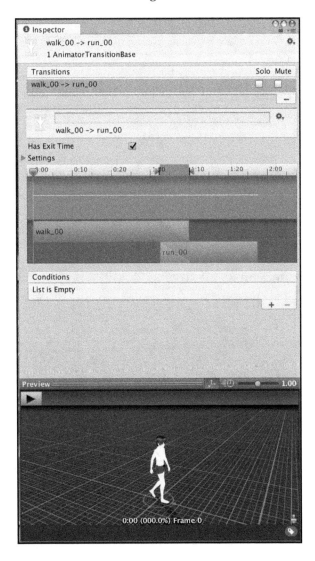

We can also click on the animation that we want to configure, such as the IDLE animation, and then a new window opens with all the animations connected to this one. We can select the link that we want to allow the next animation to play. This is demonstrated in the following screenshot:

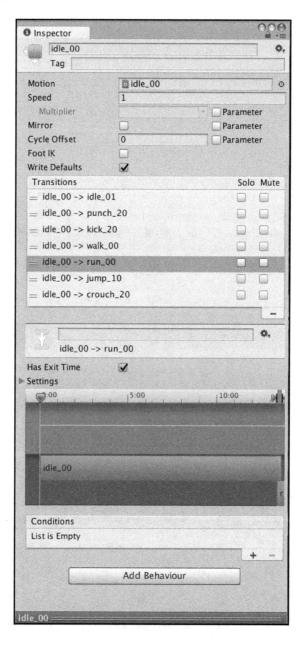

We have clicked on **idle** to **walk** and added the condition that we previously created, **currentSpeed**:

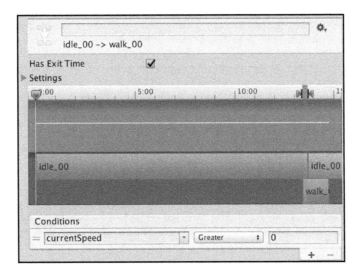

Here, we can choose if the value needs to be **Greater** or **Less** than the desired value that will start playing the next animation. For this example, we have set the value to be greater than **0.1**, so as soon as the character starts moving, it will stop the IDLE animation and play the WALK animation. We don't need to write anything inside the code because the animation state machine acts independently to the code:

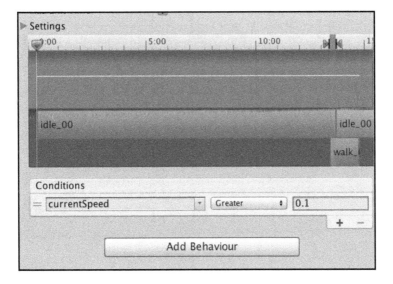

However, because we have another animation playing after the WALK animation, we need to set a limit value for the WALK animation. In this case, let's assume that our character starts running when the currentSpeed is at **5**; this means that our character stops walking at **4.9**. So, we are going to add another condition here that tells to our character that he stops walking once his currentSpeed reaches **4.9**:

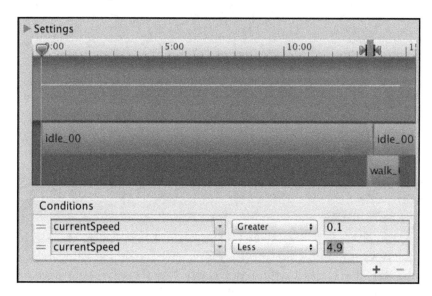

Now that we have defined when the character starts walking, we also need to do the inverse, to define when it's time to stop walking and play the IDLE animation. We need to remember that this does not affect the gameplay, so it means that if we start the game at this point, the character will start playing the WALK animation because we have already set that to happen. But even if we hadn't, the character would move in the environment even without the animation. We are simply using the values that are stored in our code to connect with the animation states, and we need to define what animation will be played at a certain value. If we forget to set that value to all animations, the character will still perform the behavior, but without the correct animation. So with that said, we need to check if all the links have conditions assigned to them.

Now to make the character go back to the IDLE animation once he stops moving, we click on the link that goes from the WALK to IDLE, and we add a new condition that expresses if the currentSpeed is Less than 0.1, he stops playing the WALK animation and starts playing the IDLE animation:

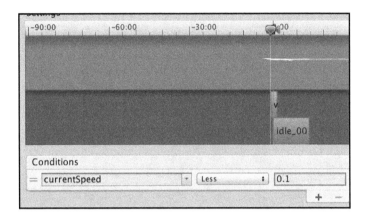

Now we can do this for the rest of the animations that use the currentSpeed value and finish the Locomotion states. Once we have all of that ready, we can move on to the **Crouch** animations. They use the **currentSpeed** value as well, but we need to have an additional value that invalidates the WALK animation and enables the **Crouch** animation. There are two ways of doing this: by pressing a **Crouch** button at the same time that we move forward, or to define zones on the map where the character goes directly to CROUCH mode. For this example, and because we are working on an AI character, we'll be using the second option and define zones on the map that will make the character enter CROUCH mode:

In this example, let's assume that the character shouldn't be walking on the grass, and for that reason he tries to hide by crouching. We could also choose a small location that is impossible to enter if he was walking upright, and for that reason the character automatically starts to walk in the crouch position.

So, to do this we need to create trigger positions on our map that change the animations according to the position that the character is currently in. In the code, we create a new Boolean variable and call it `steppingGrass`, right after the line where we connect the `currentSpeed` value with the animation state machine. We are going to add a new line that connects this Boolean to a new parameter that we are going to create on the animation state machine as well. We can start by creating the new parameter:

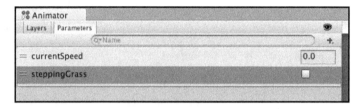

In our code, we are going to add collision detection that will turn on this value once our character is on the grass, and turn it off soon as he leaves that area:

```
public Animator characterAnimator;
public int Health;
public int Stamina;
public float movementSpeed;
public float rotationSpeed;
public float maxSpeed;
public float jumpHeight;
public float jumpSpeed;

private float currentSpeed;
private bool Dead;
private bool steppingGrass;

void Start () {

}

void Update () {

    // Sets the movement speed of the animator, to change from
    // idle to walk and walk to run
    characterAnimator.SetFloat ("currentSpeed", currentSpeed);
```

```
    // Sets the stepping grass Boolean to the animator value
    characterAnimator.SetBool("steppingGrass",steppingGrass);

    // USING XBOX CONTROLLER
    transform.Rotate(0,Time.deltaTime * (rotationSpeed *
    Input.GetAxis ("xboxlefth")), 0);

    if(Input.GetAxis ("xboxleft") > 0){
        transform.position += transform.forward * Time.deltaTime *
    currentSpeed;
        currentSpeed = Time.deltaTime * (Input.GetAxis
    ("xboxleft") * movementSpeed);
    }

    else{
        transform.position += transform.forward * Time.deltaTime *
        currentSpeed;
        currentSpeed = Time.deltaTime * (Input.GetAxis
        ("xboxleft") * movementSpeed/3);
    }

    if(Input.GetKeyDown("joystick button 18") && Dead == false)
    {

    }

    if(Input.GetKeyUp("joystick button 18") && Dead == false)
    {

    }

    if(Input.GetKeyDown("joystick button 16") && Dead == false)
    {

    }

    if(Input.GetKeyUp("joystick button 16") && Dead == false)
    {

    }

    if(Health <= 0){
        Dead = true;
    }
}

void OnTriggerEnter(Collider other) {
```

```
        if(other.gameObject.tag == "Grass")
        {
            steppingGrass = true;
        }
    }

    void OnTriggerExit(Collider other) {

        if(other.gameObject.tag == "Grass")
        {
            steppingGrass = false;
        }
    }
}
```

Now, we can proceed and add this new parameter to the CROUCH animations. We start by choosing the link between the IDLE to CROUCH animation and set the `currentSpeed` value and the new `steppingGrass` parameter. Because we have a **Crouch Idle** animation, even if the character is not moving, it will play that animation instead of the normal IDLE animation:

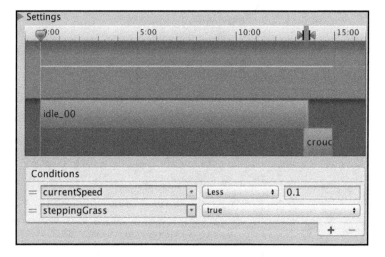

We have set the `currentSpeed` to be less than 0.1, which means that the character is not moving, and the `steppingGrass` set to **true**, which stops the normal IDLE animation and starts playing the **Crouch Idle** animation. The rest of the CROUCH animations follow the same principles as the WALK and RUN animation. Once the character starts to move, that represents the `currentSpeed` value, the **Crouch Idle** stops and the Crouch Walk plays. At the end, we link **Crouch Idle** to IDLE and Crouch Walk to WALK, making sure that if the character is walking away from the grass, the WALK animation doesn't stop and the character keeps walking upright.

Regarding the attacks, we will be using integers to randomize a number between 1 to 10, and if the number is higher than 5 it will play the KICK animation. If the number is below 5 it will play the PUNCH animation. So, when the character enters fight mode against an opponent, it will play different attacks. Once again, using this method allows us to add more animations in the future, increasing the diversity of attacks.

Once again, we create a new parameter, and for this example we are going to create an integer parameter and call it `attackRandomNumber`:

In our code, we are going to add a new variable and give it the same name (it is not necessary to create it with the same name, but it does make everything organized). Right after the lines with which we previously connected the variables with the animation state machine parameters, we are going to create a new one that connects to the `attackRandomNumber` value. Then we create a function that randomizes a number once the character enters fight mode:

```
public Animator characterAnimator;
public int Health;
public int Stamina;
public float movementSpeed;
public float rotationSpeed;
public float maxSpeed;
public float jumpHeight;
public float jumpSpeed;

private float currentSpeed;
private bool Dead;
private bool steppingGrass;
private int attackRandomNumber;

void Start () {

}

void Update () {

    // Sets the movement speed of the animator, to change from
    idle to walk and walk to run
    characterAnimator.SetFloat("currentSpeed",currentSpeed);
```

```
// Sets the stepping grass Boolean to the animator value
characterAnimator.SetBool("steppingGrass",steppingGrass);

// Sets the attackrandomnumber to the animator value
characterAnimator.SetInteger("attackRandomNumber",
    attackRandomNumber);

// USING XBOX CONTROLLER
transform.Rotate(0,Time.deltaTime * (rotationSpeed *
Input.GetAxis ("xboxlefth")), 0);

if(Input.GetAxis ("xboxleft") > 0){
    transform.position += transform.forward * Time.deltaTime *
currentSpeed;
    currentSpeed = Time.deltaTime * (Input.GetAxis
("xboxleft") * movementSpeed);
}

else{
    transform.position += transform.forward * Time.deltaTime *
currentSpeed;
    currentSpeed = Time.deltaTime * (Input.GetAxis
("xboxleft") * movementSpeed/3);
}

if(Input.GetKeyDown("joystick button 18") && Dead == false)
{
    fightMode();
}

if(Input.GetKeyUp("joystick button 18") && Dead == false)
{

}

if(Input.GetKeyDown("joystick button 16") && Dead == false)
{

}

if(Input.GetKeyUp("joystick button 16") && Dead == false)
{

}

if(Health <= 0){
    Dead = true;
}
```

```
    }

    void OnTriggerEnter(Collider other) {

        if(other.gameObject.tag == "Grass")
        {
            steppingGrass = true;
        }
    }

    void OnTriggerExit(Collider other) {

        if(other.gameObject.tag == "Grass")
        {
            steppingGrass = false;
        }
    }

    void fightMode ()
    {
        attackRandomNumber = (Random.Range(1, 10));
    }
```

After doing this, we need to assign the values to the animations. The process is the same as the previous animations, only this time we are using a different value. If `attackRandomNumber` is higher than 1, it means that he is attacking, and the attack animations should start playing. Because we have two different attacks, we decided to use them randomly, but if it was a player controlling the character, we could manually assign the number inside the code, and when the player pressed a specific button on the gamepad, the character would punch or kick.

Smooth transitions

Another important aspect that is worth mentioning is the smooth transition between animations. It is very important to maintain the integrity of the animations, so that every action performed by the character looks fluid, helping the virtual immersion of the player.

On this subject, 2D and 3D animations have considerable differences. If we are using 2D sprites, we need to draw the necessary frames that will be used for every transition, and every time we want the character to change from one animation to another, the transition animation will be played.

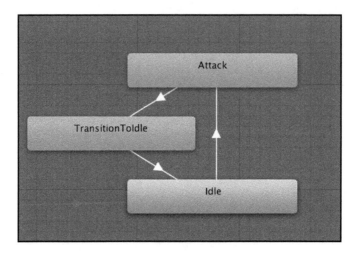

On the other hand, with 3D characters we can use the bone structure to create the transitions automatically, where the coordinates for each bone will move from the previous animation to the new one. Even if we choose to use the bone structure to help create the transitions, sometimes it might be necessary, or it would be a better option, to manually create new animations that will be used as transitions. This is a common process if the character is using an object or weapon that needs to be saved before playing the next animation.

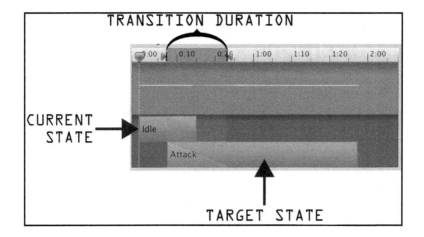

To create a smooth transition, we need the first frame of the next animation to be equal to the last frame of the current animation. We need to start the next animation from the same position of the current one. This is crucial to avoid noticing any cut in between the transition. Then we can use the game engine to our advantage and use the transition system for the animations. This will help to create a smoother transition. As we can see on the image above, we can adjust how long the transition will take, we can make a quick transition or a longer one, always experimenting with what looks better for the results that we want.

Sometimes we would need to sacrifice a smoother transition in order to have a better gameplay experience. One example of this is during a fighting game, where it's more important to have quick transitions rather than smooth ones, and for that reason we need to take in consideration the time that it takes for the character to change from one state to another.

Summary

This chapter has described how to use 2D or 3D animations to complement the actions of a character. Animations play an important part in the development of a believable AI character, and by using them correctly, the character can transmit to the player a real sensation that the character is alive and that they react autonomously. Even if the character has limited actions, we can use animations to fake or hide some of them, giving the impression that it is reacting that way because it thinks for itself.

In the next chapter, we'll be talking about navigation behavior and pathfinding, that is how to program the AI character to walk towards the desired position and choose the best route.

6
Navigation Behavior and Pathfinding

In this chapter, we'll be explaining in detail how the AI character moves around and understands where he can go and where he cannot. For different types of games, there are different solutions and we'll be addressing those solutions in this chapter, exploring common methods that can be used to develop a character that can move correctly on the map. Also we want our character to calculate the best trajectory to arrive at a certain destination, avoiding obstacles and accomplishing goals while doing it. We will introduce how to create a simple navigation behavior, then we will move on to a point to point movement and finally explore in depth how to create a more complex point to point movement (RTS/RPG system).

Navigation behavior

When we talk about navigation behavior, we are referring to the actions of a character that is confronted with a situation where they need to calculate where to go or what to do. A map can have many points where it is necessary to jump or climb stairs in order to arrive at the final destination. The character should know how to use these actions to keep moving correctly; otherwise, he will fall down a hole or keep walking into a wall where he should be climbing some stairs. To avoid that, we need to plan all of the possibilities available for the character while he is moving, making sure that he can jump or perform any other movement necessary to keep moving into the right direction.

Choosing a new direction

One important aspect that the AI character should have is choosing a new direction when he is confronted by an object that is blocking his way and that he cannot pass through. The character should be aware of the objects that are in front of him and, if he cannot keep moving forward in that direction, he should be able to choose a new direction, avoid colliding against the object and keep walking away from it.

Avoid walking against walls

If our character is facing a wall, he will need to know that he cannot pass through that wall and should choose another option. Unless we allow the character to climb the wall or destroy it, the character will need to face a new direction that is not blocked and walk in that new unblocked direction.

We will start with a simple approach that i can be often very useful, and is perhaps the best option, depending on the type of game that we are creating. In the example that we'll be demonstrating, the character in question needs to keep moving around the level just like the *Pac-Man* enemies. Starting with a basic example, we give our character the freedom to choose which direction to move in, and later on we will add more information to our character's AI so he can pursue a specific objective on the map using this method.

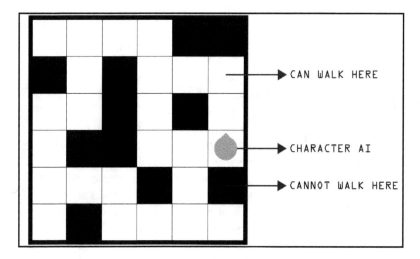

We have created a grid and painted in black the squares where the character AI is not allowed to walk. Now we are going to program our character to move forward until he finds a black square in front of him; then, he will need to choose to turn right or left, making that decision randomly. This will allow our character to move freely on the map without any specific pattern. The code for this is as follows:

```
public float Speed;
public float facingLeft;
public float facingRight;
public float facingBack;
public static bool availableLeft;
public static bool availableRight;

public bool aLeft;
public bool aRight;

void Start ()
{

}

void Update ()
{

    aLeft = availableLeft;
    aRight = availableRight;

    transform.Translate(Vector2.up * Time.deltaTime * Speed);

    if(facingLeft > 270)
    {
        facingLeft = 0;
    }

    if(facingRight < -270)
    {
        facingRight = 0;
    }

}

void OnTriggerEnter2D(Collider2D other)
{

    if(other.gameObject.tag == "BlackCube")
    {
        if(availableLeft == true && availableRight == false)
```

```
            {
                turnLeft();
            }

            if(availableRight == true && availableLeft == false)
            {
                turnRight();
            }

            if(availableRight == true && availableLeft == true)
            {
                turnRight();
            }

            if(availableRight == false && availableLeft == false)
            {
                turnBack();
            }
        }
    }

    void turnLeft ()
    {
        facingLeft = transform.rotation.eulerAngles.z + 90;
        transform.localRotation = Quaternion.Euler(0, 0, facingLeft);
    }

    void turnRight ()
    {
        facingRight = transform.rotation.eulerAngles.z - 90;
        transform.localRotation = Quaternion.Euler(0, 0, facingRight);
    }

    void turnBack ()
    {
        facingBack = transform.rotation.eulerAngles.z + 180;
        transform.localRotation = Quaternion.Euler(0, 0, facingBack);
    }
```

For this example, we added colliders to the black squares to let the character know when he is touching them. This way, he will keep moving until colliding with a black square, and at that point there will be three options: turn left, turn right, or go back. To know which directions are unblocked, we created two separate colliders and added them to our character. Each collider has a script that gives the information to the character to let it know whether that side is free or not.

The `availableLeft` Boolean corresponds to the left side, and `availableRight` corresponds to the right side. If the left or right collider is in contact with the black square, the value is set to `false`. Otherwise, it is set to `true`. We are using `aLeft` and `aRight` simply to check in real time if the values are working correctly. This way, we can see whether there are any issues:

```
public bool leftSide;
public bool rightSide;

void Start ()
{
    if(leftSide == true)
    {
        rightSide = false;
    }

    if(rightSide == true)
    {
        leftSide = false;
    }
}
void Update () {
}

 void OnTriggerStay2D(Collider2D other)
 {

    if(other.gameObject.tag == "BlackCube")
    {
        if(leftSide == true && rightSide == false)
        {
            Character.availableLeft = false;
        }

        if(rightSide == true && leftSide == false)
        {
            Character.availableRight = false;
        }
    }
 }

 void OnTriggerExit2D(Collider2D other)
 {

    if(other.gameObject.tag == "BlackCube")
    {
        if(leftSide == true)
```

```
        {
            Character.availableLeft = true;
        }

        if(rightSide == true)
        {
            Character.availableRight = true;
        }
    }
}
```

When we start the game, we can see that the character AI starts moving around on the white tiles and turning left or right every time he faces a black tile:

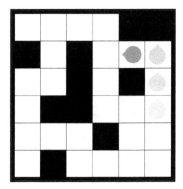

But if we let the game run for a couple of minutes, we realize that the character keeps making the same decisions, and for that reason he will just be walking around a small portion of the map. This is due to the fact that he only makes a decision when colliding with a black tile, ignoring the other opportunities to turn:

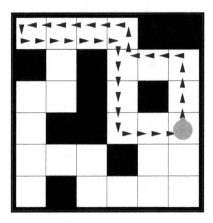

As we can see in the preceding image, the character always follows the same pattern, not an ideal situation if we want him to constantly choose different paths.

Choosing an alternative path

Our character successfully chooses a new direction every time that he approaches a wall, and now we want him to be able to move around all over the map. To make that happen, we are going to add more information into the character to let him know that if there's an available option to turn to the left or right, even if the forward path is free, the character is free to turn. We can use probabilities to determine whether the character is going to turn or not, and for this example we have chosen to give a 90% chance of choosing a new direction if one is available. That way, we can see the results happening very quickly:

```
public float Speed;
public float facingLeft;
public float facingRight;
public float facingBack;
public static bool availableLeft;
public static bool availableRight;

public static int probabilityTurnLeft;
public static int probabilityTurnRight;public int probabilitySides;

public bool forwardBlocked;

public bool aLeft;
public bool aRight;
```

After adding the variables we can move on to the `Start` method, everything that will be called on the first frame of the game.

```
void Start ()
{
    availableLeft = false;
    availableRight = false;
    probabilityTurnLeft = 0;
    probabilityTurnRight = 0;
}
```

Then we can move on the the `Update` method, everything that will be called every frame of the game.

```
void Update ()
{
    aLeft = availableLeft;
    aRight = availableRight;

    transform.Translate(Vector2.up * Time.deltaTime * Speed);

    if(facingLeft > 270)
    {
        facingLeft = 0;
    }

    if(facingRight < -270)
    {
        facingRight = 0;
    }

    if (forwardBlocked == false)
    {
        if (availableLeft == true && availableRight == false)
        {
            if (probabilityTurnLeft > 10)
            {
                turnLeft();
            }
        }

        if (availableLeft == false && availableRight == true)
        {
            if (probabilityTurnRight > 10)
            {
                turnRight();
            }
        }

        if (availableLeft == true && availableRight == true)
        {
            probabilityTurnLeft = 0;
            probabilityTurnRight = 0;
        }
    }

}
```

Here we add the trigger functions, what happens when he enters/collides against a 2D object:

```
void OnTriggerEnter2D(Collider2D other)
{

    if(other.gameObject.tag == "BlackCube")
    {
        forwardBlocked = true;

        if(availableLeft == true && availableRight == false)
        {
            turnLeft();
        }

        if(availableRight == true && availableLeft == false)
        {
            turnRight();
        }

        if(availableRight == true && availableLeft == true)
        {
            probabilitySides = Random.Range(0, 1);
            if(probabilitySides == 0)
            {
                turnLeft();
            }

            if(probabilitySides == 1)
            {
                turnRight();
            }

        }

        if(availableRight == false && availableLeft == false)
        {
            turnBack();
        }
    }
}

void OnTriggerExit2D(Collider2D other)
{
    forwardBlocked = false;
}
```

```
void  turnLeft ()
{
    probabilityTurnLeft = 0;
    facingLeft = transform.rotation.eulerAngles.z + 90;
    transform.localRotation = Quaternion.Euler(0, 0, facingLeft);
}

void turnRight ()
{
    probabilityTurnRight = 0;
    facingRight = transform.rotation.eulerAngles.z - 90;
    transform.localRotation = Quaternion.Euler(0, 0, facingRight);
}

void turnBack ()
{
    facingBack = transform.rotation.eulerAngles.z + 180;
    transform.localRotation = Quaternion.Euler(0, 0, facingBack);
}
```

We have added four new variables to our character AI script, the `probabilityTurnLeft` static variable, which calculates the probability of the character turning left; `probabilityTurnRight`, which calculates the probability of the character turning right; a new probability generator, `probabilitySides`, which will decide which way to turn when both are available and the forward path is blocked; and finally, a Boolean, `forwardBlocked`, to check whether the forward path is blocked or not. The character needs to check whether the forward path is blocked to know if he can turn or not. This will prevent the character from turning more than once when he is facing a black tile.

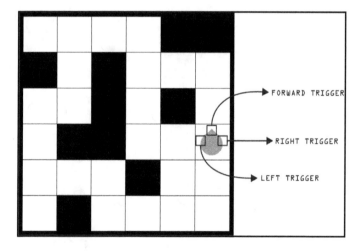

In the script that controls the side triggers, we added a new variable called
`probabilityTurn`, which gives the character information about the probabilities. Every
time the trigger exits the collider, he calculates the probability and sends a message to the
character telling it that the side is free and he can make the decision to turn to that side:

```
public bool leftSide;
public bool rightSide;
public int probabilityTurn;

void Start ()
{
    if(leftSide == true)
    {
        rightSide = false;
    }

    if(rightSide == true)
    {
        leftSide = false;
    }
}

void Update ()
{

}

void OnTriggerEnter2D(Collider2D other)
{
    if(other.gameObject.tag == "BlackCube")
    {
        if(leftSide == true && rightSide == false)
        {
            Character.availableLeft = false;
            probabilityTurn = 0;
            Character.probabilityTurnLeft = probabilityTurn;
        }

        if(rightSide == true && leftSide == false)
        {
            Character.availableRight = false;
            probabilityTurn = 0;
            Character.probabilityTurnRight = probabilityTurn;
        }
    }
}
```

```
void OnTriggerStay2D(Collider2D other)
{

    if(other.gameObject.tag == "BlackCube")
    {
        if(leftSide == true && rightSide == false)
        {
            Character.availableLeft = false;
            probabilityTurn = 0;
            Character.probabilityTurnLeft = probabilityTurn;
        }

        if(rightSide == true && leftSide == false)
        {
            Character.availableRight = false;
            probabilityTurn = 0;
            Character.probabilityTurnRight = probabilityTurn;
        }
    }
}

void OnTriggerExit2D(Collider2D other)
{

    if(other.gameObject.tag == "BlackCube")
    {
        if(leftSide == true)
        {
            probabilityTurn = Random.Range(0, 100);
            Character.probabilityTurnLeft = probabilityTurn;
            Character.availableLeft = true;
        }

        if(rightSide == true)
        {
            probabilityTurn = Random.Range(0, 100);
            Character.probabilityTurnRight = probabilityTurn;
            Character.availableRight = true;
        }
    }
}
```

If we play the game, we can see the new changes implemented to the character. Now he is unpredictable, choosing different paths every time and moving all around the map, contrary to what we had before. Once this is completed, we can create as many maps as we wish because the character will always find the right path and avoid colliding with the walls.

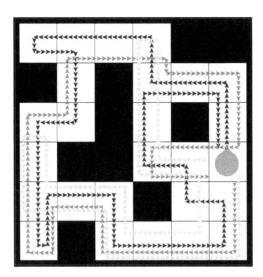

Testing on a bigger map, the character reacts the same way, moving around the whole map. This means that our main objective has been completed and now we can easily create new maps and use the character as the main enemy of the game so that he will always move differently and does not follow any pattern.

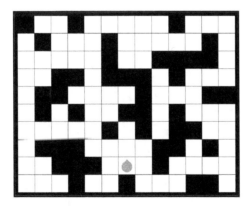

We can adjust the percentage values according to the way we want the character to react, and also implement more variables to make it unique to our game idea.

Point to point movement

Now that we understand the basics of how to create a character that can move freely in a maze genre game, we will take a look at the opposite: how to create a movement pattern from point to point. This is also an important aspect of AI movement, because later on we can combine both techniques to create a character that goes from one point to another, avoiding walls and obstacles.

Tower defense genre

Once again, the principle that we will be using to make our character move from one point to another can be applied to both 2D and 3D games. In this example, we'll explore how to create the main characteristic of a Tower Defense game: the enemy pattern. The objective is to have the enemies spawning at a start point and following a path so they can reach the final point. The enemies in a tower defense game usually just have this in mind, so it is a perfect example to test how to create point to point movement.

A *Tower Defense* game usually consists of two areas: the area where the enemies walk from their start position to the final position, and the area where the player is allowed to build towers that attack the enemies, trying to stop them reaching the final position. Because the player is not allowed to build anything inside the path where the enemies will pass, the AI does not need to be aware of its surroundings because it will always be free to pass through, and because of that we only need to focus on the point to point movement of the characters.

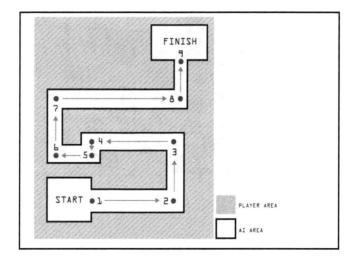

After importing the map and characters that we'll be using in the game, we need to configure the **waypoints** that will be used by the character so they know where they need to go. We can do this by manually adding the coordinates into our code, but to simplify the process we'll create objects in the scene that will serve as waypoints and we delete the 3D mesh because it won't be necessary.

Now we group all the waypoints that we have created and name the group waypoints. Once we have the waypoints in place and grouped together, we can start creating the code that will tell our character how many waypoints it needs to follow. This code is very useful because we can create different maps, using as many waypoints we need, without needing to update the character's code:

```
public static Transform[] points;

void Awake ()
{
    points = new Transform[transform.childCount];
    for (int i = 0; i < points.Length; i++)
    {
        points[i] = transform.GetChild(i);
    }
}
```

This code will be assigned to the group that we have created, and will count the number of waypoints that he has inside of it and ordering them.

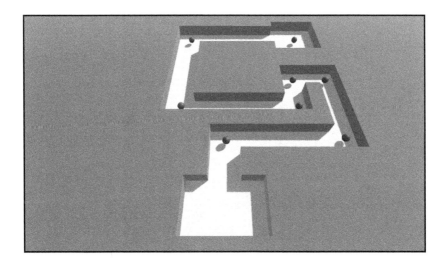

The blue spheres that we can see in the preceding image represent the 3D meshes that we have used as waypoints. For this example, the character will follow eight points until he finishes the path. Now let's move on to the AI character code and see how we can make the character move from point to point using the points that we have created.

We start by creating the basic functions of the character, the health and speed. Then we can create a new variable that will tell the character the next position that he needs to move to, and another variable that will be used show which waypoint it needs to follow:

```
public float speed;
public int health;

private Transform target;
private int wavepointIndex = 0;
```

Now we have the basic variables that are needed to make an enemy character move from point to point until he dies or reaches the end. Let's see how to use these to make it playable:

```
public float speed;
public int health;

private Transform target;
private int wavepointIndex = 0;


void Start ()
{
    target = waypoints.points[0];  speed = 10f;
}

void Update ()
{
    Vector3 dir = target.position - transform.position;
    transform.Translate(dir.normalized * speed * Time.deltaTime,
        Space.World);

    if(Vector3.Distance(transform.position, target.position) <= 0.4f)
    {
        GetNextWaypoint();
    }
}

void GetNextWaypoint()
{
```

```
if(wavepointIndex >= waypoints.points.Length - 1)
{
    Destroy(gameObject);
    return;
}

wavepointIndex++;
target = waypoints.points[wavepointIndex];
}
```

In the `Start` function, the first waypoint that the characters needs to follow is the waypoint number zero, that is, the first on the Transform list that we created in the `waypoints` code. Also, we have determined the velocity of the character, and for this example we have chosen `10f`.

Then in the `Update` function the character will calculate the distance between the next position and the current position, using the Vector 3 `dir`. The character will constantly be moving, so we have created a line of code that serves as movement for the character, `transform.Translate` in this case. Knowing the distance and the speed information, the character will know how far it is from the next position, and once he reaches the desirable distance from that point, he can then move on to the next point. To make this happen, we create an `if` statement that will tell to the character that, if he reaches 0.4f (for this example) from the point that he is moving towards, it means that he has already arrived at that destination and can start moving on to the next point, `GetNextWaypoint()`.

In the `GetNextWaypoint()` function, the character will try to confirm if he has arrived at the final destination. If the character has arrived at the final waypoint, then the object can be destroyed; if not, it can continue to the next waypoint. Here, `wavepointIndex++` will add one number to the index every time the character arrives at a waypoint, moving from 0>1>2>3>4>5, and so on.

Now we assign the code to our character and place the character on the start position and test the game to see if it is working properly:

Everything is working as expected: the character will move from one point to another until he arrives at the last one, and then he disappears from the game. However, there are still some improvements we need to make, because the character is facing always the same direction; he does not rotate when he changes direction. Let's take the opportunity to also create the instantiating code that will keep spawning enemies into the map.

In the same way we created an object to define the waypoint, we'll do the same for the start position, creating an object that will simply serve as position, so we can spawn the enemies from that point. To make that happen, we create a simple code just to test the gameplay without it being necessary to manually add the characters to the game:

```
public Transform enemyPrefab;
public float timeBetweenWaves = 3f;
public Transform spawnPoint;

private float countdown = 1f;
private int waveNumber = 1;

void Update ()
{
    if(countdown <= 0f)
```

```
    {
        StartCoroutine(SpawnWave());
        countdown = timeBetweenWaves;
    }

    countdown -= Time.deltaTime;
}

IEnumerator SpawnWave ()
{
    waveNumber++;

    for (int i = 0; i < waveNumber; i++)
    {
        SpawnEnemy();
        yield return new WaitForSeconds(0.7f);
    }
}

void SpawnEnemy ()
{
    Instantiate(enemyPrefab, spawnPoint.position,
        spawnPoint.rotation);
}
```

At this moment, we already have a wave spawner working as well, spawning a new wave of enemies every three seconds. This will help us visualize the gameplay that we are creating for our AI character. We have five variables. enemyPrefab is the character that we are creating, so the code can spawn him. timeBetweenWaves represents the time that it will wait before spawning a new wave. The spawnPoint variable determines the position where the character will appear, the start position. Here, countdown is the time that we wait before the first wave appears. waveNumber is the last variable, and serves to count the current wave (usually, this is used to differentiate the enemy difficulty from one wave to another).

If we run the game now, we can see that the number of characters appearing in the game is much more than just one, increasing every three seconds. Doing this at the same time as we develop our AI character is very useful, because if our characters have special abilities or if they have different speeds, we can fix it right away while we are developing them. Because we are just creating a small example, it is expected to work smoothly without any bugs.

Let's test it out now to see what happens:

It looks much more interesting now! We can see that the point to point movement is working as intended, and all the characters spawned into the game know where they need to go, following the right path.

We can now update the character code so it can turn to face the next point position while going around corners. To create this, we add a few more lines to the enemy code:

```
public float speed;
public int health;
public float speedTurn;

private Transform target;
private int wavepointIndex = 0;


void Start ()
{
    target = waypoints.points[0];
    speed = 10f;
    speedTurn = 0.2f;
}

void Update ()
```

```
{
    Vector3 dir = target.position - transform.position;
    transform.Translate(dir.normalized * speed * Time.deltaTime,
        Space.World);

    if(Vector3.Distance(transform.position, target.position) <= 0.4f)
    {
        GetNextWaypoint();
    }

    Vector3 newDir = Vector3.RotateTowards(transform.forward, dir,
        speedTurn, 0.0F);

    transform.rotation = Quaternion.LookRotation(newDir);
}

void GetNextWaypoint()
{
    if(wavepointIndex >= waypoints.points.Length - 1)
    {
        Destroy(gameObject);
        return;
    }

    wavepointIndex++;
    target = waypoints.points[wavepointIndex];
}
```

As we can see in the preceding code, we have added a new variable called speedTurn, which will represent the velocity of our character when turning, and in the start function we have determined the speed value as 0.2f. Then, in the update function, we calculate the velocity by multiplying this number by Time.deltaTime, giving a constant value regardless of the FPS number that the player is experiencing. Then we have created a new Vector3 variable called newDir, which will make our character turn towards the target position.

Now if we test the game once more, we can see that the characters turn towards their next point position:

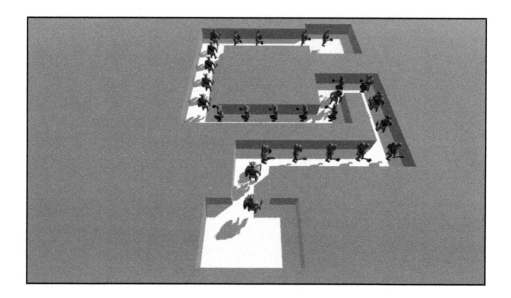

At this point, we can see that the AI characters are reacting correctly, moving from point to point as intended and turning towards their next position. Now we have the basics of a tower defense game and, we could add unique code to create a new and enjoyable game.

Racing genre

Point to point movement is a method that can be applied to practically any game genre and it has been extensively used over the years. Our next example is a racing game, where the AI drivers use point to point movement to compete against the player. To create this, we would need a road and a driver and then we'll place the waypoints on the road and tell our AI driver to follow that path. It's very similar to what we have done before but with some behavior differences in our character because we don't want it to look rigid when he is turning and also there will be other drivers on the same map and they cannot overlap one on top of another.

Without further ado let's start, first we need to establish the map, which in this case is the race track:

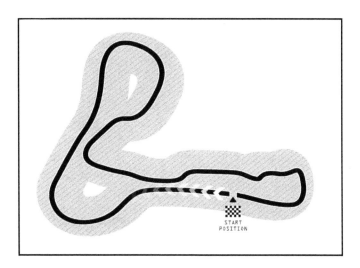

After designing our race track, we need to define every point position that our drivers need to go to, and because we have a lot of curves, we need to create more point positions than we had before so that the car follows the road smoothly.

We have done the same process as before, creating objects inside the game and using them as position references only:

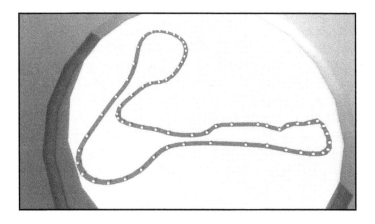

This is our map with the waypoints in place, and as we can see, there are more points on the curves. This is very important if we want to achieve a smooth transition from one point to another.

Now let's group all the waypoints again, and this time we'll create a different code. Instead of creating a code that manages the waypoints, we will be implementing that calculation inside of our AI driver code and creating a simple code to apply to each waypoint to specify the next position to follow.

 There are many ways that we can develop our code, and depending on our preferences or the game genre that we are working on, some methods can work better than others. In this case, we have found that using the code we developed for our Tower Defense character does not fit with this game genre.

Starting with the AI driver code, we have used ten variables, as shown in the following code block:

```
public static bool raceStarted = false;

public float aiSpeed = 10.0f;
public float aiTurnSpeed = 2.0f;
public float resetAISpeed = 0.0f;
public float resetAITurnSpeed = 0.0f;

public GameObject waypointController;
public List<Transform> waypoints;
public int currentWaypoint = 0;
public float currentSpeed;
public Vector3 currentWaypointPosition;
```

The first one, `raceStarted`, is a static Boolean that will tell our driver whether the race has started. This takes into consideration the fact that the race only begins when the green light appears; if not, `raceStarted` is set to `false`. Next, we have `aiSpeed`, which represents the velocity of the car. This is a simplified version for test proposes; otherwise, we would need speed functions to determine how fast can the car is going according to the gear that is set. `aiTurnSpeed` represents the velocity of the car when he is turning, how fast we want the car to steer when he is facing a new direction. Next, we have the `waypointController`, which will be linked to the waypoints group; and the `waypoints` list, which will be taken from that group.

Here, `currentWaypoint` will tell our driver which waypoint number he is currently following. The `currentSpeed` variable will show the current velocity of the car. Finally, `currentWaypointPosition` is the Vector 3 position of the waypoint that the car will be following:

```
void Start ()
{
        GetWaypoints();
        resetAISpeed = aiSpeed;
        resetAITurnSpeed = aiTurnSpeed;
}
```

In our `start` function, we have only three lines of code: `GetWaypoints()`, which will access all of the waypoints that exist inside of the group, and `resetAISpeed` and `resetAITurnSpeed`, which reset the speed values because they will influence the rigid body placed on the car:

```
void Update ()
{
        if(raceStarted)
        {
            MoveTowardWaypoints();
        }
}
```

In the update function, we have a simple `if` statement that checks whether the race has started or not. If the race has started, then he can proceed to the next step, which is the most important for our AI driver, `MoveTowardWaypoints()`. For this example, we have not stated anything while the car is waiting for the green light, but we could have implemented the engine starting and the pre-acceleration of the car, for example:

```
void GetWaypoints()
{
  Transform[] potentialWaypoints = waypointController.
      GetComponentsInChildren<Transform>();

  waypoints = new List<Transform>();

  for each(Transform potentialWaypoint in potentialWaypoints)
    {
        if(potentialWaypoint != waypointController.transform)
        {
            waypoints.Add(potentialWaypoint);
```

```
        }
    }
}
```

Next, we have GetWaypoints(), which was instantiated in the Start function. Here, we access the waypointController group and retrieve all the position information regarding the waypoints that are stored inside it. Because we will be ordering the waypoints in a different code, we don't need to do that here:

```
void MoveTowardWaypoints()
{
    float currentWaypointX = waypoints[currentWaypoint].position.x;
    float currentWaypointY = transform.position.y;
    float currentWaypointZ = waypoints[currentWaypoint].position.z;

    Vector3 relativeWaypointPosition = transform.
        InverseTransformPoint (new Vector3(currentWaypointX,
        currentWaypointY, currentWaypointZ));
    currentWaypointPosition = new Vector3(currentWaypointX,
         currentWaypointY, currentWaypointZ);

    Quaternion toRotation = Quaternion.LookRotation
        (currentWaypointPosition - transform.position);
    transform.rotation = Quaternion.RotateTowards
        (transform.rotation, toRotation, aiTurnSpeed);

    GetComponent<Rigidbody>().AddRelativeForce(0, 0, aiSpeed);

    if(relativeWaypointPosition.sqrMagnitude < 15.0f)
    {
        currentWaypoint++;

        if(currentWaypoint >= waypoints.Count)
        {
            currentWaypoint = 0;
        }
    }

    currentSpeed = Mathf.Abs(transform.
      InverseTransformDirection
      (GetComponent<Rigidbody>().velocity).z);

    float maxAngularDrag = 2.5f;
    float currentAngularDrag = 1.0f;
    float aDragLerpTime = currentSpeed * 0.1f;
```

```
    float maxDrag = 1.0f;
    float currentDrag = 3.5f;
    float dragLerpTime = currentSpeed * 0.1f;

    float myAngularDrag = Mathf.Lerp(currentAngularDrag,
        maxAngularDrag, aDragLerpTime);
    float myDrag = Mathf.Lerp(currentDrag, maxDrag, dragLerpTime);

    GetComponent<Rigidbody>().angularDrag = myAngularDrag;
    GetComponent<Rigidbody>().drag = myDrag;
}
```

Finally, we have the `MoveTowardsWaypoints()` function. Because the car has more depth in terms of mobility than a simple Tower Defense character, we decided to expand and implement more content in this part of the code.

First, we retrieve the Vector 3 position of the current waypoint that is being used. We have chosen to retrieve this information and assign the axis separately, and for that reason we have `currentWaypointX` for the X axis, `currentWaypointY` for the Y axis, and `currentWaypointZ` for the Z axis.

Then we create a new Vector 3 direction called `relativeWaypointPosition`, which will calculate the distance between the waypoint and the current position of the car and convert from World Space to Local, and in this case we have used `InverseTransformDirection`.

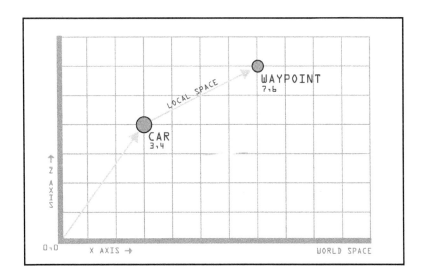

As we can see represented on the preceding graphic, we want to calculate the distance in local space between the car and the waypoint. This will tell to our driver if the waypoint is at his right or left side. This is recommended because the wheels command the car speed and they have an independent rotation value and if we kept working on this game, it would be one feature that would still need to be developed.

To smooth the rotation between one waypoint to another, we have used the following code:

```
Quaternion toRotation = Quaternion.LookRotation
        (currentWaypointPosition - transform.position);
transform.rotation = Quaternion.RotateTowards
        (transform.rotation, toRotation, aiTurnSpeed);
```

This is an updated version of what we used in the Tower Defense. It will make our car move smoothly towards the waypoint that the car is traveling toward. This gives the effect of the car turning; otherwise, he would turn right away towards the waypoint and it would look unrealistic:

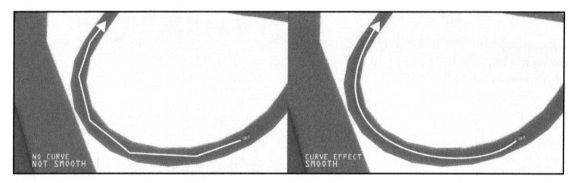

As we can see, straight lines do not fit the genre that we are currently creating. It works perfectly in other genres, like Tower Defense game, but for a racing game it is necessary to redefine the code to adjust to the situation that we are creating.

The rest of the code is exactly that, adjustments for the situation that we are creating, which is a car moving on a race track. There are force elements such as `drag`, which is the friction between the car and the road, represented in this code. When we turn the car, it will slide according to the velocity of the car at that moment, and these details are taken into consideration here, creating a more realistic point to point movement where we can see that the car is reacting according to physics.

This is the full code that we have used in our example:

```
public static bool raceStarted = false;

public float aiSpeed = 10.0f;
public float aiTurnSpeed = 2.0f;
public float resetAISpeed = 0.0f;
public float resetAITurnSpeed = 0.0f;

public GameObject waypointController;
public List<Transform> waypoints;
public int currentWaypoint = 0;
public float currentSpeed;
public Vector3 currentWaypointPosition;

void Start ()
{
    GetWaypoints();
    resetAISpeed = aiSpeed;
    resetAITurnSpeed = aiTurnSpeed;
}

void Update ()
{
   if(raceStarted)
   {
       MoveTowardWaypoints();
   }
}

void GetWaypoints()
  {
    Transform[] potentialWaypoints =
      waypointController.GetComponentsInChildren<Transform>();

    waypoints = new List<Transform>();

    foreach(Transform potentialWaypoint in potentialWaypoints)
    {
        if(potentialWaypoint != waypointController.transform)
        {
            waypoints.Add(potentialWaypoint);
        }
    }
}

void MoveTowardWaypoints()
```

```
{
        float currentWaypointX = waypoints[currentWaypoint].position.x;
        float currentWaypointY = transform.position.y;
        float currentWaypointZ = waypoints[currentWaypoint].position.z;

        Vector3 relativeWaypointPosition = transform.
            InverseTransformPoint (new Vector3(currentWaypointX,
            currentWaypointY, currentWaypointZ));
        currentWaypointPosition = new Vector3(currentWaypointX,
            currentWaypointY, currentWaypointZ);

        Quaternion toRotation = Quaternion.
            LookRotation(currentWaypointPosition - transform.position);
        transform.rotation = Quaternion.RotateTowards
            (transform.rotation, toRotation, aiTurnSpeed);

        GetComponent<Rigidbody>().AddRelativeForce(0, 0, aiSpeed);

        if(relativeWaypointPosition.sqrMagnitude < 15.0f)
        {
            currentWaypoint++;

            if(currentWaypoint >= waypoints.Count)
            {
                currentWaypoint = 0;
             }
        }

        currentSpeed = Mathf.Abs(transform.
            InverseTransformDirection
            (GetComponent<Rigidbody>().velocity).z);

        float maxAngularDrag = 2.5f;
        float currentAngularDrag = 1.0f;
        float aDragLerpTime = currentSpeed * 0.1f;

        float maxDrag = 1.0f;
        float currentDrag = 3.5f;
        float dragLerpTime = currentSpeed * 0.1f;

        float myAngularDrag    = Mathf.Lerp(currentAngularDrag,
            maxAngularDrag, aDragLerpTime);
        float myDrag = Mathf.Lerp(currentDrag, maxDrag, dragLerpTime);

        GetComponent<Rigidbody>().angularDrag = myAngularDrag;
        GetComponent<Rigidbody>().drag = myDrag;
}
```

If we start the game and test it, we can see that he is working fine. The car drives by itself, turns smoothly, and completes the track as intended.

Now that we have the basic point to point movement completed, we could implement more functions for the AI driver and start developing the game as we want. It is always recommended to start with the main functions of the gameplay before developing any details. This will help identify any ideas that we had planned for the game that do not work as well as we thought.

MOBA genre

Point to point movement is one of the most commonly used methods to control the movement of a character. It is self-explanatory why it is widely used, because the character moves from one point to another and usually that's we want; we want the character to arrive at certain destination or follow another character. One game genre that also requires this type of movement is the Multiplayer Online Battle Arena (MOBA) games that have become very popular recently. Usually, there are NPC characters that spawn at the start position and follow a predetermined path towards the enemy towers, similar to the Tower Defense enemies, but in this case the AI characters move in the same terrain as the players and can interfere with each other.

The map is divided into two equal parts, where one side needs to fight the other, and for each part it spawns a different platoon that is composed of small enemies called Minions or Creeps. When they are following their path, if one platoon finds the other, they stop moving forward and start attacking. After the battle, the survivors keep moving forward:

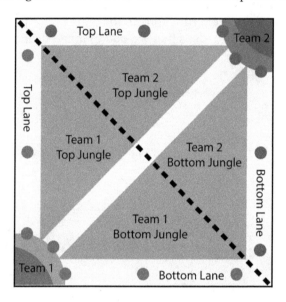

In this example we are going to re-create that portion of the game, where the platoon spawns at the start position, follows their path, stops when they find the enemies and keep moving towards their next direction until they win the fight. Then we will create the basic movement of the hero character that is controlled by the player or the computer: both have the freedom to move around the map and the characters needs to follow the direction that is directed by the player or computer while avoiding all obstacles.

We will start by importing the map into our game. We have chosen a generic MOBA style map, like we can see on the following screenshot:

The next step is to create waypoints in the map. Here we will have six different waypoints groups, because each team has three different paths and each platoon can only follow one path. We start from the base position and then we add more waypoints until we reach the enemy base. The following image shows an example of what we have created.

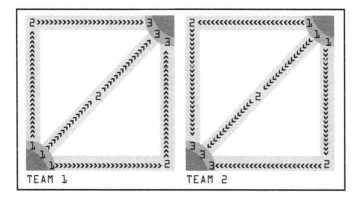

We need to create three different waypoint groups for each team, because there will be three different spawn positions as well; they will work independently from one another. After setting the waypoints, we can group them and assign the code that will gather the position information and the order that the platoon should follow. For this example, we can use the same code that we used for the Tower Defense waypoints, because the way that the enemies follow their path is similar:

```
public static Transform[] points;

void Awake ()
{
    points = new Transform[transform.childCount];
    for (int i = 0; i < points.Length; i++)
    {
        points[i] = transform.GetChild(i);
    }
}
```

Because we have six different waypoint groups, it is necessary to duplicate the same code six times and rename them accordingly. Our `spawnable` enemies will later access the right path for them, so it is recommended to rename the groups and codes so that we can easily understand which group represents which lane, for example, 1_Top/1_Middle/1_Bottom and 2_Top/2_Middle/2_Bottom. The number represents their team and the position name represents the position. In this case, we change the name `points` in our code to the correct names that represent each lane:

Lane Team 1 Top:

```
public static Transform[] 1_Top;

void Awake ()
{
    1_Top = new Transform[transform.childCount];
    for (int i = 0; i < 1_Top.Length; i++)
    {
        1_Top[i] = transform.GetChild(i);
    }
}
```

Lane Team 1 Middle:

```
public static Transform[] 1_Middle;

void Awake ()
{
    1_Middle = new Transform[transform.childCount];
    for (int i = 0; i < 1_Top.Length; i++)
    {
        1_Middle[i] = transform.GetChild(i);
    }
}
```

Lane Team 1 Bottom:

```
public static Transform[] 1_Bottom;

void Awake ()
{
    1_Bottom = new Transform[transform.childCount];
    for (int i = 0; i < 1_Top.Length; i++)
    {
        1_Bottom[i] = transform.GetChild(i);
    }
}
```

Lane Team 2 Top:

```
public static Transform[] 2_Top;

void Awake ()
{
    2_Top = new Transform[transform.childCount];
    for (int i = 0; i < 1_Top.Length; i++)
    {
        2_Top[i] = transform.GetChild(i);
    }
}
```

Lane Team 2 Middle:

```
public static Transform[] 2_Middle;

void Awake ()
{
    2_Middle = new Transform[transform.childCount];
    for (int i = 0; i < 2_Middle.Length; i++)
    {
        2_Middle[i] = transform.GetChild(i);
    }
}
```

Lane Team 2 Bottom:

```
public static Transform[] 2_Bottom;

void Awake ()
{
    2_Bottom = new Transform[transform.childCount];
    for (int i = 0; i < 2_Bottom.Length; i++)
    {
        2_Bottom[i] = transform.GetChild(i);
    }
}
```

Now that we have created all the groups and codes for each of them, we can move on to the character AI that will follow their path towards the enemy base. We can choose to duplicate the code for each team or integrate everything inside the same code, using `if` statements to decide which path the character should follow. For this example, we have chosen to integrate everything in the same code. That way, we can update the character code once and it will work for both teams at the same time. Once again, we can start by using the same code that we used in the enemies from the Tower Defense game. We can change the code so he will fit in the game that we are currently creating:

```
public float speed;
public int health;
public float speedTurn;

private Transform target;
private int wavepointIndex = 0;


void Start ()
```

```
{
    target = waypoints.points[0];
    speed = 10f;
    speedTurn = 0.2f;
}

void Update ()
{
    Vector3 dir = target.position - transform.position;
    transform.Translate(dir.normalized * speed * Time.deltaTime,
        Space.World);

    if(Vector3.Distance(transform.position, target.position) <= 0.4f)
    {
        GetNextWaypoint();
    }

    Vector3 newDir = Vector3.RotateTowards(transform.forward, dir,
        speedTurn, 0.0F);

    transform.rotation = Quaternion.LookRotation(newDir);
}

void GetNextWaypoint()
{
    if(wavepointIndex >= waypoints.points.Length - 1)
    {
        Destroy(gameObject);
        return;
    }

    wavepointIndex++;
    target = waypoints.points[wavepointIndex];
}
```

With this code, we can make the character follow the path and turn smoothly when changing from one point to another. At this point we just need to change the code to make him fit the game genre that we are creating. To do that the first thing we need to consider is changing the name points to the names that we've previously created, and add `if` statements to choose which side the character needs to follow.

Let's start by adding the information that distinguish the characters of one team from another. To do that, we need to create two new Boolean variables:

```
public bool Team1;
public bool Team2;
```

This will let us decide if the character is from Team1 or Team2, both cannot be true at the same time. Now we can implement more details into the character code, to let him know which lane he should walk on:

```
public bool Top;
public bool Middle;
public bool Bottom;
```

We have added three more Booleans that will indicate the lane that the character needs to follow. After working out which team the character is spawning from, another `if` statement will be added to determine the lane that the character will follow.

Once we have added those variables, we need to assign the waypoint groups that we created before according to the lane that the character will follow. We can implement that right in the `start` function:

```
if(Team1 == true)
 {
          if(Top == true)
          {
              target = 1_Top.1_Top[0];
          }

          if(Middle == true)
          {
              target = 1_Middle.1_Middle[0];
          }

          if(Bottom == true)
          {
              target = 1_Bottom.1_Top[0];
          }
 }

if(Team2 == true)
 {
          if(Top == true)
          {
              target = 2_Top.2_Top[0];
          }

          if(Middle == true)
          {
              target = 2_Middle.2_Middle[0];
          }
```

```
            if(Bottom == true)
            {
                target = 2_Bottom.2_Top[0];
            }
    }
```

This allows the character to question the team that it is representing, the lane where it spawned, and the path that he will follow. We need to adjust the rest of the code so it will work for this example. The next modification will be in the GetNextWaypoint() function. We need to add the if statements to let the character know the correct next waypoint that he needs to follow, similar to what we did in the Start function:

```
void GetNextWaypoint()
{
    if(Team1 == true)
    {
        if(Top == true)
        {
            if(wavepointIndex >= 1_Top.1_Top.Length - 1)
            {
                Destroy(gameObject);
                return;
            }

            wavepointIndex++;
            target = 1_Top.1_Top[wavepointIndex];
        }

        if(Middle == true)
        {
            if(wavepointIndex >= 1_Middle.1_Middle.Length - 1)
            {
                Destroy(gameObject);
                return;
            }

            wavepointIndex++;
            target = 1_Middle.1_Middle[wavepointIndex];
        }

        if(Bottom == true)
        {
            if(wavepointIndex >= 1_Bottom.1_Bottom.Length - 1)
            {
                Destroy(gameObject);
                return;
```

```
                        }

            wavepointIndex++;
            target = 1_Bottom.1_Bottom[wavepointIndex];
        }
    }

    if(Team2 == true)
    {
      if(Top == true)
      {
          if(wavepointIndex >= 2_Top.2_Top.Length - 1)
          {
              Destroy(gameObject);
              return;
           }

           wavepointIndex++;
           target = 2_Top.2_Top[wavepointIndex];
        }

        if(Middle == true)
        {
           if(wavepointIndex >= 2_Middle.2_Middle.Length - 1)
           {
              Destroy(gameObject);
              return;
            }

            wavepointIndex++;
            target = 2_Middle.2_Middle[wavepointIndex];
        }

        if(Bottom == true)
        {
            if(wavepointIndex >= 2_Bottom.2_Bottom.Length - 1)
            {
              Destroy(gameObject);
              return;
            }

            wavepointIndex++;
            target = 2_Bottom.2_Bottom[wavepointIndex];
        }
    }
}
```

At this point, if we add a character to the game and assign it the AI code, it will follow the chosen path:

It is working properly, and we are ready to implement more features to create the perfect platoon that follows a path toward the enemy tower and that stops to fight the other platoon or the hero. Any details or uniqueness that we want to add to our platoon can be applied now that we have the basic movement working. Here, we have attached the complete code for the platoon AI character:

```
public float speed;
public int health;
public float speedTurn;

public bool Team1;
public bool Team2;

public bool Top;
public bool Middle;
public bool Bottom;

private Transform target;
private int wavepointIndex = 0;
```

After updating the variables in the preceding code we can move on to the `Start` method that will be called on the first frame:

```
void Start ()
{
   if(Team1 == true)
   {
      if(Top == true)
      {
         target = 1_Top.1_Top[0];
      }

      if(Middle == true)
      {
         target = 1_Middle.1_Middle[0];
      }

      if(Bottom == true)
      {
         target = 1_Bottom.1_Top[0];
      }
   }

   if(Team2 == true)
   {
      if(Top == true)
      {
         target = 2_Top.2_Top[0];
      }

      if(Middle == true)
      {
         target = 2_Middle.2_Middle[0];
      }

      if(Bottom == true)
      {
         target = 2_Bottom.2_Top[0];
      }
   }
   speed = 10f;
   speedTurn = 0.2f;
}
```

Here is the `Update` method that will be called every frame of the game:

```
void Update ()
{
   Vector3 dir = target.position - transform.position;
   transform.Translate(dir.normalized * speed * Time.deltaTime,
      Space.World);

   if(Vector3.Distance(transform.position, target.position) <= 0.4f)
   {
       GetNextWaypoint();
   }

   Vector3 newDir = Vector3.RotateTowards(transform.forward, dir,
      speedTurn, 0.0F);

   transform.rotation = Quaternion.LookRotation(newDir);
}

void GetNextWaypoint()
{
   if(Team1 == true)
   {
     if(Top == true)
     {
       if(wavepointIndex >= 1_Top.1_Top.Length - 1)
       {
         Destroy(gameObject);
         return;
       }

       wavepointIndex++;
       target = 1_Top.1_Top[wavepointIndex];
     }

     if(Middle == true)
     {
       if(wavepointIndex >= 1_Middle.1_Middle.Length - 1)
       {
          Destroy(gameObject);
          return;
        }

        wavepointIndex++;
        target = 1_Middle.1_Middle[wavepointIndex];
     }
```

```
        if(Bottom == true)
        {
            if(wavepointIndex >= 1_Bottom.1_Bottom.Length - 1)
            {
                Destroy(gameObject);
                return;
            }

            wavepointIndex++;
            target = 1_Bottom.1_Bottom[wavepointIndex];
        }
    }

    if(Team2 == true)
    {
        if(Top == true)
        {
            if(wavepointIndex >= 2_Top.2_Top.Length - 1)
            {
                Destroy(gameObject);
                return;
            }

            wavepointIndex++;
            target = 2_Top.2_Top[wavepointIndex];
        }

        if(Middle == true)
        {
            if(wavepointIndex >= 2_Middle.2_Middle.Length - 1)
            {
                Destroy(gameObject);
                return;
            }

            wavepointIndex++;
            target = 2_Middle.2_Middle[wavepointIndex];
        }

        if(Bottom == true)
        {
            if(wavepointIndex >= 2_Bottom.2_Bottom.Length - 1)
            {
                Destroy(gameObject);
                return;
            }

            wavepointIndex++;
```

```
                target = 2_Bottom.2_Bottom[wavepointIndex];
        }
    }
}
```

Another important aspect of a MOBA game is the hero's movement. Even if it's controlled by the player, the character has AI to determine the path that he needs to follow in order to arrive at the chosen destination. To complete this task, we will introduce the point to point method first; then we will continue the same example but using an advanced method that will make our character decide the best path to arrive at the final destination without implementing any waypoints.

This example will also serve as an example of how to create a character that follows the player. To do this, we need to set all the possible paths that the character is allowed follow. We want the AI to avoid colliding with objects or passing through walls, for example:

Let's focus on this area of the map. As we can see, there are walls and trees blocking a portion of the map, and the characters should not be allowed to pass through them. Using the waypoints method, we will create points on the map that the character should follow if he wants to reach a certain destination. he won't have any specific order like the previous examples that we have created, because the character can move in any direction, and for that reason we cannot predict the path that it will choose.

We start by positioning the waypoints on the walkable positions. This will prevent the character from moving on the non-walkable area:

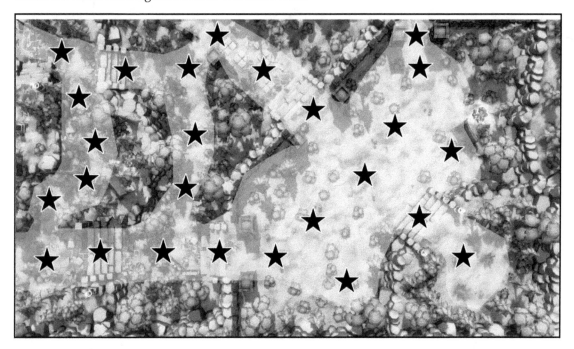

The stars that we see on the map represent the waypoints that we have created, so we should only place them in the areas that the character is able to walk in. If the character wants to move from one position to another, it must follow the waypoints until it gets to the closest waypoint to the desired destination.

In the gameplay mechanics, we can choose why the character needs to reach a certain destination, such as following the player, going to the base to recover health points, moving towards the enemy wall to destroy it, and many others choices. Independently of what the character AI needs to achieve, it needs to move correctly on the map, and this waypoints system will work in any circumstance.

Here we can find the full code that will make this work. Then we'll explain everything in detail to better understand how to replicate this code so it can work in a different game genre:

```
public float speed;
private List <GameObject> wayPointsList;
private Transform target;
private GameObject[] wayPoints;

void Start ()
{

    target = GameObject.FindGameObjectWithTag("target").transform;
    wayPointsList = new List<GameObject>();

    wayPoints = GameObject.FindGameObjectsWithTag("wayPoint");

    for each(GameObject newWayPoint in wayPoints)
    {
       wayPointsList.Add(newWayPoint);
     }
 }

void Update ()
{
   Follow();
}

void Follow ()
{
   GameObject wayPoint = null;

   if (Physics.Linecast(transform.position, target.position))
   {
      wayPoint = findBestPath();
    }

    else
    {
       wayPoint = GameObject.FindGameObjectWithTag("target");
     }

    Vector3 Dir = (wayPoint.transform.position -
            transform.position).normalized;
    transform.position += Dir * Time.deltaTime * speed;
    transform.rotation = Quaternion.LookRotation(Dir);
   }
```

```
GameObject findBestPath()
{
    GameObject bestPath = null;
    float distanceToBestPath = Mathf.Infinity;

    for each(GameObject go in wayPointsList)
    {
        float distToWayPoint = Vector3.
            Distance(transform.position, go.transform.position);
        float distWayPointToTarget = Vector3.
            Distance(go.transform.position,
            target.transform.position);
        float distToTarget = Vector3.
            Distance(transform.position, target.position);
        bool wallBetween = Physics.Linecast
            (transform.position, go.transform.position);

        if((distToWayPoint < distanceToBestPath)
            && (distToTarget > distWayPointToTarget)
                && (!wallBetween))
        {
            distanceToBestPath = distToWayPoint;
            bestPath = go;
        }

        else
        {
            bool wayPointToTargetCollision = Physics.Linecast
                (go.transform.position, target.position);
            if(!wayPointToTargetCollision)
            {
                bestPath = go;
            }
        }
    }
    return bestPath;
}
```

If we assign this code into our character and hit the **play** button, we can test the game and see that what we have created works perfectly. The character should use the waypoint positions to move across the map to reach the desired destination. This method can be used for NPC characters and playable characters as well, because for both cases the characters need to avoid colliding with the wall and obstacles:

If we continue the example and expand the waypoints across the whole map, we have a basic MOBA game working properly, with a platoon of monsters spawning at each base and following the right path, and hero characters that can move freely on the map without colliding with walls.

Point to point movement and avoiding dynamic objects

Now that we have characters that can follow the right path and avoid static objects, we are ready to move on to the next level and make those characters avoid dynamic objects while moving from point to point. We will revise the three different examples created in this chapter and see how we can add the avoiding technique to the AI characters in those examples.

Those three methods should cover almost every game genre that uses point to point movement as their primary method of locomotion, and we will be able to create new ideas with these examples as a guideline:

Let's start with the racing game, where we have a car that drives around the track until he finishes the race. If the car drives alone and there's nothing obstructing the path, it won't be necessary to avoid any obstacles, but usually obstacles make the game more interesting or challenging, especially when they are spontaneous and we don't expect them. A great example of this is the Mario Kart game, where they throw bananas and other objects to destabilize the opposing players, and the objects don't have any pre-defined position so the characters can't predict where they're going to be. So it is important for the drivers to have the necessary functions to avoid colliding with those objects and be able to do that in real time.

Assuming that two objects appeared unexpectedly on the road while the AI character was following the next waypoint, we want the character to anticipate the collision and turn around to avoid crashing against the object. The method that we will be using here is a combination of the waypoint movement with the maze movement. The character can only obey one order at a time, he can either respect the waypoint movement or the maze movement, and that's exactly what we need to add on to our code so the character AI can choose the best option according the current situation that he is facing:

```
public static bool raceStarted = false;
```

```
public float aiSpeed = 10.0f;
public float aiTurnSpeed = 2.0f;
public float resetAISpeed = 0.0f;
public float resetAITurnSpeed = 0.0f;

public GameObject waypointController;
public List<Transform> waypoints;
public int currentWaypoint = 0;
public float currentSpeed;
public Vector3 currentWaypointPosition;

public static bool isBlocked;
public static bool isBlockedFront;
public static bool isBlockedRight;
public static bool isBlockedLeft;
```

After updating the preceding variables, we can move on to the Start method. This will be called in the first frame:

```
void Start ()
{
      GetWaypoints();
      resetAISpeed = aiSpeed;
      resetAITurnSpeed = aiTurnSpeed;
}
```

Here is the Update method that will be called every frame of the game:

```
void Update ()
  {
    if(raceStarted && isBlocked == false)
    {
      MoveTowardWaypoints();
    }

    if(raceStarted && isBlockedFront == true
        && isBlockedLeft == false && isBlockedRight == false)
    {
        TurnRight();
    }

    if(raceStarted && isBlockedFront == false
        && isBlockedLeft == true && isBlockedRight == false)
    {
        TurnRight();
    }
```

```
    if(raceStarted && isBlockedFront == false
        && isBlockedLeft == false && isBlockedRight == true)
    {
        TurnLeft();
    }
}

void GetWaypoints()
  {
        Transform[] potentialWaypoints = waypointController.
            GetComponentsInChildren<Transform>();

        waypoints = new List<Transform>();

        for each(Transform potentialWaypoint in potentialWaypoints)
          {
            if(potentialWaypoint != waypointController.transform)
            {
                waypoints.Add(potentialWaypoint);
            }
          }
  }

void MoveTowardWaypoints()
{
    float currentWaypointX = waypoints[currentWaypoint].position.x;
    float currentWaypointY = transform.position.y;
    float currentWaypointZ = waypoints[currentWaypoint].position.z;

    Vector3 relativeWaypointPosition = transform.
        InverseTransformPoint (new Vector3(currentWaypointX,
        currentWaypointY, currentWaypointZ));
    currentWaypointPosition = new Vector3(currentWaypointX,
        currentWaypointY, currentWaypointZ);

    Quaternion toRotation = Quaternion.
        LookRotation(currentWaypointPosition - transform.position);
    transform.rotation = Quaternion.
        RotateTowards(transform.rotation, toRotation, aiTurnSpeed);

    GetComponent<Rigidbody>().AddRelativeForce(0, 0, aiSpeed);

    if(relativeWaypointPosition.sqrMagnitude < 15.0f)
    {
        currentWaypoint++;

        if(currentWaypoint >= waypoints.Count)
        {
```

```
                            currentWaypoint = 0;
                }
        }

        currentSpeed = Mathf.Abs(transform.
            InverseTransformDirection(GetComponent<Rigidbody>().
            velocity).z);

        float maxAngularDrag = 2.5f;
        float currentAngularDrag = 1.0f;
        float aDragLerpTime = currentSpeed * 0.1f;

        float maxDrag = 1.0f;
        float currentDrag = 3.5f;
        float dragLerpTime = currentSpeed * 0.1f;

        float myAngularDrag = Mathf.Lerp(currentAngularDrag,
            maxAngularDrag, aDragLerpTime);
        float myDrag = Mathf.Lerp(currentDrag, maxDrag,
            dragLerpTime);

        GetComponent<Rigidbody>().angularDrag = myAngularDrag;
        GetComponent<Rigidbody>().drag = myDrag;
}

void TurnLeft()
{
    //turning left function here
}

void TurnRight()
{
    //turning right function here
}
```

We have added four new static variables to our code: `isBlocked`, `isBlockedFront`, `isBlockedRight`, and `isBlockedLeft`. This will check if the path in front of the car is free from obstacles or not. The car will continue following the waypoint path until something appears and the car needs to turn left or right to pass the obstacle. To make this work, we need to add at least three sensors in front of the car. When they interact with some object, the sensor gives that information to the AI driver, and at this point it will choose the best option according to that information:

As we can see in the preceding image, the car now has three sensors attached to it. In this example, the right sensor will report that it is blocked by an obstacle and the driver will turn left until that side is free again. Once the three sensors report that nothing is obstructing the driver's path, the car will return to following the waypoint that it was previously moving towards. If we notice that the driver doesn't recognize some obstacles, it is recommended to increase the number of sensors to cover a larger area.

Now let's move on to the platoon characters that we created for the MOBA example. Here, we will need to create a different method, because the characters will move towards the next waypoint until they find something, but this time we don't want them to move away. Instead, we want the character to move towards the character that they have found.

To create this, we will add a circular or spherical collider to our character. This will serve as detection. If something triggers that zone, the character will stop moving towards its waypoint and use the position of the hero that triggered the collider as a waypoint to pursue:

```
public float speed;
public int health;
public float speedTurn;

public bool Team1;
public bool Team2;
public bool Top;
public bool Middle;
public bool Bottom;

private Transform target;
private int wavepointIndex = 0;

static Transform heroTarget;
static bool heroTriggered;
```

After updating the preceding variables, we can move on to the `Start` method, which will be called on the first frame:

```
void Start ()
{
    if(Team1 == true)
    {
        if(Top == true)
        {
            target = 1_Top.1_Top[0];
        }

        if(Middle == true)
        {
            target = 1_Middle.1_Middle[0];
        }

        if(Bottom == true)
        {
            target = 1_Bottom.1_Top[0];
        }
    }

    if(Team2 == true)
    {
        if(Top == true)
        {
            target = 2_Top.2_Top[0];
        }

        if(Middle == true)
        {
            target = 2_Middle.2_Middle[0];
        }

        if(Bottom == true)
        {
            target = 2_Bottom.2_Top[0];
        }
    }
    speed = 10f;
    speedTurn = 0.2f;
}
```

Here is the `Update` method that will be called every frame of the game:

```
void Update ()
{
   Vector3 dir = target.position - transform.position;
   transform.Translate(dir.normalized * speed * Time.deltaTime,
      Space.World);

   if(Vector3.Distance(transform.position, target.position) <=
         0.4f && heroTriggered == false)
   {
      GetNextWaypoint();
   }

   if(heroTriggered == true)
   {
      GetHeroWaypoint();
   }

   Vector3 newDir = Vector3.RotateTowards(transform.
         forward, dir, speedTurn, 0.0F);

   transform.rotation = Quaternion.LookRotation(newDir);
}
```

This `GetNextWaypoint` method is used to gather the information regarding the next waypoint that the character needs to follow:

```
void GetNextWaypoint()
{
   if(Team1 == true)
   {
      if(Top == true)
      {
         it(wavepointIndex >= 1_Top.1_Top.Length - 1)
         {
            Destroy(gameObject);
            return;
         }

         wavepointIndex++;
         target = 1_Top.1_Top[wavepointIndex];
      }

      if(Middle == true)
      {
```

```
      if(wavepointIndex >= 1_Middle.1_Middle.Length - 1)
      {
        Destroy(gameObject);
        return;
       }

       wavepointIndex++;
       target = 1_Middle.1_Middle[wavepointIndex];
    }

    if(Bottom == true)
    {
       if(wavepointIndex >= 1_Bottom.1_Bottom.Length - 1)
       {
          Destroy(gameObject);
          return;
       }

        wavepointIndex++;
        target = 1_Bottom.1_Bottom[wavepointIndex];
    }
}

if(Team2 == true)
{
   if(Top == true)
   {
      if(wavepointIndex >= 2_Top.2_Top.Length - 1)
      {
         Destroy(gameObject);
         return;
      }

      wavepointIndex++;
      target = 2_Top.2_Top[wavepointIndex];
   }

   if(Middle == true)
   {
       if(wavepointIndex >= 2_Middle.2_Middle.Length - 1)
       {
          Destroy(gameObject);
          return;
       }

       wavepointIndex++;
       target = 2_Middle.2_Middle[wavepointIndex];
   }
```

```
            if(Bottom == true)
            {
                if(wavepointIndex >= 2_Bottom.2_Bottom.Length - 1)
                {
                    Destroy(gameObject);
                    return;
                }

                wavepointIndex++;
                target = 2_Bottom.2_Bottom[wavepointIndex];
            }
        }
    }
```

In the `GetHeroWaypoint` method, we set what happens when the character needs to follow the Hero direction, like attacking or any other function:

```
    void GetHeroWaypoint()
    {
        target = heroTarget.transform;
    }
```

We've added a spherical collider to the character that gives the trigger information to the character, to know if a hero character has entered that zone. If no hero triggered that zone, the character will continue following the waypoint, otherwise it will focus his attention to the hero and use him as a target point.

With this example we learned the core features of the artificial intelligence movement that can be found in a MOBA game and now we can re-create this popular game genre. From this chapter onwards we can create simple to complex navigation systems and use them to make our AI character more active in the game, constantly pursuing an objective even if that objective is moving.

Summary

In this chapter, we have introduced point to point movement, a method that is widely used in many games today, and we can adapt the codes that we have created to work in practically any game. At this point ,we are able to re-create many popular games and add our personal touch to them. In the next chapter, we'll continue talking about movement, but we will be focusing on an advanced aspect called the Theta algorithm. This will serve as a continuation of what we have learned in this chapter, and we will be able to create a character AI that, without any previous information or positions, will be able to find for itself the best path to follow in order to arrive at a certain destination.

7
Advanced Pathfinding

In this chapter, we will take a look at the advanced pathfinding methods that can be used in a wide range of games. The main objective of this chapter is to learn the foundations of how to create an advanced AI element that can analyze the map and process all the necessary information in order to decide the best path that needs to be taken. Advanced pathfinding methods can be found in many popular game titles that require the AI character to choose the best path in real time, and we will analyze some of the most famous examples and how can we replicate the same results.

Simple versus advanced pathfinding

As we discovered in the previous chapter, pathfinding is used by AI characters to discover the direction that they need to move and how to do it correctly. Depending on the game that we are working on, we could use a simple pathfinding system or a complex one. Both can be very useful. There are situations where a simple pathfinding system is enough to accomplish the task that we are looking for, but in other cases we need a different alternative to the methods that we have covered before in order to achieve the complexity and realism that is necessary for our AI character.

Before talking about any advanced system of creating a pathfinding method, let's discover why we need to use it and in what circumstances it is necessary to update our character and make it more intelligent and aware. Using our previous examples, we will be looking at the limitations that exist for a normal pathfinding method. Understanding the limitations of a simple pathfinding system will help us acknowledge what is missing and what challenges we will face when we are about to create a more complex system. So it is a good start to first learn how we can set up a simple pathfinding system and then we can move on to a more complex one. Because games have evolved at the same rate as the technology available to create them, our first example will be an older game, and then we'll see how the same game has evolved, in particular AI pathfinding.

Open world maps are now very common, and many games from different genres use this to create a rich experience, but it wasn't always like this. Let's take the first **Grand Theft Auto** (**GTA**) game as an example. Analyzing the pattern of the cars that are driving on the map, we can see that they don't have a complex system, and the drivers are stuck to the predefined route or lap that each of them is assigned to follow. Obviously, this AI pathfinding system was very advanced at that time and even if we play it today, we don't feel discouraged by the AI characters because it works wonderfully for that game.

The AI drivers follow their path and stop every time the player is in their way. This demonstrates that they have a collision detector in front of each car to tell them if there is something blocking the path. If there is something in front of the car, the driver stops immediately, and until the path is unblocked, it won't drive again. This is a sign that the drivers have some sort of pathfinding system that couldn't solve different situations where it was not possible for them to keep driving in the same direction. For that reason and to avoid any errors or glitches in the game, the programmers have chosen to make the drivers stop when that happens.

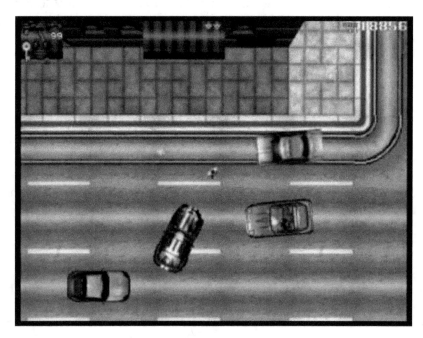

The preceding case scenario, where the drivers stop when it's not possible for them to keep moving forward, became one of the biggest strengths in their future games. Many things have evolved in the GTA games, and the AI is definitely one of them. They have refined the AI drivers, making them aware of the situation and their surroundings. Let's analyze *GTA San Andreas,* which is also available to play on mobile phones. In this game, if we stop our car in front of the AI driver, the results are completely different. Depending on the personality of the AI driver, it will react differently; for example, some of them will simply honk the horn and wait a little bit, and if the player keeps blocking their way, the driver will outrun the player. Others might react more aggressively, getting out of the car to confront the player physically.

If the AI driver notices that the environment is getting dangerous by hearing shots, they speed up and choose the fastest path to get out of that situation. This type of behavior demonstrates that the AI characters have a more complex and refined pathfinding system in conjunction with a possibility map, where the surrounding situation will reflect which path they end up choosing.

As we can see, the drivers now have a presence that's much more noticeable than in the first game. In the previous chapter, we studied how to create a simple pathfinding system, very similar to what we analyzed in the first GTA game. Now, we'll look in depth at how to create an AI character that can get away from any unexpected situation.

This is one of those things that still isn't perfect, and many developers are trying new ways of creating AI characters that can behave almost like a human person would if trapped in the same situation. Some companies are getting close to that--one big example is Rockstar Games with their GTA franchise, and for that reason we have chosen to start with their example.

A* search algorithm

Unpredictable situations usually lead to a large amount of hours coding the extensive possibilities that the characters have. For this reason, it was necessary to think on a new way to create a better pathfinding system, where the characters could analyze the surroundings for themselves in real time and choose the best path to take. One method that has become very popular for this effect is using **theta algorithms**, which allows the characters to constantly search for the best path without it being necessary to manually set which points they need to follow.

The Theta search algorithm (A*) is a widely used search algorithm that can be used to find solutions for many problems and pathfinding is one of them. Using this algorithm to solve pathfinding problems is very common due to the uniform-cost search and heuristic search. The Theta search algorithm examines every corner of the map to help the character determine if it is possible to use that location or not, while trying to reach the desired destination.

How it works

The map or scene of the game needs to be prepared or pre-analyzed before the theta algorithm can work. The environment that includes all the assets of the map will be handled as a graph. This means that the map will be broken into different points and locations, which are called nodes. These nodes are used to record all the progress of the search. While memorizing the map location, each individual node has other attributes, such as fitness, goal, and heuristic, usually represented by the letters f, g, and h. The purpose of the fitness, goal, and heuristic attributes is to put in order how good a path is according to the current node.

Different values are assigned to the paths between the nodes. These values usually represent the distances between the nodes. The value between the nodes doesn't necessarily have to be distance. The value can also be time; this will help us find the fastest path instead of the shortest one, for example. The Theta algorithm uses two lists, an open list and a closed list. The open list contains the nodes that were totally explored. Marker arrays can also be used to find out whether a state is in the open list or the closed list.

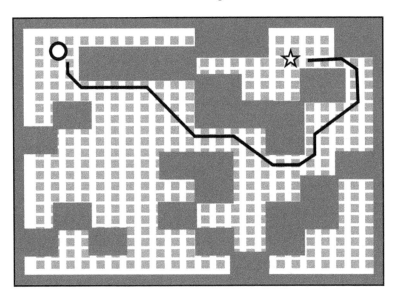

This means that the character will constantly be searching for the best nodes to follow in order to achieve the fastest or shortest results. As we can see in the preceding screenshot, the map was pre-analyzed, the walkable area is represented by the small gray squares, while the big squares represent the area that is blocked by some object or environment asset. The AI character represented by the black and white circle needs to move node by node until it reaches the star object. If for some reason one of the nodes is blocked, the character will rapidly switch to the closest one and then continue on its way.

As we can see, this pathfinding method's theory is very similar to what we have created before, where the character follows point by point until it arrives at the final destination. The main difference is that with the Theta algorithm, the points are generated automatically by the AI, making it the best choice when developing big or complex scenes.

Disadvantages of using A*

The Theta algorithm is not the perfect solution that can be used everywhere or in every game, and we should keep that thought in mind. Because the AI character is constantly searching for the best path to follow, a significant portion of the CPU is being used exclusively for that task. Because tablets and mobile devices are very popular gaming platforms nowadays, it is worth mentioning that developing a game for these platforms requires paying special attention to the CPU and GPU usage, and for that reason, A* pathfinding can be a disadvantage here.

But hardware limitation isn't the only disadvantage. When we let the AI assume all the work without any human control, bugs are highly likely. That is one reason why modern games that prefer using open world maps encounter a lot of bugs and weird AI reactions, because it is extremely difficult to narrow down all the possible outcomes in a massive gameplay area.

" says bugs in the latest demo are natural for open world games"
–Final Fantasy XV director

The director of Final Fantasy XV commented about this issue, stating that bugs are expected in every open world game. This summarizes perfectly why using theta algorithms for AI pathfinding is a popular and efficient approach when developing open world games, but it is not perfect and bugs will definitely occur.

Now that we have a basic understanding of the theta algorithm and the pros and cons of it, let's move on to the practical section.

Going directly from A to B

We are going to start with a simple example, without any obstacles between one point and another. This will help us visualize how the algorithm finds the best path. Then we will be adding an obstacle and observing how the algorithm chooses the best path when contouring the obstacle at the same time.

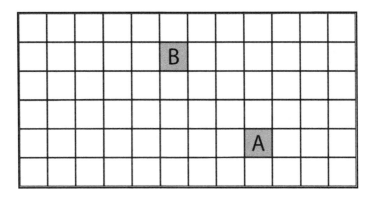

On this grid we have two points, **A** that is the starting point and **B** that is the end point. We want to find the shortest path between the two. To help us solve this problem, we will be using the A* algorithm and we'll see how it manages to find the shortest path.

So, the algorithm calculates every step to find the shortest one. To calculate this, the algorithm uses two nodes, as we discovered before, the G node and the H node. G represents the distance from the starting point, so it calculates how far it is from the **A** position. H represents the distance from the end point, so it calculates how far it is from the **B** position. If we sum both nodes $(G + H = F)$, we get the F node value, which represents the shortest path.

In this case, the shortest number is **42**, so we can move to that position and calculate again every available hypothesis.

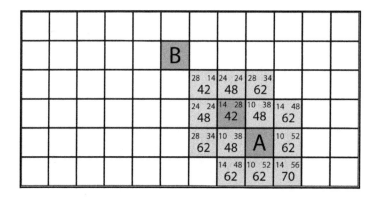

Once again, the algorithm calculates the best options that are available from the position that we are in. We are getting close to B, and for that reason the values for the H nodes are getting smaller while the values for the G nodes are getting bigger, and that is perfectly fine. From all the possibilities that we currently have, the number 42 is once again the lowest number and the best option to take. So the natural decision is to move towards that position.

And finally, we have arrived at the **B** point. Once the algorithm finds that the H node value is zero, that means that it has already arrived at the desired destination and there's no need to keep searching for a better path.

From point A to B with obstacles in the way

This is exactly how the A* pathfinding works; it goes from point to point evaluating the best options and pursuing the shortest path until it reaches the final destination. The earlier example was simple, and now we are going to make it more interesting to see how it works if we add obstacles to the map.

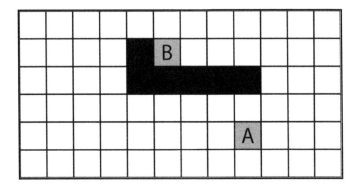

Using the same map, we have painted some squares in black, representing that those positions can't be used. Now, it starts getting slightly more interesting, because if we try to guess what the best path to take would be, we might be wrong. Once again, let's calculate what the best options are, as follows:

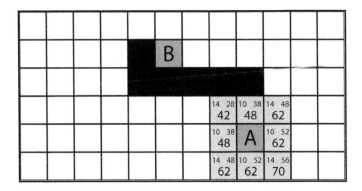

The results that we get are exactly the same as the first test and this is normal, because none of the points that are surrounding the **A** position are positioned on the black squares. Once again, we can move towards the lowest number that is **42**.

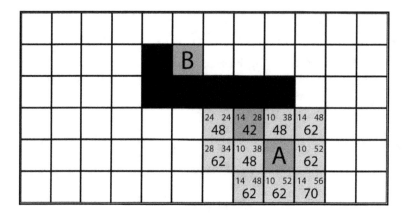

Now that we have made our first move and calculated the best options that are available from that point, we are in an interesting situation. At this moment, we have the three lowest numbers and we have to choose one. We need to find the shortest path that leads us to the **B** position and because the three lowest numbers are the same, we need to make the decision according to the H node only, which represents the distance between our current position and the B position. Two of the positions have the H value of **38** while just one of them has the value of **24**, making it the lowest H value of the three. So let's move on in that direction, which seems to be closer to the final destination.

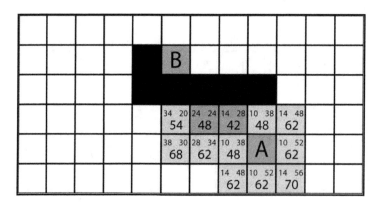

From now on we can notice that the F values are getting higher, which represents the shortest path value. This is due to the black squares that we have added to the map. Because of them, we need to go around, increasing the length of the path that we need to take. This is how the AI will perceive the walls; they know for a fact that the final destination is close, but in order to arrive there, they can't pass through the wall, so they need to go around until they find an open door or something similar.

Now, the lowest values are in the other direction, which means that we need to go back in order to find a better path. This is a very important aspect of the algorithm, because if we have the character walking around searching for the best path at the same time that it is walking, we will have a more human-like result. It will look like that he is searching for the correct path to arrive at the desired destination, like a person would if they didn't know the right path. On the other hand, the character can be programmed to make all the calculations before it starts moving, and in that case we would see a character going directly to the right path until it reaches the final point. Both methods are valid and can be used for different purposes and different games.

Continuing our pathfinding, we need to keep choosing the lowest value, so at this point we need to go back and choose between the two lowest values, **48**. Both have the same G and H values, so the only way to find out which is the best path to take is to randomly choose one of the points or pre-calculate them to see which of them will have the lowest value. So let's choose one randomly to see the values that come up.

After choosing one of the two shortest possibilities, we found that the values are getting higher, and for that reason we need to go back and calculate the other value as well to see if there is a lower value after that. Because we can already see the map and we already know where the **B** point is placed, we know for a fact that the lowest value is actually further away than the **68** value that appeared just now. But if we didn't know where the B point was, we still needed to check that **48** value, to see if the destination point was near that position or not. That is what the AI character will decide in the gameplay it will constantly check the lowest F value.

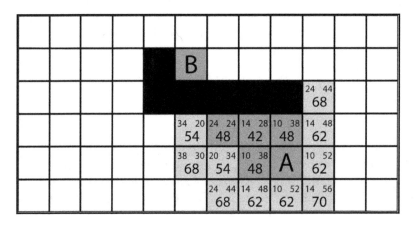

After choosing the new position, we can see that it didn't provide any better opportunities, and we need to keep searching for a better path, which in this case is going to be a point that we have already discovered, but whose outcomes we didn't calculate. Once again, we have the two lowest F values and we will be choosing the lowest H value, that is, **20**.

After calculating the new possibilities, we notice that we need to choose **54** again to see if the final destination is closer to that point. This is exactly the process that will occur when we program the AI to find the shortest path that it will need to take in order to arrive at the final destination. The calculations need to be solved in real time, and as will start to notice, they can get very complex. This is why it consumes a significant portion of the CPU power, because it is the hardware component designated to this function (calculus).

Now, we will be selecting the number **54**, because it is the lowest number on the map.

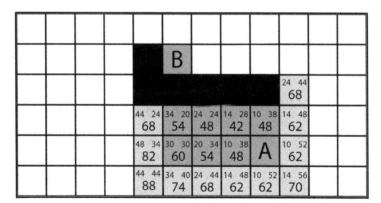

If we keep moving down, the values will get higher, which means that we are getting farther away from where we need to be. If we were the AI and didn't know that the final destination is at the top, we would need to check the number **60**, because it is the most promising of them all at the moment. So, let's calculate the outcomes.

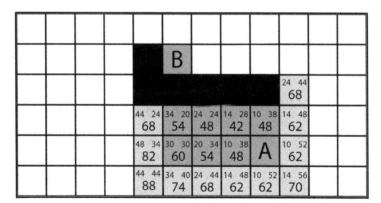

Now, we can see that there are a lot of identical lowest numbers, which are **62**, so we need to explore them all and keep calculating until the character finds the right path. For the purposes of the example we will be moving to every lowest number that we can see on the map now.

					B			38 30 / 68	34 40 / 74	38 50 / 88
		58 24 / 82							24 44 / 68	28 54 / 82
		54 28 / 82	44 24 / 68	34 20 / 54	24 24 / 48	14 28 / 42	10 38 / 48	14 48 / 62	24 58 / 82	
		58 38 / 96	48 34 / 82	30 30 / 60	20 34 / 54	10 38 / 48	A	10 52 / 62	20 62 / 82	
			44 44 / 88	34 40 / 74	24 44 / 68	14 48 / 62	10 52 / 62	14 56 / 70	24 66 / 90	

After exploring all the lowest possibilities, we can see that we are getting closer to the final destination. At this point, the lowest value available is **68**, and after that it will be easy to reach the final point.

					72 10 / 82	62 14 / 76	52 24 / 76	48 34 / 82	52 44 / 96	
					68 0 / 68	58 10 / 68	48 20 / 68	38 30 / 68	34 40 / 74	38 50 / 88
		58 24 / 82							24 44 / 68	28 54 / 82
		54 28 / 82	44 24 / 68	34 20 / 54	24 24 / 48	14 28 / 42	10 38 / 48	14 48 / 62	24 58 / 82	
		58 38 / 96	48 34 / 82	30 30 / 60	20 34 / 54	10 38 / 48	A	10 52 / 62	20 62 / 82	
			44 44 / 88	34 40 / 74	24 44 / 68	14 48 / 62	10 52 / 62	14 56 / 70	24 66 / 90	

Finally, we have arrived at the point **B** destination. This is the visual aspect of A* algorithm, where the darker gray area represents the positions that the computer has visited and the lighter gray area represents the outcome calculations of those areas that we visited.

The computer can calculate the best path in real time, or the developers can also choose to let the AI calculate the best options before exporting the game. So the AI will automatically know which path it needs to follow when the game starts, saving some CPU power.

To explain how this works in the programming language, we will be using pseudo code to demonstrate this example. This way we can understand from start to finish how we can create the search method in any programming language and how we can adapt it ourselves:

```
OPEN // the set of nodes to be evaluated
CLOSED // the set of nodes already evaluated

Add the start node to OPEN

loop
    current = node in OPEN with the lowest f_cost
    remove current from OPEN
    add current to CLOSED

    if current is the target node // path has been found
        return

    foreach neighbor of the current node
        if neighbor is not traversable or neighbor is in CLOSED
            skip to the next neighbor

if new path to neighbor is shorter OR neighbor is not in OPEN
    set f_cost of neighbor
    set parent of neighbor to current
    if neighbor is not in OPEN
        add neighbor to OPEN
```

Let's analyze each line of code that we used to create the example. We have divided the grid map into two different categories: OPEN and CLOSED. The OPEN ones are the squares that we have already explored, represented on the image by the dark gray blocks. While the CLOSED are the white blocks that we didn't explore yet. This will allow the AI to distinguish between the explored and not explored blocks, going from point to point finding the best path:

```
Add the start node to OPEN
```

Then we assigned the first block that is considered OPEN; this will set the starting point and it will automatically start calculating the best options from that position:

```
loop
    current = node in OPEN with the lowest f_cost
    remove current from OPEN
    add current to CLOSED
```

After that, we need to create a loop, and inside our loop we have a temporary variable called `current`; this is equal to the node in the OPEN list that has the lowest F cost. Then it will be removed from the OPEN list and added to the CLOSED list:

```
if current is the target node // path has been found
        return
```

Then, if the current node is the target node, the code assumes that the final destination has been explored and we can just exit out of the loop:

```
foreach neighbor of the current node
        if neighbor is not traversable or neighbor is in CLOSED
            skip to the next neighbor
```

Otherwise, we must go through each of the `neighbor` nodes of the current node. If it is not traversable, meaning that we cannot pass that position or if it was previously explored and is on the CLOSED list, the code can skip to the next neighbor. This part sets where it is possible to move and also tells the AI to not take into consideration positions that were previously explored:

```
if new path to neighbor is shorter OR neighbor is not in OPEN
    set f_cost of neighbor
    set parent of neighbor to current
    if neighbor is not in OPEN
        add neighbor to OPEN
```

If it is not the case, then we can move on and check a couple of things. If the new path to the `neighbor` is shorter than the old path or if the `neighbor` is not on the OPEN list, then we set the `f_cost` of the `neighbor` by calculating the `g_cost` and the `h_cost`. We see the new possible blocks have children from the current block, so we can trace the steps that are being taken. And finally, if the `neighbor` is not on the OPEN list, we can add it.

Looping this, the code will constantly be searching for the best options and moving towards the closest values until it arrives at the target node value.

The same principles that we have just learned can be found in pedestrians of the *GTA 5*. Many other games use this method, obviously, but we wanted to use this game as an example of the two pathfinding systems that can be found in most games. If we applied this system to AI police in order to search and find the player, we would have more or less the same results that can be seen in the actual gameplay.

It takes more than just searching for the final destination, and this is just a small portion of the final code, but we would see an AI character avoiding walls and getting closer to the player position, step by step. On top of that, it would be necessary to add more content to the AI code, letting the character know what to do in multiple situations that can occur, such as having water in the middle of the path, stairs, moving cars, and many others.

Generating grid nodes

Now we are going to implement what we have learned so far into a practical exercise. Let's start by creating or importing our scene into the game editor.

For this example, we are going to use buildings as non-walkable objects, but it can be anything that we choose, then we need to separate the objects that we just imported from the ground. To do this, we are going to assign them to a separate layer, and we are going to call it **unwalkable**.

Then we can start creating our first class of the game, and we are going to start from the node class:

```
public bool walkable;
 public Vector3 worldPosition; public Node(bool _walkable, Vector3
      _worldPos, int _gridX, int _gridY) {
      walkable = _walkable;
      worldPosition = _worldPos;
```

We have seen that the nodes have two different states, either they are walkable or non-walkable, so we can start by creating a Boolean called walkable. Then we need to know in what point in the world the node represents, so we create a Vector 3 for the worldPosition. Now, we need some way to assign these values when we create a node, so we create the Node variable that will contain all the important information regarding the nodes.

After creating the essential part of this class, we can move on to the `grid` class:

```
Node[,] grid;
public LayerMask unwalkableMask;
public Vector2 gridWorldSize;
publicfloatnodeRadius;
void OnDrawGizmos()
{
        Gizmos.DrawWireCube(transform.position,new
    Vector3(gridWorldSize.x,1,gridWorldSize.y));
}
```

First of all, we need a two-dimensional array of nodes that represents our grid, so let's create a two-dimensional array of nodes, and we can call it `grid`. Then we can create a `Vector2` that will define the area in world coordinates that this grid covers and call it `gridWorldSize`. We also need a `float` variable to define how much space each individual node covers, which in this class is called `nodeRadius`. Then we need to create a `LayerMask` to define the area that is non-walkable and give it the name `unwalkableMask`.

In order to visualize the grid that we just created in our game editor, we decided to use `OnDrawGizmos` method; using this is useful but not mandatory:

```
public LayerMask unwalkableMask;
public Vector2 gridWorldSize;
public float nodeRadius;
Node[,] grid;

float nodeDiameter;
int gridSizeX, gridSizeY;

void Start() {
    nodeDiameter = nodeRadius*2;
    gridSizeX = Mathf.RoundToInt(gridWorldSize.x/nodeDiameter);
    gridSizeY = Mathf.RoundToInt(gridWorldSize.y/nodeDiameter);
    CreateGrid();
}

void CreateGrid(){
    grid = new Node[gridSizeX,gridSizeY];
    Vector3 worldBottomLeft = transform.position - Vector3.right *
gridWorldSize.x/2 - Vector3.forward * gridWorldSize.y/2;
    }
```

Let's create a Start method, and we are going to add some basic calculations. The main thing that we need to figure out is how many nodes can we fit in to our grid. We start by creating a new float variable called nodeDiameter and new int variables called gridSizeX and gridSizeY. Then, inside of our Start method we are going to add the value of the nodeDiameter that is equal to nodeRadius*2. gridSizeX is equal to gridWorldSize.x/nodeDiameter,and this will tell us how many nodes can fit in the gridWorldSize.x. Then we will be rounding the number to fit into an integer number, so we will be using Mathf.RoundToInt to make this possible. After creating the calculus for the x axis, we can duplicate the same code and change it to make it work for the y axis. To finalize our Start method, we create a new function, we are going to call CreateGrid():

```
public LayerMask unwalkableMask;
public Vector2 gridWorldSize;
public float nodeRadius;
Node[,] grid;

float nodeDiameter;
int gridSizeX, gridSizeY;

void Start(){
        nodeDiameter = nodeRadius*2;
        gridSizeX = Mathf.RoundToInt(gridWorldSize.x/nodeDiameter);
        gridSizeY = Mathf.RoundToInt(gridWorldSize.y/nodeDiameter);
        CreateGrid();
}

void CreateGrid()
{
        grid = new Node[gridSizeX,gridSizeY];
        Vector3 worldBottomLeft = transform.position - Vector3.right *
        gridWorldSize.x/2 - Vector3.forward * gridWorldSize.y/2;

        for (int x = 0; x < gridSizeX; x ++) {
            for (int y = 0; y < gridSizeY; y ++) {
                Vector3 worldPoint = worldBottomLeft + Vector3.right *
                (x * nodeDiameter + nodeRadius) + Vector3.forward * (y
                * nodeDiameter + nodeRadius);
                bool walkable = !(Physics.CheckSphere(worldPoint,
                                nodeRadius,unwalkableMask));
                grid[x,y] = new Node(walkable,worldPoint);
            }
        }
}
```

Here we add the value of the `grid` variable, `grid = new Node[gridSizeX, gridSizeY];`. Now we need to add collision detection that will establish the walkable and non-walkable areas of the map. To do this, we create a loop that can be seen in the code demonstrated previously. We simply added a new `Vector3` variable to get the bottom left corner of the map, which is called `worldBottomLeft`. Then we assigned the collision detection, which will search for any objects that are colliding with the walkable area by using `Physics.Check`:

```
void OnDrawGizmos() {
        Gizmos.DrawWireCube(transform.position,new
        Vector3(gridWorldSize.x,1,gridWorldSize.y));


        if (grid != null) {
            foreach (Node n in grid) {
                Gizmos.color = (n.walkable)?Color.white:Color.red;
                Gizmos.DrawCube(n.worldPosition, Vector3.one *
                (nodeDiameter-.1f));
            }
        }
    }
```

Before testing it out, we need to update our `OnDrawGizmos` function, so that we can see the grid on top of the map. To make the grid visible, we assigned the colors red and white and the form of the cubes by using the `nodeDiameter` value to set the dimension of each cube. If the node is walkable, the color will be set to white; otherwise, it will be set to red. Now we can test it out:

The results are wonderful; now we have a grid that auto-analyses the map and indicates the walkable and non-walkable areas. With this part completed, the rest will be easier to implement. Before moving on to the next part, we need to add a method that will tell our character which node it is standing in. In our code, we will be adding a function called `NodeFromWorldPoint` that will make this possible:

```
public LayerMask unwalkableMask;
public Vector2 gridWorldSize;
public float nodeRadius;
Node[,] grid;

float nodeDiameter;
int gridSizeX, gridSizeY;

void Start(){
        nodeDiameter = nodeRadius*2;
        gridSizeX = Mathf.RoundToInt(gridWorldSize.x/nodeDiameter);
        gridSizeY = Mathf.RoundToInt(gridWorldSize.y/nodeDiameter);
        CreateGrid();
}

void CreateGrid()
{
        grid = new Node[gridSizeX,gridSizeY];
        Vector3 worldBottomLeft = transform.position - Vector3.right *
            gridWorldSize.x/2 - Vector3.forward * gridWorldSize.y/2;

        for (int x = 0; x < gridSizeX; x ++) {
            for (int y = 0; y < gridSizeY; y ++) {
                Vector3 worldPoint = worldBottomLeft + Vector3.right *
                (x * nodeDiameter + nodeRadius) + Vector3.forward * (y
                * nodeDiameter + nodeRadius);
                bool walkable = !(Physics.CheckSphere(worldPoint,
                                    nodeRadius,unwalkableMask));
                grid[x,y] = new Node(walkable,worldPoint);
            }
        }
}
public Node NodeFromWorldPoint(Vector3 worldPosition) {
        float percentX = (worldPosition.x + gridWorldSize.x/2) /
        gridWorldSize.x;
        float percentY = (worldPosition.z + gridWorldSize.y/2) /
        gridWorldSize.y;
        percentX = Mathf.Clamp01(percentX);
        percentY = Mathf.Clamp01(percentY);

        int x = Mathf.RoundToInt((gridSizeX-1) * percentX);
```

```
        int y = Mathf.RoundToInt((gridSizeY-1) * percentY);
        return grid[x,y];
    } void OnDrawGizmos() {
        Gizmos.DrawWireCube(transform.position,new
        Vector3(gridWorldSize.x,1,gridWorldSize.y));


        if (grid != null) {
            foreach (Node n in grid) {
                Gizmos.color = (n.walkable)?Color.white:Color.red;
                Gizmos.DrawCube(n.worldPosition, Vector3.one *
                (nodeDiameter-.1f));
            }
        }
    }
}
```

And we have finally completed the first part of our example. We have a code that can work in any scene–we just need to define the scale of the map in which we want the code to search for the walkable and non-walkable areas, and the dimensions of each node in case we want to change the precision of the pathfinding remember that if we increase the number of nodes on the map, more CPU power will be required to calculate the pathfinding system).

Pathfinding implementation

The next step is to set the character to search for the final destination that we want. Let's start by creating a new class, which we will call **pathfinding**. This class will manage the search for the best path in order to reach the final destination. It will calculate in real time the shortest path that the character needs to follow and it will be updated every second, so if the final destination is moving, it will keep following and recalculating the best path.

We start by adding the AI character into our game editor that will eventually search for another character of the game. For test purposes, we will simply add some basic functions to our character that will let him move around the map, but we can also use a simple cube to test whether the pathfinding system is working.

After importing our character into the game, we can start creating the class that will be assigned to it:

```
Grid grid;

void Awake(){
      requestManager = GetComponent<PathRequestManager>();
      grid = GetComponent<Grid>();
 }

void FindPath(Vector3 startPos, Vector3 targetPos)
{
Node startNode = grid.NodeFromWorldPoint(startPos);
 Node targetNode = grid.NodeFromWorldPoint(targetPos);
 }
```

We start by creating a function called `FindPath` that will store all the necessary values to calculate the distance between the start position and the target position. Then we add a `Grid` variable that will have the same value as the `grid` that we have previously created. Then we used the `Awake` function to access to the `grid` values:

```
void FindPath(Vector3 startPos, Vector3 targetPos)
{
Node startNode = grid.NodeFromWorldPoint(startPos);
Node targetNode = grid.NodeFromWorldPoint(targetPos);

List<Node> openSet = new List<Node>();
HashSet<Node> closedSet = new HashSet<Node>();
openSet.Add(startNode);
 }
```

Then we need to create a list that will contain all of the nodes present in the game, as we have demonstrated before. One list contains all the OPEN nodes, and another one will contain all the CLOSED nodes:

```
public bool walkable;
public Vector3 worldPosition;

public int gCost;
public int hCost;
public Node parent;
public Node(bool _walkable, Vector3 _worldPos, int _gridX, int _gridY)
```

```
{
        walkable = _walkable;
        worldPosition = _worldPos;
}

public int fCost
{
        get {
                return gCost + hCost;
        }
}
```

Now we have opened the Node class, and we added new variables called gCost and hCost. The idea is that this class calculates the shortest path value, and as we saw previously, in order to get the fCost that represents the shortest path, we need to sum the values of the g and h nodes.

$f(n)=g(n)+h(n)$.

Once the Node class is edited, we can go back to our pathfinding class and continue implementing the lines of code that will make our AI character search for the optimal path:

```
Grid grid;

void Awake()
{
        grid = GetComponent<Grid> ();
}

void FindPath(Vector3 startPos, Vector3 targetPos)
{
    Node startNode = grid.NodeFromWorldPoint(startPos);
    Node targetNode - grid.NodeFromWorldPoint(targetPos);

    List<Node> openSet = new List<Node>();
    HashSet<Node> closedSet = new HashSet<Node>();
    openSet.Add(startNode);

    while (openSet.Count > 0)
{
        Node node = openSet[0];
        for (int i = 1; i < openSet.Count; i ++) {
        if (openSet[i].fCost < node.fCost || openSet[i].fCost ==
        node.fCost) {
```

```
                    if (openSet[i].hCost < node.hCost)
                        node = openSet[i];
            }
        }
```

Back to our pathfinding class; we need to define the current node that the character is positioned in. To make this happen, we added `Node currentNode = openSet[0];` this will set 0 as the default node. Then we create the loop that will compare the `fCost` of the possible nodes to choose which one is the best option, `openSet[i].fCost < node.fCost || openSet[i].fCost == node.fCost`. This is the code that we have used to achieve the desirable results for this example, but it can still be optimized if necessary:

```
Grid grid;
void Awake()
{
        grid = GetComponent<Grid> ();
}

void FindPath(Vector3 startPos, Vector3 targetPos)
{
    Node startNode = grid.NodeFromWorldPoint(startPos);
    Node targetNode = grid.NodeFromWorldPoint(targetPos);

    List<Node> openSet = new List<Node>();
    HashSet<Node> closedSet = new HashSet<Node>();
    openSet.Add(startNode);

    while (openSet.Count > 0)
    {
            Node node = openSet[0];
            for (int i = 1; i < openSet.Count; i ++)
    {

            if (openSet[i].fCost < node.fCost || openSet[i].fCost ==
            node.fCost){
                    if (openSet[i].hCost < node.hCost)
            node = openSet[i];
                }
            }

            openSet.Remove(node);
            closedSet.Add(node);

            if (node == targetNode) {
                    RetracePath(startNode,targetNode);
                    return;
            }
```

Continuing our loop, we have now defined when the current node is set to OPEN or CLOSED and established that if the current node value is equal to the target node value, it means that the character already has arrived at the final destination if (currentNode == targetNode):

```
public List<Node> GetNeighbors(Node node)
{
    List<Node> neighbors = new List<Node>();

    for (int x = -1; x <= 1; x++) {
        for (int y = -1; y <= 1; y++) {
            if (x == 0 && y == 0)
                continue;

            int checkX = node.gridX + x;
            int checkY = node.gridY + y;

            if (checkX >= 0 && checkX < gridSizeX && checkY >= 0 &&
            checkY < gridSizeY) {
                neighbors.Add(grid[checkX,checkY]);
                }
            }
        }
    }
```

Now we need to loop through each of the neighbor nodes of the current node. To do this, we have decided to add this to our grid code, so we need to open the grid class that we created at the beginning of the example and add the List function demonstrated previously. Then we will be adding the necessary values to the Node class (gridX and gridY):

```
public bool walkable;
public Vector3 worldPosition;
public int gridX;
public int gridY;

public int gCost;
public int hCost;
public Node parent;
public Node(bool _walkable, Vector3 _worldPos, int _gridX, int _gridY)
{
    walkable = _walkable;
    worldPosition = _worldPos;
    gridX = _gridX;
    gridY = _gridY;
}
```

```
public int fCost
{
    get
{
        return gCost + hCost;
    }
}
```

Here, we have added the final content for the `Node` class that contains the `gridX` and `gridY` values that will be used by the `grid` code. This is the final look at the `Node` class. Now, we can move on to the pathfinding class again:

```
foreach (Node neighbor in grid.GetNeighbors(node)) {
if (!neighbor.walkable || closedSet.Contains(neighbor))
{
            continue;
}
}
```

Here, we have added a `foreach` loop that will loop through the neighbors to check if they are walkable or non-walkable.

To better understand the next step that we are going to take, there will be some example diagrams of what we want to achieve to complete the pathfinding system:

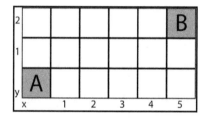

We first need to count along the **X** axis to know how many nodes away we are from the final position on the **X** axis, and then we count along the **Y** axis to find out how many nodes away we are from the final position on the **Y** axis:

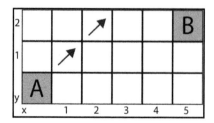

In this example, we can see that in order to get to the **B** position we need to move upwards two points. Because we are always searching for the shortest path, at the same time we are going upwards, we move on the **X** axis:

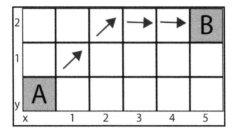

To calculate how many either vertical or horizontal moves are necessary to reach the **B** position, we just subtract the lower number from the higher number. For example, before going on a straight line to the **B** position, it is necessary to calculate *5-2 = 3*, which gives us how many horizontal moves we need to reach the final destination.

Now, we can get back to the pathfinding code and add the equation that we have just learned:

```
int GetDistance(Node nodeA, Node nodeB)
{
    int dstX = Mathf.Abs(nodeA.gridX - nodeB.gridX);
    int dstY = Mathf.Abs(nodeA.gridY - nodeB.gridY);

    if (dstX > dstY)
            return 14*dstY + 10* (dstX-dstY);
    return 14*dstX + 10 * (dstY-dstX);
}
```

Here, we just added the lines of code that will tell us how many horizontal and vertical steps the AI needs to take in order to arrive at the target destination. Now, if we look back at the pseudo code that we created at the very beginning of this chapter to check what is left to create, we can see that we have followed the same structure and that we are almost finished. The pseudo code is as follows:

```
OPEN // the set of nodes to be evaluated
CLOSED // the set of nodes already evaluated

Add the start node to OPEN

loop
    current = node in OPEN with the lowest f_cost
    remove current from OPEN
    add current to CLOSED
```

```
if current is the target node // path has been found
      return

foreach neighbor of the current node
      if neighbor is not traversable or neighbor is in CLOSED
            skip to the next neighbor

if new path to neighbor is shorter OR neighbor is not in OPEN
   set f_cost of neighbor
   set parent of neighbor to current
   if neighbor is not in OPEN
         add neighbor to OPEN
```

So, let's keep adding more important content into our code and keep moving towards the conclusion of the pathfinding class.

We need to set the neighbor's `f_cost` and as we already know, to calculate this value, we need to use the `g_Cost` and `h_Cost` of the neighbor node:

```
foreach (Node neighbor in grid.GetNeighbors(node))
{
    if (!neighbor.walkable || closedSet.Contains(neighbor)) {
        continue;
    }

    int newCostToNeighbor = node.gCost + GetDistance(node, neighbor);
    if (newCostToNeighbor < neighbor.gCost ||
    !openSet.Contains(neighbor)) {
        neighbor.gCost = newCostToNeighbor;
        neighbor.hCost = GetDistance(neighbor, targetNode);
        neighbor.parent = node;
    }
}
```

In the pathfinding class we have added the following code, which will calculate the neighbor nodes to check for their `f_cost`:

```
void RetracePath(Node startNode, Node endNode) {
        List<Node> path = new List<Node>();
        Node currentNode = endNode;

        while (currentNode != startNode) {
                path.Add(currentNode);
                currentNode = currentNode.parent;
        }
        path.Reverse();

        grid.path = path;
}
```

Before exiting from the loop, we will be calling a function called `RetracePath`, and we can give it `startNode` and `targetNode`. Then we have to create that new function with the same name and assign a list of the nodes that we have already explored. In order to visualize the pathfinding to see if it is working properly or not, we also have a path that we will be creating in the `grid` class:

```
public List<Node> path;
void OnDrawGizmos()
{
Gizmos.DrawWireCube(transform.position,new
Vector3(gridWorldSize.x,1,gridWorldSize.y));

        if (grid != null) {
                foreach (Node n in grid) {
                        Gizmos.color = (n.walkable)?Color.white:Color.red;
                        if (path != null)
                                if (path.Contains(n))
                                        Gizmos.color = Color.black;
                        Gizmos.DrawCube(n.worldPosition, Vector3.one *
(nodeDiameter-.1f));
                }
        }
}
```

This section of the `grid` class was updated, now containing the `List`, `path`, and a new gizmo that will show on the editor view, the path between the AI position and the target position:

```
public Transform seeker, target;

Grid grid;

void Awake()
{
    grid = GetComponent<Grid> ();
}

void Update()
{
    FindPath (seeker.position, target.position);
}
```

And finally, to conclude our example, we add a `void Update()` into our pathfinding class that will make the AI constantly search for the target position.

Now we can move on to our game editor and assign the code pathfinding that we have created to the grid. Then we simply assign the AI character and the target position that we want:

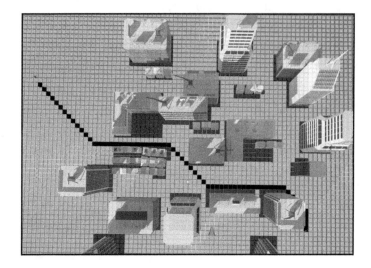

If we test the pathfinding system, we can see that it is working perfectly. In the preceding screenshot, the top left point is the AI character's position, and in the bottom right is the target destination. We can see that the character planned the shortest path and one that avoids colliding with the buildings:

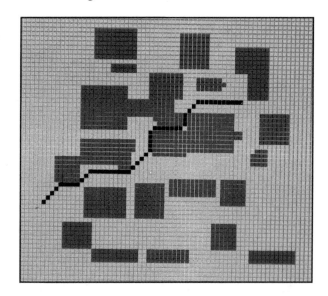

Then we have disabled the mesh from the buildings to have a better look at the walkable and unwalkable areas of the map. We can see that the character only chooses the walkable areas and avoids any obstacles in its way. It is complicated to demonstrate it using still images, but if we change the target location in real time, we can see the pathfinding adjusting the route that the character needs to take, and it always chooses the shortest path.

The advanced pathfinding system that we have just created can be found in many popular games that everybody loves. Now that we have learned how to create a complex pathfinding system, we are able to re-create some parts of the most advanced AI characters of modern games such as GTA or Assassins Creed. Talking about Assassins Creed, it will be our next game, reference for the next chapter because its AI characters link perfectly between A* pathfinding and realistic crowd interactions, as we can see in the preceding screenshot.

Summary

In this chapter, we revisited how to create point-to-point movement, but instead of using a simple method, we have studied how huge and successful game studios manage to solve one of the most complicated features of a AI, pathfinding. Here, we have learned how to use theta algorithms to recreate an human feature that helps us search and move in the right direction in order to arrive at the desired destination.

In the next chapter, we will be talking about realistic crowd interactions, a very important aspect when trying to make an AI character as realistic as possible. We will be studying different approaches used in different types of game, and also we will be looking at how humans and animals interact in their environments and how we can use that in our AI code.

8
Crowd Interactions

After understanding how to develop an AI character that can move freely around the map, searching for the best paths to arrive at certain destinations, we can start working on the interaction between characters. In this chapter, we will be looking at realistic crowd interactions, how to develop a believable crowd behavior, and how a character should perceive the rest of the group. The goal of this chapter is to keep giving information to our AI character about the environment, and in this particular case, about the other intelligent agents of the game. On this chapter, we will be talking about AI coordination, communication and crowd collision avoidance.

What is crowd interaction

Crowd interaction is a real-life subject that usually refers to multiple organisms sharing the same space. One big example is the human life, how humans interact with other humans and also other species. The decisions that we make most of the time involve other people, from the simple decisions to the most advanced and complicated ones. Let's assume that we want to buy a ticket for the cinema and the movie starts at 3pm. If we were the only ones interested in watching that movie, we could arrive only 2 minutes before it starts to buy a ticket and we would be on time to watch the movie. But if more than 100 people are interested in watching that same movie, we need to anticipate that and arrive much earlier at the cinema so we have time to buy the ticket. Once we arrive at the cinema, there are rules about how we should wait until it is our turn to buy the ticket. Usually we wait behind the last person that is in the line. This behavior is an example of crowd interactions. We live surrounded by other humans, and for that reason we need to adapt our goals accordingly.

In video games, we also can find this type of interaction, and can go from simple behaviors to advanced and complex ones. If we have more than one AI character in the game and they share the same space, there will be times where one will collide with another. It's up to the creators to think about that, about what would happen if two characters try to do the same thing at the same time, if it makes sense or if it will result in bugs. To solve these problems, we need to think about them and implement decisions that will help characters share the same space together, avoiding errors and behaving more realistically.

Video games and crowd interactions

As we have discovered before, crowd interactions are a real-life matter, but it can be found in video games, especially those that relies on human-like aspects. Because of the popularity of open-world maps, crowd interactions became a very important aspect when developing the game, because the AI agents of the game are constantly sharing the same space. This means that almost every open world game has the necessity to plan a crowd interaction system.

Assassin's Creed

A very popular case of crowd interaction system on a video game can be found in the Assassin's Creed series. The non-playable characters walk around the map in groups, and in a simple way they avoid collisions and interact with the environment. This helps create a realistic atmosphere to the game, a crucial point that can make the game believable and submerging the player into a virtual world:

Not only can we see group interaction in the general population of the game, but also in the guards and especially in the combat. From time to time, the player needs to fight against a few guards, and usually there is more than one guard ready to attack the player. One interesting point is that the guards don't attack at the same time; they evaluate the situation and wait for a better opportunity to attack.

This concept gives a sense of interaction between the multiple non-playable characters:

Grand Theft Auto (GTA)

The Grand Theft Auto game series is a source of many interesting lessons that we can learn with it. The constant seek to keep improving the game every time by trying to make it more realistic and believable changed the focus of the player to the surroundings, instead of simply looking at the main character. To make the surroundings more appealing and realistic, the creators of the game started to spend more time developing AI agents, how they move, how they react, and how they interact. The interaction between the AI characters was groundbreaking at the time.

The player could see characters stopping to talk with each other, confronting physically with each other in more dramatic events, and all of that made the environment much more alive:

As we can see on the preceding screenshot, the streets of the game are populated by distinct individuals that are interacting with each other. We can see a man taking his dog for a walk, two girls talking, a young woman taking a picture of another woman, and all of this does not contribute in any way to the gameplay but it makes the experience much more vivid and realistic.

The Sims

Another great example of crowd interaction can be found in the real-life simulator game, *The Sims*. Once again we are mentioning this game because it shaped the way developers create their games, and in terms of AI, they have contributed a lot about it.

Non-playable characters do not mean that they simply need to be in idle position, waiting for something to happen. Here we can see that all the characters have unique personalities and that they interact with each other. Even if the player sets aside the controller and just watches the game, there will be many interesting things going on, and all of that comes from the AI characters:

Previously in this book we have analyzed the priorities of *The Sims* characters, and we know that they can decide not to do one thing if another is more important at the time. And now that we know how pathfinding works, we can even implement a more advanced system into the characters, for example, letting them organize their priorities, taking in consideration the time that its necessary for them in order to reach the specific destination that lets them conclude the task. But all of that will be explored in a moment.

FIFA/Pro evolution soccer

Another example that is extremely important to mention is the AI character that can be found in multiple sports games. Even if from the outside it doesn't look a game genre that is complex, sports games are probably the most advanced in terms of AI development.

The reason is that the games are based on real-life sports, and many of them are team sports. The difficulties in developing a realistic and functional team sports game are numerous, and for that reason it is a great case study:

The preceding screenshot shows gameplay footage of FIFA 17. Here we can see that only one character has the possession of the ball, while all the others are spread apart, either waiting for the character to pass the ball or anticipating the character's position in order to attempt win the ball from him. In total, that makes one ball for twenty-two characters in the game (eleven for each side). This is the reason why sports games require well-developed AI characters, because they are constantly working even if they don't have the ball. Individually, they have a position/role that they play, defending or attacking, left, right, or middle position, and many more. In the group, they all need to follow a strategy together and obey the rules of the game. If our teammate has the ball and is running forward, we can support him by running in the same direction, making it easy for him to pass, or we can stay behind because if that player loses the ball, someone needs to catch it back.

The interactions between the other characters are happening constantly, and it's not only about running after the ball to see who can get it first, it's about sharing a lot of information between them and trying to win the game.

Planning crowd interactions

Sometimes we put aside the planning phase while creating a game and think that all we need to create an awesome game is to have an idea and everything will flow smoothly from our head. Successful games are successful because every step of the development is planned to the smallest detail, and we should remember that when creating our own games. At this point, we have a strong technical knowledge to develop a challenging and interesting game with plenty of AI features in it, so our next step is to combine the ability to create games with a plan to make them look better.

Now that we've analyzed some popular examples of crowd interaction systems in video games, we can take a look at how to plan these types of interaction. We will follow the examples from before and see how we can plan similar crowd interaction into our games.

Group fight

Let's create a scenario where we have multiple AI characters fighting the player. We start by implementing the combat features into the character code, such as attacking with one hand, attacking with two hands, defending, going after the player, and all of that. Once we have that implemented, the character is able to fight the player and that's the starting point. If we didn't plan anything and we had four characters fighting the player, they all would attack at the same time to defeat the player.

That would have worked with a few bugs here and there, but it would do the job if we didn't have time to create a better system. What we are looking for is to get some interaction between the AI characters so they won't look stupid attacking the player at the same time without analyzing the situation:

So, now that we have the game running and we have enemy characters that follow the player and attack him, we want to plan the interaction between the AI characters to let them decide who should attack first and when the others can attack too.

We can choose from numerous factors that the characters will have in consideration to make this decision, and the more we plan, more developed and challenging the AI character become:

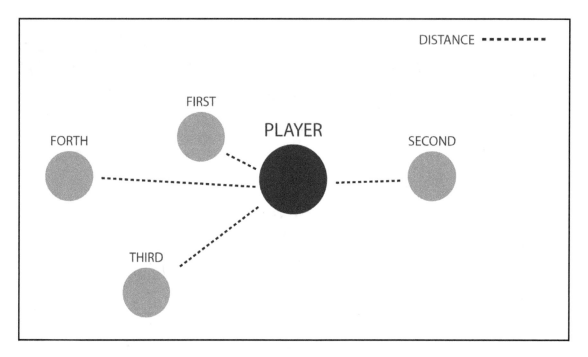

For this example, we used the distance between the AI characters and the player to determine which one will attack first. We want the closest character to attack first and all the others will wait until that one has low HP. Once that character has low HP, the second closest character will intervene in the fight and attack the player.

Now that we have our first criteria set on our characters to decide which one should be the first to attack, we can move on to determine what happens to the other characters while they are waiting. We also need to take into consideration that the player can decide to attack any other character at any time, and we don't want the AI character to stay on idle position just because it's not his time to attack. So the idea is to think about different situations that can happen and plan how the AI would behave in those situations, in particular, especially how they will interact with each other:

```
public static int attackOrder;
public bool nearPlayer;
public float distancePlayer;
public static int charactersAttacking;
private bool Attack;
```

```
private bool Defend;
private bool runAway;
private bool surpriseAttack;

void Update ()
{

    if(distancePlayer < 30f)
    {
        nearPlayer = true;
    }

    if(distancePlayer > 30f)
    {
        nearPlayer = false;
    }

    if(nearPlayer == true && attackOrder == 1)
    {
        Attack = true;
    }

    else
    {
        Defend = true;
    }

}
```

We can start with a simple code just to determine the behavior of the character according to the situation that we are working with, and then we can keep adding more content as necessary to make it work as we want to. For this example, we have created a static integer called attackOrder that will contain the attack order of each character, so they know if it's their time to attack or not. After that, we have a public Boolean called nearPlayer, which will check whether the player is close the player character or not. We can have 30 characters on the map but we just want the closest ones to attack the characters. For this example, the others will simply ignore the player. To determine whether the AI character is near or not, we have a public float called distancePlayer, which will be the result of the distance between the AI character and the player. Then we have added a public static int called charactersAttacking, where the number will increase each time a new character arrives near the player. We can use this to give information to the other characters about how many skeletons are currently attacking the player.

A small and simple code such as this one can make a huge difference for the crowd interaction that we are working on, because we can use the information about how many characters are attacking the player to decide what they will do. For example, we can determine that if there's only two characters attacking, one will constantly defend the player's attacks while the other attacks, and when the player switches from one character to another, they will do the same thing and swap their roles, making it harder for the player to defeat the enemies:

This can be seen in the preceding screenshot, where one of the skeletons tells the other that it will be defending and that the other one can attack the player from behind. This is exactly what crowd interaction is, one character giving information to another about what it can do or how it should behave. The more information the characters share with the others, the more options they have of what they can do, and the more realistic their interactions will look because they are not acting alone.

As we can see, even with simple codes we can achieve complex results, but it's necessary to think about it and plan everything ahead, and obviously the code will get bigger every time we add more details and options to it.

Communication (attention zones)

Continuing with the same example, where we have a few skeletons on the map that will start attacking the player if the player gets near them, we can add one more feature that will make them interact even more one with another. Another thing that will make the characters behave like a group instead of single characters placed on the game is the communication. For example, here we have the skeletons that will only attack if the player is near, but what happens if one of the skeletons that is near the player yells that he saw the player character? We can assume that all the AI characters around that area will hear the yell and will start running in that direction in order to help their friend.

Once again, we can use simple lines of code in order to achieve this, but if we don't plan the interactions and how the characters should behave has a group, this type of element will be missing from the AI characters and they will behave independently, which will make it not so smart.

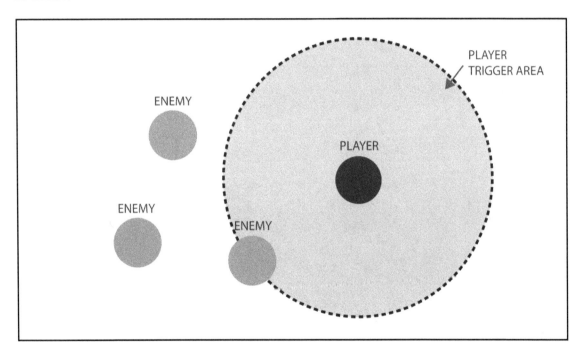

As we can see, this is the system that we have right now. The AI characters don't communicate with each other and so the only skeletons that are aware of the player's position are the ones that are close enough to the player. If we are trying to create a crowd system, we need to plan situations like this one. Just because the other ones don't see the player character, doesn't necessarily mean that they have to react like nothing is happening.

Let's think about a real-life situation. For example, we have one person inside a house and another one outside. The person that is outside of the house sees an incredible beautiful bird while the person that is inside doesn't see it, so it will remain inside of the house. If the person that saw the bird doesn't communicate with the other one, the person that is inside the house will never know about it. So, normally what would happen is the person that sees the bird will call the other one to come outside so it can see the beautiful bird as well. This is a realistic behavior that can be implemented in our crowd interaction system.

To change this non-interaction situation to a more realistic version, we need to add one more feature to our characters that will make them communicate with each other. At this point, we just need simple communication, and we could use a similar code to what we have used to determine if the character can see the player or not:

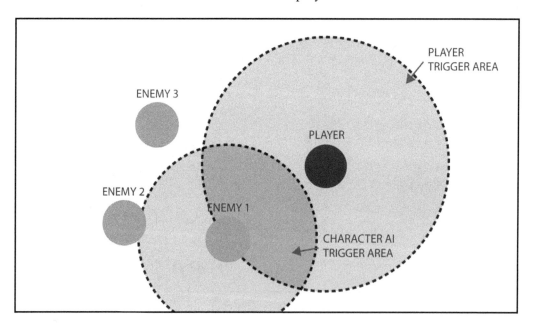

So now we have a AI character that has entered on the player trigger area, and for that reason he will yell so the others AI characters that are near are aware of the player's position as well. In the preceding diagram, we can see that now not only the player has a trigger area, but the enemy that has spotted the player has one as well. This new trigger area will serve to alert the other characters, and it's meant to represent a yell. So when we play the game, and the enemy spots us, we will hear a yell that will give a sense of communication between the AI characters:

```
public static int attackOrder;
public bool nearPlayer;
public bool nearEnemyAttacked;
public float distancePlayer;
public static int charactersAttacking;
private bool Attack;
private bool Defend;
private bool runAway;
private bool surpriseAttack;

void Update ()
{

    if(distancePlayer < 30f)
    {
        nearPlayer = true;
    }

    if(distancePlayer > 30f)
    {
        nearPlayer = false;
    }

            if(nearPlayer == true && attackOrder == 1)
                {
                    Attack = true;
                }

            else
                {
                    Defend = true;
                }

        if(nearEnemyAttacked == true)
        {
            runPlayerDirection();
        }
    }
```

To make this happen, we simply added new Boolean called `nearEnemyAttacked`. In conjunction with this, we add a trigger detection to check if there are some skeletons near that have spotted the player. If it's triggered, the Boolean turns true; otherwise, it will remain false.

Once it gets triggered, it's time for that same AI character to call for any other ones that are around:

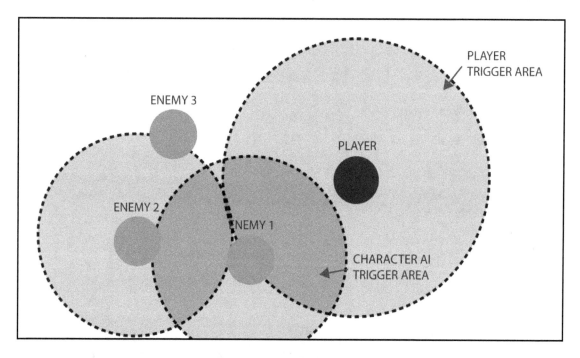

As we can see in the preceding diagram, due to the communication system we have implemented, we now have three characters that are fully aware of the player's position. The last character will also yell, trying to tell others about the player's position, but if the trigger area doesn't overlap an AI character, nothing will happen:

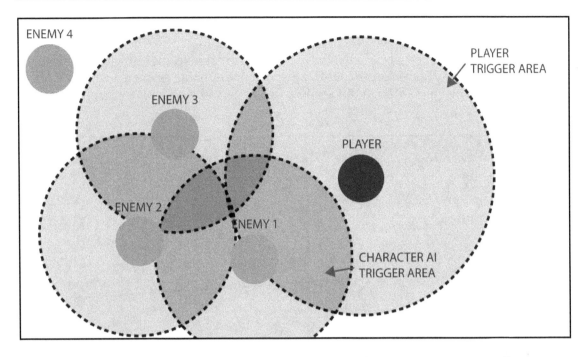

For example, **ENEMY 4** is far too away to be affected by the trigger zone, so it will remain in that position until the player gets near his location; otherwise, he won't know what is happening.

The trick of this example is to have characters talking to each other, yelling or trying to get the attention of characters that are near. This will give a sense of communication turning simple and individual actions into a more appealing group interaction.

Communication (talking to other AI characters)

There are many other examples that can be shown in terms of communication, because it's always possible to find new ways to communicate between characters; just like in real life, we are constantly finding new ways of communicating. But for now, we will stick to the basic form of communication, talking.

If we plan to have a lot of AI characters in the game, it will rapidly take a big part of the game, where the focus of the player will be set directly or indirectly to them. Probably not every game that we will be creating will have characters that react instantly to the presence of the player, and maybe the player could be just one more character in the game, and for that reason could be ignored. So in this section, will be excluding the player part and we will exclusively plan the AI character interactions:

Let's create a city with a lot of people and assign a few details to them so they can behave like a realistic crowd. We can start by adding basic movement information into our character, such as walking, running, idle, and pathfinding. With that implemented in our character, we have an individual character that can walk around the city that avoids colliding with the buildings and walks on the sidewalk.

Now our first suggestion for this example is to add a simple trigger detection so the characters are aware when another characters passes nearby:

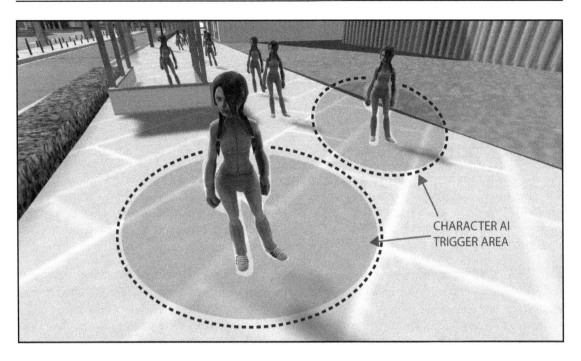

After adding the trigger area to the characters, we can advance to the next step and work on the interaction between them. Our plan here is to have a probability map to determine a probability to find a known person that can start a conversation with:

```
If(probabilityFriendly > 13)
{
  // We have 87% of chance
  talkWith();
}
```

To make this work, we added an integer function that for this example we called it probabilityFriendly. This refers to the probability of finding a friendly person. When a new character enters the trigger area, the calculation will be made randomly, and if the number fits our percentage, both characters will stop walking around and will start a conversation. After that, we can keep adding more details to this situation, such as when they end the conversation, we could make them walk side by side while talking, and endless other options that could derive from this small trigger detection and probability map.

The idea behind this is to have characters that can interact with each other randomly. From the player's point of view, it would look like the characters are friends and they simply have stopped to talk because they know each other. This helps create a realistic atmosphere, and it's not so much about a technical point but instead about planning every possible interaction between characters.

Team sports

As we saw previously while explaining some popular examples of crowd interaction systems in video games, sports games have a well-developed AI system that works specifically well in team sports. Now we will take an in-depth look at some of the core features of team sports video games and see how they have achieved some interesting results, making the AI characters of those games very challenging and realistic.

If we analyze the real-life sport football, we have two teams each composed of eleven individual players. In order to win the game, the team needs to score more goals than the opponent, so the game can be divided into two basic forms: attacking, where the focus is scoring goals; and defending, where the focus is avoiding conceding goals. There is just one ball in the game, so a lot of the players' time is spent without having the possession of the ball, and that time can be very important to the end result of the game. Either the player tries to take the ball from the opponent or get in a good position to receive the ball. That's the two basic forms when the player doesn't have the possession of the ball.

The video game tries to mimic every detail of the sport, and because it is a team sport, there is a lot of work on the development of the AI group interaction. The mindset of the AI characters needs to be more on team play and less on simple individual play. So they only make certain decisions, if those decisions follow the group objectives.

If we watch a football match, we can hear the players talking to each other to pass them the ball, to move forward, to go backwards, and so on. The idea is to have that type of communication inside of the video game as well. It does not necessarily need to be about verbal communication, but the rather about actions that makes the game much more realistic.

Let's analyze step-by-step the basic AI decisions that the characters make while playing the game. We will start by taking a look the organization of the characters on the field, as shown in the following diagram:

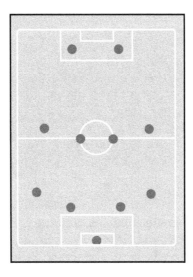

This is one example of a simple formation of a football team on the field. At the bottom, we can see just one circle, and that represents the goalkeeper, the one that is responsible for defending the goal. This character is the only one that remains constantly around this area; all the others can move freely if they want to. Now that we have a visual representation of how a football team is distributed on the field, we can move on with the example.

Each character in the game has an individual objective. This may be passing the ball to the offensive players, shooting as much as possible to try to score goals, simply staying behind to defend, and so on. While they have these individual objectives, they also need to think about the team objectives and decide if one objective or another is more important at a certain point, and if the decision that they are making will help to achieve the objective successfully.

Let's move on to the creation of an individual player. We start from the basics, running after the ball. To create this, we can use techniques that were explained earlier in the book, such as walking towards an object's position:

```
public float speed;
public Transform ball;
public bool hasBall;

void Start ()
{
    speed = 1f;
}

void Update ()
{
```

```
if(hasBall == false)
{
    Vector3 positionA = this.transform.position;
    Vector3 positionB = ball.transform.position;
    this.transform.position = Vector3.Lerp(positionA, positionB,
        Time.deltaTime * speed);
}

if(hasBall == true)
{

}
}
```

Here we have the code that makes the character running after the ball. At this moment, we will be working on just one character and then we'll gradually add team interactions in order to have at least a basic form of what we can see on a fully developed sports game. So if we play the game with only this code, we can see that the character will move towards the ball's position, and that is the basics of the football game, to reach the ball:

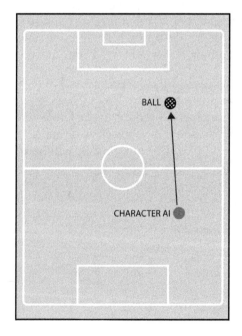

At the moment, we have an individual player working properly, and that is want we expected for now. If we added more characters into the game, all of them would run towards the ball, ignoring everything else, so no communication or interaction would be happening in the game:

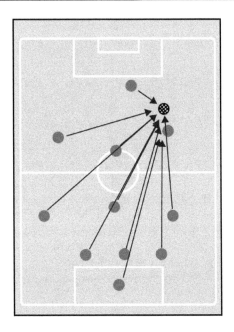

If we had all the characters in the game running towards the ball's position, as we can see in the preceding diagram, it will be like the characters don't have a perception of the others around them. So to avoid this situation, we can get the character that is closest to the ball to communicate that to the other characters, so they don't need to run for the ball as well. To create that, we can have a constant calculation between the distance of each character and the ball:

```
public float speed;
public Transform ball;
public bool hasBall;
public float ballDistance;

void Start ()
{
    speed = 1f;
}

  void Update ()
{

    if(hasBall == false)
    {
        Vector3 positionA = this.transform.position;
        Vector3 positionB = ball.transform.position;
        this.transform.position = Vector3.Lerp(positionA,
```

```
                    positionB, Time.deltaTime * speed);
        }

    if(hasBall == true)
    {

    }

    ballDistance =Vector3.Distance(transform.position,ball.position);

}
```

To achieve this, we have used the distance calculation that we have explored previously on the book. So now we have three new variables on the code, `ballDistance` that is a float that will be the measurement of how far the character is from the ball.

Now that we have this set we need to have the character verifying if he is the closest of them all from the ball and if so, he can then move on and run towards the ball position:

```
public float speed;
public Transform ball;
public bool hasBall;
public float ballDistance;
public static float teamDistance;

void Start ()
{
    speed = 1f;
}

void Update ()
{

    if(hasBall == false)
    {
        Vector3 positionA = this.transform.position;
        Vector3 positionB = ball.transform.position;
        this.transform.position = Vector3.Lerp(positionA, positionB,
            Time.deltaTime * speed);
    }

    if(hasBall == true)
    {

    }

    ballDistance =Vector3.Distance(transform.position,ball.position);
```

```
        if(teamDistance < ballDistance)
        {
            teamDistance = ballDistance;
        }

    }
```

For this example, we decided to simply add a variable that will be shared for all the characters, so we added a static float variable called `teamDistance`. This will store the value of the character that is closest to the ball. At this point, the characters will know if they are the ones that are closest to the ball. From this point, it is simple to move to the next step and have the character check if it is the closest one, and if so, it can run towards the ball. This will be the first team element that we'll be adding to our AI characters. They will check with the others to see which one should get the ball, and as we planned, it makes more sense to be the one that is closest to the ball, but we can break it down further so they can check which one will get to the ball first. However, for this example we'll stick with the principle that all of the characters run at the same velocity:

```
public float speed;
public Transform ball;
public bool hasBall;
public float ballDistance;
public static float teamDistance;
public bool nearTheBall;

public float teamdist;

void Start ()
{
    speed = 0.1f;
    teamDistance = 10;
}

void Update ()
{
    teamdist = teamDistance;

    if(hasBall == false && nearTheBall == true)
    {
        Vector3 positionA = this.transform.position;
        Vector3 positionB = ball.transform.position;
        this.transform.position = Vector3.Lerp(positionA, positionB,
            Time.deltaTime * speed);
    }

    if(hasBall == true)
    {
```

```
    }

    ballDistance =Vector3.Distance(transform.position,ball.position);

    if(teamDistance > ballDistance)
    {
        teamDistance = ballDistance;
    }

    if(teamDistance == ballDistance)
    {
        nearTheBall = true;
    }

    if(teamDistance < ballDistance)
    {
        nearTheBall = false;
    }

}
```

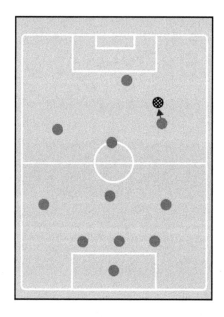

Now if we test the game, we can see that only one character is running after the ball. All the other characters have the perception that one of their team is closer to the ball, so that one will get the ball. At this moment, we already have a simple form of group interaction and we are on the right track.

The next thing that we need to work on is that the ball will be moving throughout the game, and our code works in a static scenario, but if the ball gets moved, the team distance check should be reset. The reason is that the value will be getting lower when the character AI gets closer to the ball, and that value never increases, so we need to update it. We start by creating a new script for the ball:

```
public Vector2 curPos;
public Vector2 lastPos;

public bool ballMoving;

void Update ()
{

    curPos = transform.position;

    if(curPos == lastPos)
    {
        ballMoving = false;
    }

    else
    {
        ballMoving = true;
        characterAI.teamDistance = 10;
    }

    lastPos = curPos;
}
```

After adding this script to the ball, the distance check of the players will get updated every time the ball get's moved. Now let's make sure that the ball moves. To make this happen, we need to allow the character to kick the ball.

First, we will update the ball script that we just created. We want to add a variable that will store the position where the ball will land after the character shooting it:

```
public Vector2 curPos;
public Vector2 lastPos;
public static Transform characterPos;
public float speed;

public bool ballMoving;

void Start ()
{
```

```
        characterPos = this.transform;
        speed = 2f;
    }

    void Update ()
    {
        curPos = transform.position;

        if(curPos == lastPos)
        {
            ballMoving = false;
        }

        else
        {
            ballMoving = true;
            characterAI.teamDistance = 10;
        }

        lastPos = curPos;

        Vector2 positionA = this.transform.position;
        Vector2 positionB = characterPos.transform.position;
        this.transform.position = Vector2.Lerp(positionA, positionB,
            Time.deltaTime * speed);
    }
```

So, what we have done here is give information about the landing position of the ball. To make this happen, we added a `public static Transform` variable called `characterPos`. We have chosen to have character positions here for the test, because we want the characters to pass the ball and not simply kick it:

```
public float speed;
public Transform ball;
public bool hasBall;
public float ballDistance;
public static float teamDistance;
public bool nearTheBall;
public List<Transform> teamCharacters;
public int randomChoice;
public float teamdist;
```

Then we updated the variables of the character AI script. Here, we have a list that will contain all the players' coordinates of the team. The idea is to have the character choosing a friendly teammate to pass the ball and shoot it in that direction.

So for this example, we have chosen to use the coordinates of the characters as a waypoint for the ball. To make this feature more realistic, we can add more details about the trajectory of the ball being affected by gravity or wind:

```
void Update ()
{
    teamdist = teamDistance;

    if(hasBall == false && nearTheBall == true)
    {
        Vector3 positionA = this.transform.position;
        Vector3 positionB = ball.transform.position;
        this.transform.position = Vector3.Lerp(positionA, positionB,
            Time.deltaTime * speed);
    }

    if(ballDistance < 0.1)
    {
        hasBall = true;
    }

    if(hasBall == true)
    {
        passBall();
        hasBall = false;
    }

    ballDistance =Vector3.Distance(transform.position,ball.position);

    if(teamDistance > ballDistance)
    {
        teamDistance = ballDistance;
    }

    if(teamDistance == ballDistance)
    {
        nearTheBall = true;
    }

    if(teamDistance < ballDistance)
    {
        nearTheBall = false;
    }

}

void passBall ()
{
```

```
        randomChoice = Random.Range(0, 9);
        ballScript.characterPos = teamCharacters[randomChoice];
}
```

Then we use the variables that we just added to our code to send the new direction to the ball when the character AI gets close enough to the ball. `void passBall ()` is the function that we created that will be called every time the character wants to pass the ball. At this moment, we just want the characters to pass the ball to each other, so we have assigned a random number to select a character from the list.

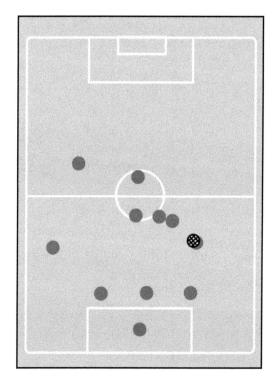

If we test the game, we can see that there is a lot more movement and interaction going on. So what we can see is that the closest character will get near the ball and when that happens, he will pass the ball to another character. The ball will move towards the character and the character will get closer to the ball so he can pass the ball to another character. Currently, this will happen forever in a loop, a character gets the ball, passes, another one gets the ball and passes, and so on.

Now we have the foundation of a simple football game, and we can simply keep adding more features like the ones we just created to make them communicate to see who's going to get the ball and pass the ball to the teammates.

Crowd collision avoidance

To finalize this chapter, we'll be talking about crowd collision avoidance. The idea of having a lot of characters in the same map is becoming a standard for open world games. But this often brings a problem, collision avoidance:

We have already discovered how advanced pathfinding works, and we know that is a powerful system when developing AI movement. But if we have a lot of characters trying to reach the same position at the same time, it will cause them to collide with each other and they will probably block the path that is needed to reach that destination. As we can see in the preceding screenshot, everything is running smoothly and without any abnormal situation because the characters are following different directions and rarely do they interfere with the others.

But what happens if all the characters try to access the same position at the same time, for example trying to get inside the house. It is only possible for one character at a time to go through the door, and that means that plenty of other characters will wait in line to enter.

The solution for this problem is still being explored, and there is not a definite answer, but there are some ways to get around this.

Currently crowd dynamics solutions usually involve two different layers, one for the pathfinding and another one for the local collision avoidance. Using this approach, we have a few benefits, it will produce a high quality movement and also it will have avoidance on a small scale, it is a very common method used on multiple games.

There are different alternatives to achieve this with a satisfactory result. A popular choice for many games is the combination of the Theta Algorithm A* with the velocity obstacle. This allow us to calculate the distance between our character and the other one that will collide against us.

In high-density crowd situations, solely relying on local collision avoidance and idealized pathfinding will cause agents to pile up at popular, shared path waypoints. Collision avoidance algorithms only help to avoid local collisions in the pursuit of following the ideal path. Often, games rely on these algorithms to divert agents to less-congested, less-direct routes in high-density situations. In certain situations, collision avoidance can lead to this desired behavior, though it is always a side effect of the system and not a deliberate consideration.

Work has been done in incorporating aggregate crowd movement and crowd density into pathfinding computations. Approaches that augment pathing via crowd density do not take into account the aggregate movement or direction of movement of the crowd, which leads to overcorrection of the phenomenon, which can be seen in the following image:

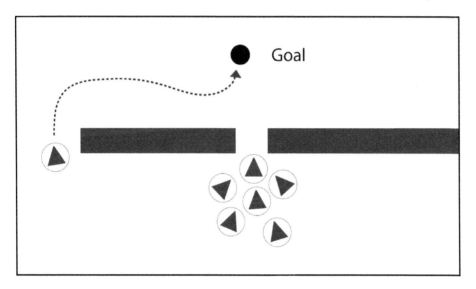

Congestion maps are similar in many ways to existing cooperative pathfinding algorithms, such as Direction Maps (DMs), but they differ in a few key respects. DMs use average crowd motion over time to encourage agents to move with the crowd. Because of this, many of the oscillations present in the congestion map approach are smoothly resolved. Conversely, this temporal smoothing prevents DMs from quickly and accurately reacting to changes in the environment and crowd behavior. Both congestion maps and DMs apply the aggregate crowd movement information to the path planning process in much the same way; however, congestion maps handle agents of varying size and shape, while DMs traditionally assume homogeneity.

The final major difference between DMs and congestion maps is that congestion maps weight movement penalties proportional to the density of the crowd. Without taking density into account, DMs display overly pessimistic pathfinding behavior, where agents are encouraged to path around sparse groups of agents blocking the ideal path.

Summary

In this chapter, we explored some popular examples of crowd interaction systems used on popular video games and we saw how important is to plan every interaction that we can think of because this is what will turn a few simple lines of code into a realistic-looking game. To conclude the chapter, we revisited the advanced pathfinding system and we saw how multiple characters in the game can share the same final destination, taking an alternative path to avoid colliding, and waiting in line for other characters to move forward.

In the next chapter, we'll be looking at AI planning and decision making. We'll see how we can have AI anticipating things, knowing in advance what it will do when arriving at a certain position or facing a certain problem.

9
AI Planning and Collision Avoidance

In this chapter, we will cover topics that will help bring a higher complexity level to our AI characters. The idea of this chapter is to give the power of planning and deciding to the characters. We have already explored some of the technical knowledge required to achieve this in the previous chapters, and now we will explore in detail the process of creating an AI character that can plan ahead their decisions.

Search

We will start by talking about searching in video games. Search can be the first decision that our characters make because in most of the times, we want the characters to search for something, either searching for the player or for something else that will lead the character to their victory.

Having our characters be able to successfully find something is very useful and can be highly important as well. This is a feature that can be found in a large number of video games, and for that reason, it is likely that we will need to use it as well.

As we saw in previous examples, most of the times we have a player who walks around the map and when they come across an enemy, that enemy changes from an idle to offensive position. Now, we want the enemy to be proactive and constantly searching for the player instead of waiting for him. In our heads, we can start thinking about the process that is required for the enemy to start searching for the player. That process that we have in our heads needs to be planned, and that plan needs to be in the AI character's head. Basically, we want the AI thoughts to be the same as our thoughts because that will look realistic, and that is exactly what we want.

Other times, we might want the search to be secondary, where the main priority of the character is something else. This is very common for real-time strategy games, where the AI characters start exploring the map, and at a certain point, they find an enemy base. The searching wasn't their priority, but even then it is a part of the game-exploring the map and getting the opponent's location. After discovering the player's location, the AI character can decide whether exploring more of it becomes a priority or not and what would be their next step.

Also, we can create realistic animals for hunting games, for example, where the main objective of the animal is to eat and drink, so they have to constantly search for food or water, and if they are not hungry or thirsty anymore, they can search for a warm place to stay. However, meanwhile if the animal finds a predator, their priority will change immediately, and the animal will start searching for a safe place to stay.

There are many decisions that can depend on a search system, and it is a feature that mimics what real life humans or animals do. We will cover the most common types of searches on video games, and the objective is to turn the AI character able to search and successfully find anything.

Offensive search

The first type of search that we will create is an offensive search. By offensive search, we mean that this is set to be the primary objective of the AI character. The idea is that the character of the game for some reason needs to find the player, similar to the hide and seek game, where one of the players has to hide and the other one needs to find them.

We have a map where the character can walk freely, only taking in consideration the collision avoidance that they have to make (trees, hills, and rocks):

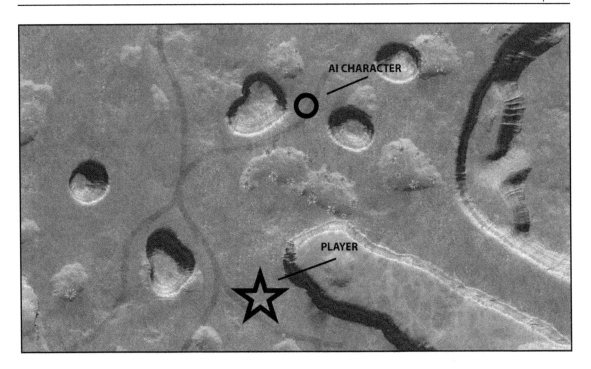

So, the first step is to create a system where the character can walk around the map. For this example, we have chosen to create a waypoint system where the character can move from point to point and explore the entire map.

After importing the map and characters that we'll use on the game, we need to configure the waypoints that will be used by the character to know where they need to go. We can do this manually adding the coordinates into our code, but to simplify the process, we'll create objects on the scene that will serve as waypoints and delete the 3D mesh, because it won't be necessary.

Now, we group all the waypoints that we have created and name the group as **waypoints**. Once we have the waypoints in place and grouped together, we can start creating the code that will tell our character how many waypoints they need to follow. This code is very useful because that way we can create different maps, using as many waypoints as we need without necessarily updating the character code:

```
public static Transform[] points;

    void Awake ()
    {
        points = new Transform[transform.childCount];
        for (int i = 0; i < points.Length; i++)
```

```
        {
            points[i] = transform.GetChild(i);
        }
    }
```

This code will be assigned to the group that we have created and will count the number of waypoints that has inside of it and ordering them.

The blue spheres that we can see in preceding image represent the 3D meshes that we have used as waypoints. For this example, the character will follow eight points until they finish the path. Now, let's move on to the AI character code and see how we can make the AI character move from point to point using the points that we have created.

We will start by creating the basic functions of the character-the health and speed-then we will create a new variable that will give them the next position and another variable that will be used to know which waypoint they need to follow:

```
public float speed;
public int health;

private Transform target;
private int wavepointIndex = 0;
```

Now, we have the basic variables that are needed to make an enemy character move from point to point until they find the player. Let's see how to use these in order to make it playable now:

```
private float speed;
public int health;

private Transform target;
private int wavepointIndex = 0;


void Start ()
{
    target = waypoints.points[0];   speed = 10f;
}

void Update ()
{
    Vector3 dir = target.position - transform.position;
    transform.Translate(dir.normalized * speed * Time.deltaTime,
Space.World);

    if(Vector3.Distance(transform.position, target.position) <= 0.4f)
    {
        GetNextWaypoint();
    }
}

void GetNextWaypoint()
{
    if(wavepointIndex >= waypoints.points.Length - 1)
    {
        Destroy(gameObject);
        return;
    }

    wavepointIndex++;
    target = waypoints.points[wavepointIndex];
}
```

In the `Start` function, we assigned the first `waypoint` that the characters need to follow that is, the `waypoint` number zero, the first on the transform list that we have created previously on the `waypoint` code. Also, we have determined the velocity of the character, and for this example, we have chosen `10f`.

Then, in the `Update` function, the character will calculate the distance between the next position and the current position, using the `Vector3 dir`. The character will constantly be moving on, so we have created a line of code that serves as movement for the character `transform.Translate` in this case. Knowing the distance and the speed information, the character will know how far it is from the next position, and once they reach the desirable distance from that point, they can move on to the next point. To make this happen, we will create an `if` statement that will tell the character when they reach `0.4f` (for this example) near from the point that he is moving into, that means that he already have arrived to that destination and he can start moving on to the next point `GetNextWaypoint()`.

In the `GetNextWaypoint()` function, the character will start to confirm whether they already have arrived at the final destination; if they have, then the object can be destroyed, if not, they can follow the next waypoint. The `wavepointIndex++` will add one number to the index every time the character arrives at the waypoint position, moving from `0>1>2>3>4>5` and so on.

Now, we assign the code to our character and place the character at the start position and test the game to check whether it is working properly:

Now, the character moves from one point to another, and this is the first and necessary step when developing a search system-the character needs to move around the map. Now, we just need to make it turn to the direction that they are facing and then we can start worrying about the search feature:

```
public float speed;
public int health;
public float speedTurn;

private Transform target;
private int wavepointIndex = 0;


void Start ()
{
    target = waypoints.points[0];
    speed = 10f;
    speedTurn = 0.2f;
}

void Update ()
{
    Vector3 dir = target.position - transform.position;
    transform.Translate(dir.normalized * speed * Time.deltaTime,
Space.World);

    if(Vector3.Distance(transform.position, target.position) <= 0.4f)
    {
        GetNextWaypoint();
    }

    Vector3 newDir = Vector3.RotateTowards(transform.forward, dir,
speedTurn,
    0.0F);

    transform.rotation = Quaternion.LookRotation(newDir);
}

void GetNextWaypoint()
{
    if(wavepointIndex >= waypoints.points.Length - 1)
    {
        Destroy(gameObject);
        return;
    }

    wavepointIndex++;
    target = waypoints.points[wavepointIndex];
```

```
}
```

Now, we have the character facing the direction that they are moving on, and we are ready to add the searching system.

So, we have a character that is walking from point to point on the map, and at this moment even if they find the player, they won't stop walking and nothing will happen. So, that's what we are going to do now.

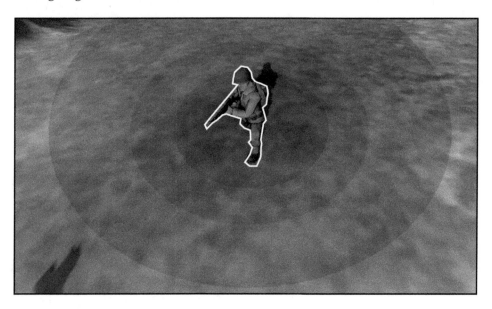

The approach that we have chosen to achieve the desired results is to add a trigger zone in form of a circle around the character, as we can see in the preceding screenshot. The character will be walking around the map, and when that trigger zone detects the player, the character has found the primary objective. Let's add that into our character code:

```
public float speed;
public int health;
public float speedTurn;
private Transform target;
private int wavepointIndex = 0;
private bool Found;

void Start ()
{
    target = waypoints.points[0];
    speed = 10f;
    speedTurn = 0.2f;
```

```
    }

    void Update ()
    {
        Vector3 dir = target.position - transform.position;
        transform.Translate(dir.normalized * speed * Time.deltaTime,
        Space.World);

        if(Vector3.Distance(transform.position, target.position) <= 0.4f)
        {
            GetNextWaypoint();
        }

        Vector3 newDir = Vector3.RotateTowards(transform.forward, dir,
        speedTurn, 0.0F);

        transform.rotation = Quaternion.LookRotation(newDir);
    }

    void GetNextWaypoint()
    {
        if(wavepointIndex >= waypoints.points.Length - 1)
        {
            Destroy(gameObject);
            return;
        }

        wavepointIndex++;
        target = waypoints.points[wavepointIndex];
    }

    void OnTriggerEnter(Collider other)
    {
        if(other.gameObject.tag =="Player")
        {
            Found = true;
        }
    }
```

So, now we added a `void OnTriggerEnter` that verifies that the trigger zone gets in touch with something else. To check whether the object that has entered on the trigger zone is the player, we have an if statement that checks whether the object of the game has the tag `Player`. If that is true, the Boolean variable `Found` is changed to true. This Boolean variable will be very useful in a moment.

Let's test the game and check whether the character passes through the player and whether at that moment the variable `Found` has changed from false to true:

The search system that we just implemented works great; the character will walk around the map searching for the player and they can find the player without any issue. The next step is to tell the character to stop searching when they already have found the player.

```
public float speed;
public int health;
public float speedTurn;
private Transform target;
private int wavepointIndex = 0;
public bool Found;

void Start ()
{
    target = waypoints.points[0];
    speed = 40f;
    speedTurn = 0.2f;
}

void Update ()
{
    if (Found == false)
    {
        Vector3 dir = target.position - transform.position;
        transform.Translate(dir.normalized * speed *
        Time.deltaTime,
        Space.World);
```

```
        if (Vector3.Distance(transform.position, target.position)
        <= 0.4f)
        {
            GetNextWaypoint();
        }

        Vector3 newDir = Vector3.RotateTowards(transform.forward,
        dir,
        speedTurn, 0.0F);

        transform.rotation = Quaternion.LookRotation(newDir);
    }
}

void GetNextWaypoint()
{
    if(wavepointIndex >= waypoints.points.Length - 1)
    {
        Destroy(gameObject);
        return;
    }

    wavepointIndex++;
    target = waypoints.points[wavepointIndex];
}

void OnTriggerEnter(Collider other)
{
    if(other.gameObject.tag == "Player")
    {
        Found = true;
    }
}
```

With these last modifications, we have an AI character that goes around the map until they find the player and when they finally find them, they stop moving around and ready to plan what to do next.

What we have done here is use the Found Boolean to determine whether the player should be searching for the player or not.

IF(FOUND == FALSE)
THEN THE CHARACTER
NEEDS TO KEEP
MOVING AROUND
SEARCHING FOR
THE PLAYER.

The preceding image represents the state of our character at the moment, and we are ready to implement more features on it to make them plan and take the best decisions.

This searching system can be applied to a lot of different game genres, and we can set it fairly quickly, which makes it a perfect way to start planning the AI character. Now, let's move on and work on the anticipation feature of the player character.

Predicting opponent actions

Now, let's make the character anticipate what is going to happen even before getting in confrontation against the player. This is the part where the character AI starts to plan the best options available to accomplish the objective.

Let's take a look at how we can implement an anticipation system into the character AI. We will continue to use the example mentioned in the preceding section, where we have a soldier searching for another one in the map. At the moment, we have a character that moves around the map and stops when they find the player.

If our character AI has found the player, most likely situation is for the player to find the character AI as well so that both characters are aware of each other. What are the chances of the player attacking the character AI? What are the chances of the player not having enough bullets to fire against the character? All of that is very subjective and very unpredictable. However, we want our character to have that in mind and anticipate the possible moves of the player.

So, let's start with a simple question: is the player facing the character?. Having the character to check this will help them to make a judgment about the possible outcomes. To achieve this result, we will be adding a trigger `Collider` in the back and another in front of each character of the game, including the player as we can see in the following screenshot:

The idea of having two extra Colliders on each character is to help the other characters identify whether they are looking at the back or front side of the character. So, let's add this to every character of the game and name the trigger `Collider` with the names `back` and `front`.

Now, let's make the character distinguish between the back and the front trigger. It can be done in two different ways-the first way is by adding a stretched trigger collider in front of the character representing the observation range:

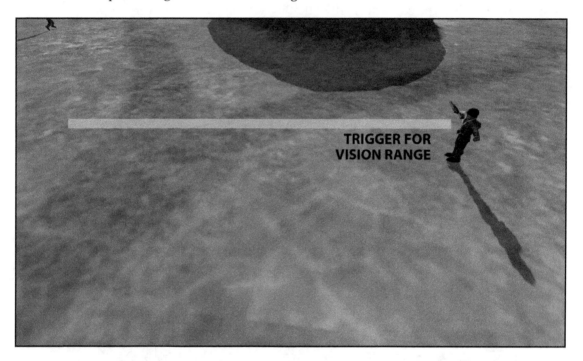

Alternatively, we can create a **RAYCAST** starting from the character's position and ending at the distance that we think is likely to be the vision range of our character as shown in the following screenshot:

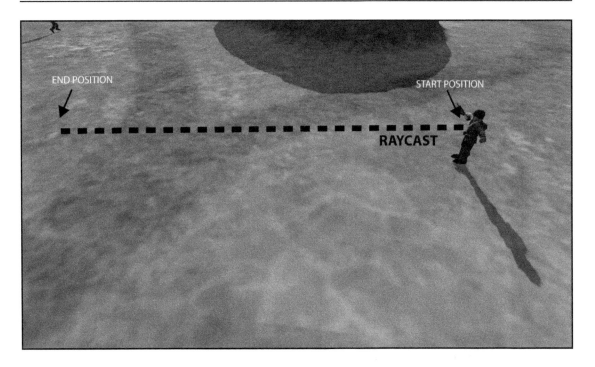

Both methods have their advantages and disadvantages, and once again, we don't necessarily need to constantly use the most complicated methods to achieve great results. So, the advice here is to use the method that we are more comfortable with, and a good choice for this example would be the trigger Collider to represent the vision range of the character.

Let's add the trigger Collider in front of the character, and then we can start working on the code to make it detect the front or back side of the characters. The first thing we need to change in our code is to make the character face the player's direction when they see him. The character wouldn't be able to anticipate anything if they are not looking at the player, so let's fix that first:

```
void Update ()
    {
        if (Found == false)
        {
            Vector3 dir = target.position - transform.position;
            transform.Translate(dir.normalized * speed *
            Time.deltaTime,
            Space.World);

            if (Vector3.Distance(transform.position, target.position)
            <= 0.4f)
```

```
        {
            GetNextWaypoint();
        }

        Vector3 newDir = Vector3.RotateTowards(transform.forward,
        dir,
        speedTurn, 0.0F);

        transform.rotation = Quaternion.LookRotation(newDir);
    }

    if (Found == true)
    {
        transform.LookAt(target);
    }
}

void GetNextWaypoint()
{
    if(wavepointIndex >= waypoints.points.Length - 1)
    {
        Destroy(gameObject);
        return;
    }

    wavepointIndex++;
    target = waypoints.points[wavepointIndex];
}

void OnTriggerEnter(Collider other)
{
    if(other.gameObject.tag == "Player")
    {
        Found = true;
        target = other.gameObject.transform;

    }
}
```

Now, we have our AI character constantly facing the player when they see them. To make this work, we added our first line of code inside the `if (Found == true)`. Here, we used the `transform.LookAt` that makes the AI face the player character. When the player is spotted by our AI character, it automatically becomes the target:

Now that, we have our AI character facing the player, we can check whether they are looking at the back or front side of the player.

It might look illogical for us to think that the character doesn't know the difference, but when developing an AI character, everything needs to be written on the code, especially details such as this one that can have a huge impact on anticipating, planning, and finally making a decision.

So, now we have to use the trigger `Collider` that we added previously to check whether our AI character is facing the front or back side of the player that is in front of them. Let's start by adding the following two new variables:

```
public bool facingFront;
public bool facingBack;
```

The variables that we added are the Boolean `facingFront` and `facingBack`. The trigger will set one of these values to true, and that way, the character AI will know which side they are looking at. So, let's configure the trigger:

```
void Update ()
    {
        if (Found == false)
        {
```

```
            Vector3 dir = target.position - transform.position;
            transform.Translate(dir.normalized * speed *
            Time.deltaTime,
            Space.World);

            if (Vector3.Distance(transform.position, target.position)
            <= 0.4f)
            {
                GetNextWaypoint();
            }

            Vector3 newDir = Vector3.RotateTowards(transform.forward,
            dir,
            speedTurn, 0.0F);

            transform.rotation = Quaternion.LookRotation(newDir);
        }

        if (Found == true)
        {
            transform.LookAt(target);
        }
    }

    void GetNextWaypoint()
    {
        if(wavepointIndex >= waypoints.points.Length - 1)
        {
            Destroy(gameObject);
            return;
        }

        wavepointIndex++;
        target = waypoints.points[wavepointIndex];
    }

    void OnTriggerEnter(Collider other)
    {
        if(other.gameObject.tag == "Player")
        {
            Found = true;
            target = other.gameObject.transform;
        }

        if(other.gameObject.name == "frontSide")
        {
            facingFront = true;
            facingBack = false;
```

```
        }

    if(other.gameObject.name == "backSide")
    {
        facingFront = false;
        facingBack = true;
    }
}
```

So, what we did was having the trigger checking whether was colliding against the back or front side of the other character. To achieve this result, we have the trigger questioning whether the collision that it has detected was the `frontSide` object or `backSide` object. Only one of them can be true at a time.

Now that, we have our character distinguishing the player's back side and front side, we want him to be able to analyze the dangers of both situations. So, the first thing we will do is to have a very distinct difference of the situation when the character finds the player facing their back and when they are facing their front. When facing the front side, the player is ready to shoot at our AI character, so it is an even more dangerous situation. We will be creating a danger meter and can start importing this situation into the equation:

```
public float speed;
public int health;
public float speedTurn;
private Transform target;
private int wavepointIndex = 0;
public bool Found;
```

```
public bool facingFront;
public bool facingBack;

public int dangerMeter;
```

In the variables section, we add a new integer called `dangerMeter`. Now, we will add the values that will help determine whether the situation that our AI character is facing has a higher or lower risk to be attacked:

```
void OnTriggerEnter(Collider other)
    {
        if(other.gameObject.tag == "Player")
        {
            Found = true;
            target = other.gameObject.transform;
        }

        if(other.gameObject.name == "frontSide")
        {
            facingFront = true;
            facingBack = false;
            dangerMeter += 50;
        }

        if(other.gameObject.name == "backSide")
        {
            facingFront = false;
            facingBack = true;
            dangerMeter += 5;
        }
    }
```

So, depending on the situation, we can add a small value that will represent a small risk or a big value that will represent a big risk. If the danger value is high, the AI character needs to anticipate a life-threatening situation, and for that reason, dramatic decisions probably will be made. On the other hand, if our character is facing a lower-risk situation, they can start planning something more precise and effective.

Plenty of factors can be added to the `dangerMeter`, such as the location where our character is positioned in relation to the player. To make this, we need to divide the map into different zones and assign a level of risk that each zones has. For example, if the character is in the middle of the forest, it can be considered a moderated risk zone, whereas if they are in the open, it can be considered a higher risk zone. How many bullets our character has, the remaining lifelines, and endless more can be added into our `dangerMeter` equation. Having this implemented into our character will help him anticipate the situations that can happen to him.

Collision avoidance

Predicting collisions is a very useful thing to have been implemented into our AI characters and can be used on crowd systems too in order to make the crowd move more organically when one character is walking on the direction as another character as we saw in the previous chapter. Now, let's take a look at a simple way to implement this feature:

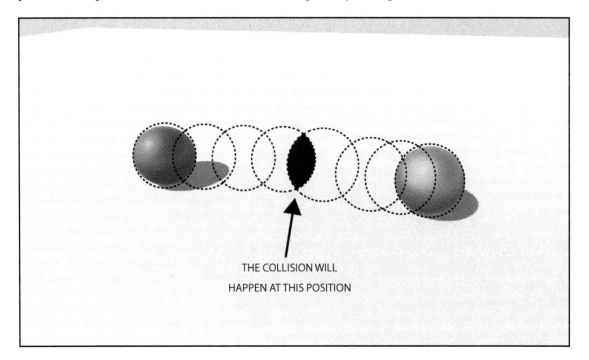

THE COLLISION WILL

HAPPEN AT THIS POSITION

To predict a collision, we need at least two objects or characters. In the preceding image, we have two spheres representing two characters and the dashed lines represent their movement. If the blue sphere moves toward the red sphere, at a certain point, they will collide with each other. The main objective here is to predict when that will happen and adjust the trajectory of the sphere so that it can avoid the collision.

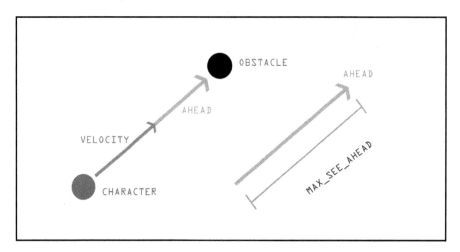

In the preceding image, we can see the representation of what we need to do if we want our character to avoid colliding with the obstacle. We need to have the velocity vector that will indicate the direction of the character. This same vector will also be used to produce a new one called `ahead`, which is a copy of the velocity vector, but with a longer length. This means that the `ahead` vector represents the line of sight of our character, and as soon they see the obstacle, they will adjust their direction to avoid colliding with it. This is how we calculate the `ahead` vector:

```
ahead = transform.position + Vector3.Normalize(velocity) * MAX_SEE_AHEAD;
```

The `ahead` is a `Vector3` variable, `velocity` is a `Vector3` variable, and `MAX_SEE_AHEAD` is a float variable that will tell how far ahead we can see. If we increase the `MAX_SEE_AHEAD` value, the earlier the character will start adjusting his direction, as demonstrated on the following diagram:

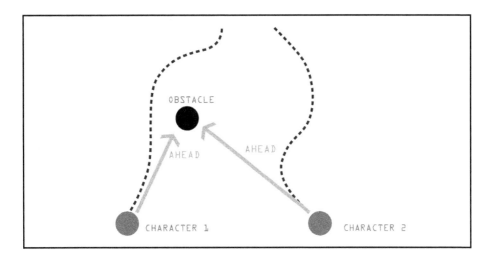

To check for the collision, one solution that can be used is the line-sphere intersection, where the line is the `ahead` vector and the sphere is the obstacle. This method works, but we'll be using a simplification of that, which is easier to understand and has identical results. So, the `ahead` vector will be used to produce another vector, and this vector will be half of its length:

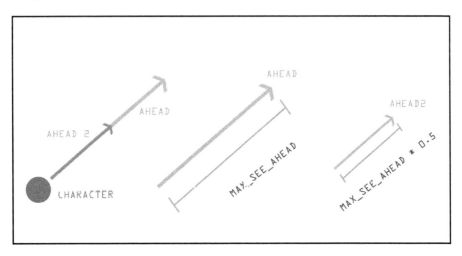

In the preceding image, we can see that `ahead` and `ahead2` goes toward the same direction, the only difference is the length between them:

```
ahead = transform.position + Vector3.Normalize(velocity) * MAX_SEE_AHEAD;
ahead2 = transform.position + Vector3.Normalize(velocity) * (MAX_SEE_AHEAD
* 0.5);
```

We need to check for a collision to know whether one of those two vectors is inside the **OBSTACLE ZONE**. To calculate that, we can compare the distance between the vectors and the obstacle center. If the distance is less or equal to the **OBSTACLE ZONE**, then that means that our vectors are inside of the **OBSTACLE ZONE** and a collision was found.

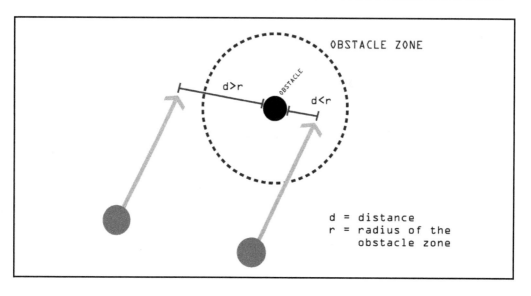

The `ahead2` vector does not appear on the preceding diagram just to simplify it.

If either of the two `ahead` vectors get inside of the **OBSTACLE ZONE**, it means that the obstacle is blocking the path, and to solve our problem, we will calculate the distance between the two points:

```
public Vector3 velocity;
public Vector3 ahead;
public float MAX_SEE_AHEAD;
public Transform a;
public Transform b;

void Start (){

    ahead = transform.position + Vector3.Normalize(velocity) *
MAX_SEE_AHEAD;
    }

void Update ()
{

    float distA = Vector3.Distance(a.position, transform.position);
```

```
        float distB = Vector3.Distance(b.position, transform.position);

        if(distA > distB)
        {
            avoidB();
        }

        if(distB > distA)
        {
            avoidA();
        }
    }

    void avoidB()
    {

    }

    void avoidA()
    {

    }
}
```

In case of having more than one obstacle blocking the path, we'll need to check which one is closer to our character, then we can start avoiding the closer obstacle first and then move on to the second obstacle:

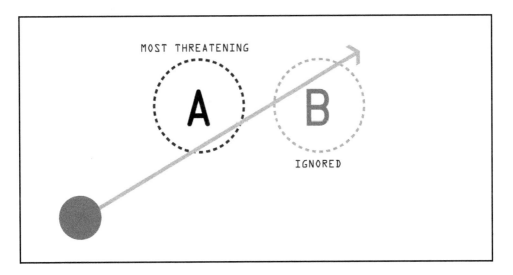

The closest obstacle, the most threatening, will be selected for calculation. Now, let's take a look at how we can calculate and perform the avoidance:

```
public Vector3 velocity;
public Vector3 ahead;
public float MAX_SEE_AHEAD;
public float MAX_AVOID;
public Transform a;
public Transform b;
public Vector3 avoidance;

void Start () {

    ahead = transform.position + Vector3.Normalize(velocity) *
MAX_SEE_AHEAD;
 }

void Update ()
{

    float distA = Vector3.Distance(a.position, transform.position);
    float distB = Vector3.Distance(b.position, transform.position);

    if(distA > distB)
    {
        avoidB();
    }

    if(distB > distA)
    {
        avoidA();
    }
}

void avoidB()
{
    avoidance = ahead - b.position;
    avoidance = Vector3.Normalize(avoidance) * MAX_AVOID;
}

void avoidA()
{
    avoidance = ahead - a.position;
    avoidance = Vector3.Normalize(avoidance) * MAX_AVOID;
}
}
```

After `avoidance` is calculated, it is normalized and scaled by `MAX_AVOID`, which is a number that is used to define the `avoidance` length. The higher the `MAX_AVOID` value is, the stronger is the avoidance, pushing our character away from the obstacle.

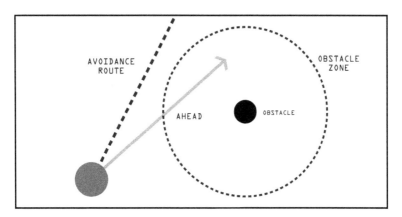

 The position of any entity can be set as vectors, so they can be used in calculations with other vectors and forces.

Now, we have the foundation to make our character predict and steer away from the obstacle position, avoiding collision with it. Using this in conjunction with a pathfinding, we can let our characters move freely in the game and enjoy the results.

Summary

We have explored how to make our AI character create and follow a plan to execute a determinate objective in this chapter. The idea is to think ahead what is going to happen and to prepare for that situation. To complete this, we have also explored how to make our AI character predict a collision with an object or another character. This will be fundamental not only to make our character move freely on the map, but also it serves as a new equation to have in mind when planning what to do. In our next chapter, we will be talking about awareness, how to develop one of the most iconic features of stealth games, and make our AI characters self-aware of what is happening around them with realistic field of view.

10
Awareness

In our last chapter, we will be looking at how we can develop AI characters that use **tactics** and awareness to accomplish their goals. Here we will be using everything that we have explored before, understanding how we can combine everything together to create artificial intelligent characters that can be used in stealth games or games that also rely on tactics or awareness.

Stealth sub-genre

Stealth games are a very popular sub-genre where the main objective of the player is to use stealth elements, being undetected by the opponents in order to complete the main goals. Even being a genre that is widely popular in military games it is possible to see this sub-genre being applied in almost any game. If we take a deep look, any game where the enemy character is triggered by noise or vision of the player, is using stealth elements. This means that at some point or another, having awareness or even tactics implemented on our AI characters can be very useful regardless of the game genre that we are working on.

About tactics

The tactics is the process that the character or a group of characters take in order to achieve certain objectives. It usually means that the characters can use all of their abilities, choosing the best ones depending on the situations, to defeat the opponent. The concept of tactics in video games is to give to the AI the power of decision, making him behave smartly while trying to reach the main goal. We can compare this to the tactics that are used by the soldiers or police officers in order to catch the bad guys of the real world.

They have a wide array of technology and human resources to catch a bandit, but in order to accomplish that task with success they need to choose wisely what they are going to do, step by step. The same principles can be applied to our AI characters; we can make them choose the best options available in order to accomplish their objective.

To create this, we can use every topic that was covered before in this book and with that, we are able to develop an AI character capable of choosing the best tactic that takes down the player or achieving his goal.

About awareness

One very important aspect that correlates with the tactics is the awareness of the character. Some common factors can make part of the awareness of an AI character such as audio, vision, and perception, for example. These factors are inspired on the human features that we all have, vision, audio, touch, and perception of what is happening around us.

Therefore, what we are looking for is to create artificial intelligent characters that can process all of that information at the same time that they are doing other things making them aware of the surroundings, making better judgment of what decisions should be taken on that given moment.

Implementing vision awareness

Before starting out with the tactics, we will take a look at how we can implement an awareness system into our characters.

Let's start by implementing a vision awareness into our game character. The idea is to simulate the human vision, where we can see very good at close range and not so good when something is really far away. Many games have adopted this system and they all have differences, some have a more complex system while others have a basic one. The basic example can be found especially on a more juvenile adventure game such as *Zelda - Ocarina of Time* for example, where the enemies will only appear or react when you reach a certain trigger zone as shown in the following screenshot:

For example, in this situation if the player goes back and exits the enemy trigger zone, the enemy will stay in an idle position, even if he is clearly able to see the player. This is a basic system of awareness and we can include it in the vision section.

Meanwhile, other games have developed their entire gameplay around this subject (vision awareness), where the vision range has an extremely important aspect on the gameplay itself. One of the several examples can be the Ubisoft title, Splinter Cell.

In this game all types of awareness systems are used, sound, vision, touch, and perception. If the player stays quiet in a shadowy area, it has less chance of being discovered than being quiet in a well-illuminated area and the same for the sound. So, for the example in the preceding screenshot, the player has approached very close to the enemy that is looking in another direction.

In order for the player to get this near, it was necessary to move very quietly and in the shadows. If the player was making noise or walking straight into illuminated areas, the enemy would have spotted him. This is a much more complex system than the *Zelda* game, but once again, it all depends on the game that we are creating and which system fits better on the gameplay that we are looking for. We will be demonstrating basic examples and then moving on to more advanced ones.

Basic vision detection

First, we start by creating and adding a scene into our game, and then we add the player.

We assign all the necessary codes into the player so it is possible for us to move and test the game. For this example, we have quickly assigned some basic movement information into our player, because that is the only interaction that will occur between the player and the AI character.

So now, we have our character moving freely on the scene and we are ready to start working on the enemy character. We want to replicate that specific moment on the *Zelda* game, where the enemy comes from the ground when the player gets near from his position and once the player gets far away, the enemy goes back into the ground.

The rabbit that we can see in the screenshot is the AI character that we have just imported into the game and now we need to define the area around him that will serve as awareness. Therefore, if the player gets near the rabbit he will detect the player and will eventually get out of his hole.

Let's say that we want the rabbit to be able to see from his hole the area that is represented by the dashed line. How can we proceed from now? We can do two things here, one is adding the trigger `Collider` into the hole object, where it will detect the player and instantiate the rabbit from the hole position, two is adding the trigger `Collider` directly to the rabbit that will be invisible (hypothetically inside the hole) and in the code we have a state for when the rabbit is inside the hole and another state for the moment when he is outside.

We decided for this example to use the hole as the main object for that moment where the rabbit is hiding and at the moment that the player enters the trigger area, the hole object instantiates the AI character.

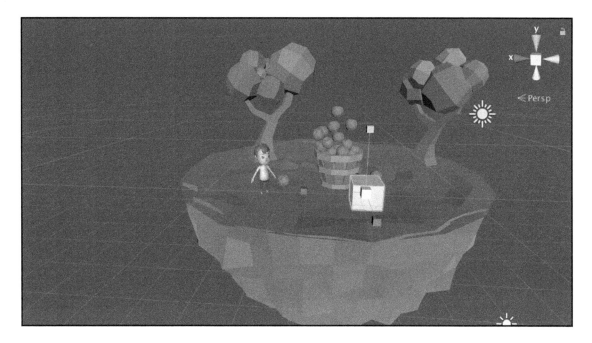

We transformed the rabbit into a prefab, so we can instantiate it later and then we removed him from the scene. Then we have created a cube inside the game and we positioned it on the hole position. Because we don't need the hole to be visible for this example, we will be turning off the mesh from this object.

Creating a cube instead of an empty object allow us to better visualize the object inside the game editor in case we need to change something or simply have a notion of where we have those objects.

At this point, we need to make this object detect the player and so we will be adding a trigger with the dimension that we previously planned to use.

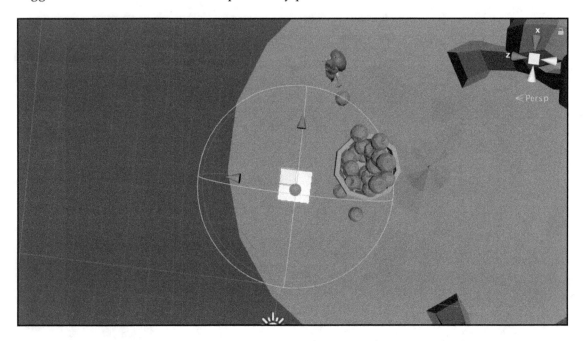

We deleted the default cube trigger that appears automatically when you create the cube and then we assigned a new sphere trigger. Why are we not using the cube trigger? We could be using the cube trigger and technically it would work too, but the covered area would be completely different from the circular area that we planned and for that reason we deleted the default trigger and assigned a new one that fits our purpose.

Now that we have the sphere trigger covering the area that we want, we need to make it detect the player. For this, we need to create the script that will be assigned to the cube/hole:

```
void OnTriggerEnter (Collider other) {

if(other.gameObject.tag == "Player")
{
Debug.Log("Player Detected");
} }
```

Inside the script, we add this line of code. It is a simple trigger check for when the object gets inside the trigger area (we have used this to demonstrate previous examples). For now we simply have the trigger to check if the player gets detected using `Debug.Log("Player Detected");`. We assign this script to the cube/hole object and then we can test it.

If we move the player into the trigger area that we created, we can see the message **Player Detected**.

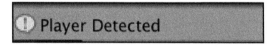

Well this is the first part of the basic example; we have the player moving around the map and the hole that is capable of detecting the player when he is near.

This method where we use the trigger Collider to detect something isn't directly associated with any kind of awareness because this is just the technical part, the way we use it is what will determine if this is meant to be the vision of our AI character or not.

Now, we can work on the rabbit, our AI character. We already have him created and set as a prefab, ready to appear in the game. So the next step is for the hole object to instantiate the rabbit, transmitting the sensation to the player that the rabbit saw him and for that reason he decided to get out of the hole. On the hole object code we update the `Player Detected` message to the `instantiate`:

```
public GameObject rabbit;
public Transform startPosition;
public bool isOut;

void Start ()
{
isOut = false;
}
void OnTriggerEnter (Collider other)
{

if(other.gameObject.tag == "Player" && isOut == false)
{
isOut = true;
Instantiate(rabbit, startPosition.position,
startPosition.rotation);
}
}
```

So what we have done is define what would be the instantiated object, which in this case is the character AI `rabbit`. Then we added the `startPosition` variable that will set the position where we want the character to appear, in alternative we could also use the hole object position that would work just fine for this example. Finally, we added a simple Boolean `isOut` to prevent the hole creating more than one rabbit at the same time.

When the player gets inside the trigger zone, the rabbit gets instantiated and jumps out of the hole.

Now, we have a rabbit that jumps out of the hole when he sees the player. Our next step is to also add the same vision to the rabbit itself, but this time we want the rabbit to constantly check if the player is inside the trigger zone, this would represent that it can see the player and if the player gets away from his vision, the rabbit cannot see him anymore and returns to the hole.

For the AI character, we can use a wider area than the hole.

So as we can see, that would be the area where the rabbit can see the player, if the player gets out of that area, the rabbit can't see the player no more.

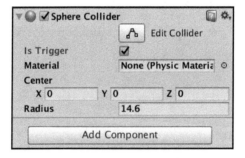

Once again, let's add a sphere `Collider`, but this time to the rabbit.

Enable the Is **Trigger option** in order to turn the Collider into activation zones. Otherwise it won't work.

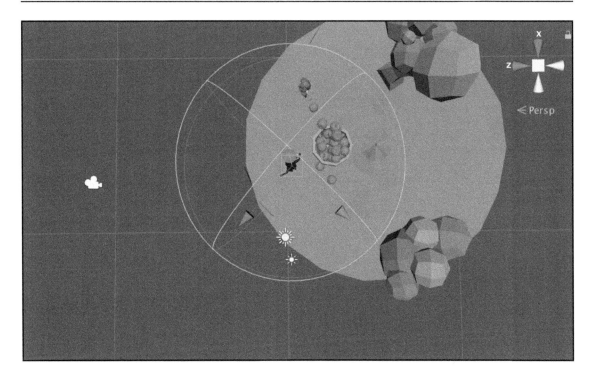

This is what we have so far, the sphere `Collider` with the dimensions that we planned and ready to receive the player position information that will serve as the vision to our AI character.

Now, what we need to do is add to the rabbit script the portion of the code that is responsible for the trigger zone:

```
void OnTriggerStay (Collider other) {

if(other.gameObject.tag == "Player")
{
Debug.Log("I can see the player");
}
}
```

What we have here is a trigger check to see if the player continues inside the trigger zone, to do this we simply use the `OnTriggerStay`, which works perfectly to this example that we are creating.

We use `Debug.Log("I can see the player");` simply to test if this is working as intended.

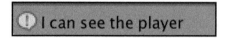

We test the game and we can notice that when the player gets inside the rabbit area, we receive the console message that we wrote and this means that it is working.

Now, let's add the second part of the rabbit vision, where the player gets out of the trigger zone and the rabbit can't see him no more. To do this we need to add another trigger check, which will serve to check if the player already left the area:

```
void OnTriggerStay (Collider other) {

if(other.gameObject.tag == "Player")
{
Debug.Log("I can see the player");
}
}

void OnTriggerExit (Collider other){

if(other.gameObject.tag == "Player")
{
Debug.Log("I've lost the player");
}
}
```

Following is the `OnTriggerStay` that we added into the AI character code, we add some new lines of code that checks if the player has left the trigger zone. To do this we use the `OnTriggerExit` that does what the name says, checks the exit of the object that has entered the trigger zone. But to make this work we need to first set an `OnTriggerEnter`, otherwise it won't count if the player entered the zone or not, it only knows if he is there or not:

```
void OnTriggerEnter (Collider other) {

if(other.gameObject.tag == "Player")
{
Debug.Log("I can see the player");
}
}

void OnTriggerStay (Collider other){

if(other.gameObject.tag == "Player")
```

```
{
Debug.Log("I can see the player");
}
}

void OnTriggerExit (Collider other){

if(other.gameObject.tag == "Player")
{
Debug.Log("I've lost the player");
}
}
```

Now, we have the trigger counting when the player gets inside the area, when he keeps inside the area, and also the moment that he exits that same area. This represents the moment that the rabbit starts seeing the player, when he keeps seeing him, and when he loses eye contact with the player.

At this point, we can test the game and see if what we have done is working correctly or not. When we start the game, we can confirm that by looking at the console messages that we wrote to see if everything is working as intended.

It is normal to see a higher number on the OnTriggerStay function because it is constantly checking every frame for the player, so as we can see in the preceding screenshot, our AI character now has the basic vision check working.

Advanced vision detection

Now that we understand how a basic vision detection that we can find in many action/adventure games works, we can move on and take a look at the advanced vision detection that can be found in stealth games. Let's take a deep look into the *Metal Gear* game and see how the AI characters have their vision developed.

If we take a look at this screenshot, we notice that the enemy AI cannot see the player, but the player is inside of the area where the enemy is well capable of seeing. So why doesn't the AI character turn to the player and start attacking him? Simply because the trigger area is set only to be in front of the enemy eyes.

For that reason, if the player is behind the enemy, he won't notice the player.

As we can see in the second screenshot, everything that is in the darker area, the enemy doesn't have any way of getting information regarding the players presence, while the light area represents the vision of the character and there he can see everything that is happening. Now we will be taking a look at how we can develop a similar system into our AI characters.

Let's start by creating a test scenario. It can be simple cube meshes for now and later on we can change them into a better looking object.

We have created a few cube meshes and placed them randomly on top of a plane (that will be the ground). The next step will be creating the character, we'll be using a capsule to represent the character.

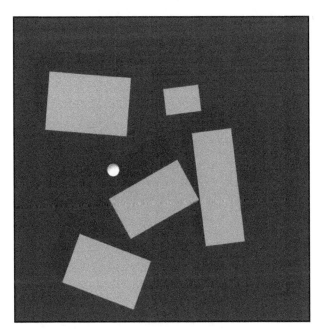

We can place the newly created capsule anywhere on the map. Now, we need to create some targets that will be spotted by our AI character.

We can distribute the target objects anywhere on the map as well. Now, we need to define two different layers, one for the obstacles and another one for the targets.

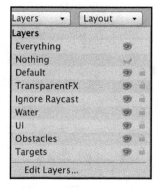

In Unity we click under the **Layers** button to expand more options, and then we click where it says **Edit Layers....**

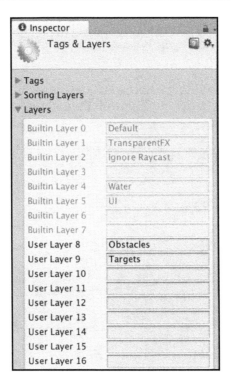

This column will open and here we can write the layers we need to create. As we can see, there's already the two layers that we need, one called **Obstacles** and the other called **Targets**. After this, we need to assign them to the objects.

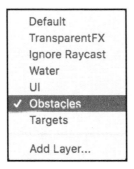

To do this we simply need to select the **Obstacles** objects and then click on the **Layers** button and choose the **Obstacles** layer. We also do the same for the **Target** objects, choosing the **Targets** layer.

The next thing to do is start adding the necessary code into our character. We will also need to add to the character a rigid body and freeze all the rotation axis demonstrated in the following screenshot:

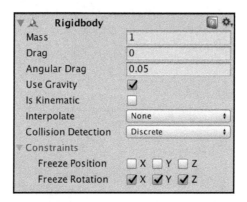

Then we can create a new script for the character:

```
public float moveSpeed = 6;

Rigidbody myRigidbody;
Camera viewCamera;
Vector3 velocity;

void Start ()
{
myRigidbody = GetComponent<Rigidbody> ();
viewCamera = Camera.main;
}

void Update ()
{
Vector3 mousePos = viewCamera.ScreenToWorldPoint (new
    Vector3(Input.mousePosition.x, Input.mousePosition.y,
    viewCamera.transform.position.y));
transform.LookAt (mousePos + Vector3.up * transform.position.y);
velocity = new Vector3 (Input.GetAxisRaw ("Horizontal"), 0,
    Input.GetAxisRaw ("Vertical")).normalized * moveSpeed;
}

void FixedUpdate ()
```

```
{
  myRigidbody.MovePosition (myRigidbody.position + velocity *
  Time.fixedDeltaTime);
}
```

What we have here is the basic movement of our character, so we can test it ourselves by controlling the character to move anywhere we want to. With this done, we are able to move around the map with the character and with the mouse we can simulate the direction in which the character is looking at.

Now, let's work on the script that simulates the vision of our character:

```
public float viewRadius;
 public float viewAngle; public Vector3 DirFromAngle(float
    angleInDegrees)
{
 }
```

We start out with two public floats, one for the `viewRadius` and another one for `viewAngle`. Then we create a public `Vector3` called `DirFromAngle` and we want the results to be in degrees and so we will be using trigonometry to solve this.

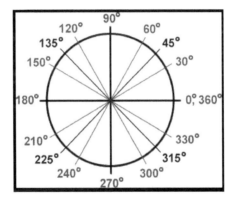

The preceding diagram represents the default trigonometry values in degrees, where it starts from the right side with the number zero and the values will increase in a counter-clockwise way.

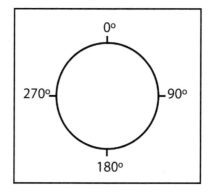

Because we are developing this example in Unity, we need to keep in mind that the trigonometry values are in a different order, as we can see in the preceding diagram. Here, the zero number starts on the top and the value increase in a clockwise way.

With this information in mind, we can now proceed with the direction angle in which our character will be looking at:

```
public float viewRadius;
public float viewAngle; public Vector3 DirFromAngle(float
    angleInDegrees)
{
    return new Vector3(Mathf.Sin(angleInDegrees *
    Mathf.Deg2Rad), 0,
    Mathf.Cos(angleInDegrees * Mathf.Deg2Rad));
}
```

Now, we have the basic foundation of our exercise done, but in order to visually see it on the game editor we need to create a new script that will show the radius of the character vision:

To do this, we go ahead and create a new folder in the project section:

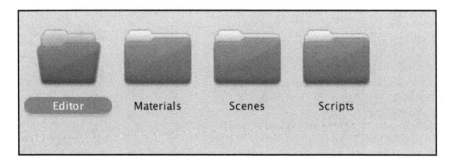

In order for the game engine to use this content that will appear in the game editor we need to name the folder as Editor. Everything inside this folder can be used/seen in the game editor, without clicking the play button, which can be very handy in many situations just like the one we are creating.

Then inside of the Editor folder that we just created, we create a new script that will be responsible for the visualization of the character field of view:

```
using UnityEngine;
using System.Collections;
using UnityEditor;
```

Because we want to use this script in editor mode, we need to specify that on the top of our script. To do that, we start by adding using UnityEditor.

Then after that we add one more line in which we will be connecting with the previous script we created to be able to use that in editor mode:

```
using UnityEngine;
using System.Collections;
using UnityEditor;

[CustomEditor (typeof (FieldOfView))]
```

And now let's work on what is going to appear on the screen to represent the field of view that we created:

```
using UnityEngine;
using System.Collections;
using UnityEditor;

[CustomEditor (typeof (FieldOfView))]
public class FieldOfViewEditor : Editor{

void OnSceneGUI(){
FieldOfView fow = (FieldOfView)target; } }
```

We created a `void OnSceneGUI()` and this will contain all the information that we want to be visible on our game editor. We start by adding the target of the field of view; this will get the field of view object reference:

```
using UnityEngine;
using System.Collections;
using UnityEditor;

[CustomEditor (typeof (FieldOfView))]
public class FieldOfViewEditor : Editor{

void OnSceneGUI(){
FieldOfView fow = (FieldOfView)target; Handles.color = color.white; } }
```

Next we define the color that we want to represent the vision of our character, to do this we added the `Handles.color` and we have chosen the color to be white. This won't be visible on the export version of our game, so we can choose the color that is easier for us to see in the editor:

```
using UnityEngine;
using System.Collections;
using UnityEditor;

[CustomEditor (typeof (FieldOfView))]
public class FieldOfViewEditor : Editor{

void OnSceneGUI(){
FieldOfView fow = (FieldOfView)target; Handles.color = color.white;
Handles.DrawWireArc (fow.transform.position, Vector3.up,
Vector3.forward, 360, fow.viewRadius); } }
```

What we have done now is give a form to the visualization that we are creating. The form is set to be in an arch and that is why we use `DrawWireArc`. Now, let's take a look at what we have done so far:

On the script that we created and assigned to the character, we need to change the value of **View Radius** to any desired value.

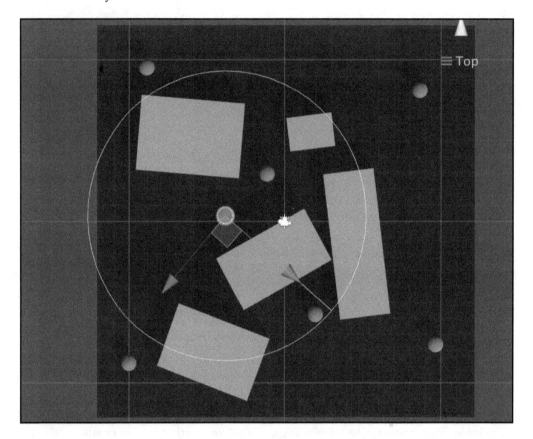

When increasing that value, we will notice a circle growing around the character, this means that our script is working well so far. The circle is representing the vision of our character and now let's change a few things to make it look like the *Metal Gear Solid* image that we used as a reference.

Let's open the character `FieldOfView` script again to add new modifications:

```
public float viewRadius;
[Range(0,360)]
public float viewAngle;
public Vector3 DirFromAngle(float angleInDegrees, bool angleIsGlobal)
  {
   if(!angleIsGlobal)
  {
   angleInDegrees += transform.eulerAngles.y;
```

```
}
return new Vector3(Mathf.Sin(angleInDegrees * Mathf.Deg2Rad), 0,
Mathf.Cos(angleInDegrees * Mathf.Deg2Rad));
}
```

We added a range for the `viewRadius` so that way we can make sure that the circle does not surpass the `360` degrees mark. Then we added a Boolean parameter to `public Vector3 DirFromAngle` to check if the angle value is set to global, so that way we can control the direction that our character is facing.

Then we are going to open the `FieldOfViewEditor` script once again to add the `viewAngle` information:

```
using UnityEngine;
using System.Collections;
using UnityEditor;

[CustomEditor (typeof (FieldOfView))]
public class FieldOfViewEditor : Editor
{
void OnSceneGUI()
{
 FieldOfView fow = (FieldOfView)target;
 Handles.color = color.white;
 Handles.DrawWireArc (fow.transform.position, Vector3.up,
 Vector3.forward, 360, fow.viewRadius);
 Vector3 viewAngleA =
 fow.DirFromAngle(-fow.viewAngle/2, false);
 Handles.DrawLine(fow.transform.position, fow.transform.position +
 viewAngleA * fow.viewRadius);
 Handles.DrawLine(fow.transform.position,
 fow.transform.position +
 viewAngleB * fow.viewRadius);
 }
 }
```

Now, let's test it again to see the new modifications that we have done:

On the `View Angle` option we are going to change the value from zero to any other to see what it is doing:

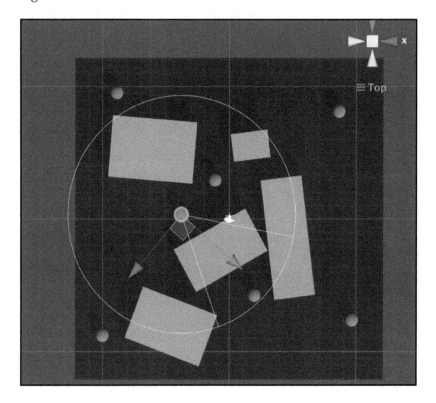

Now, if we look at the circle that is around the character, we will notice a triangular shape inside. The size of that shape can be controlled precisely with the `View Angle` option, and the triangle shape represents the vision of our character, so at this moment we can notice that the character is looking slightly to the bottom right.

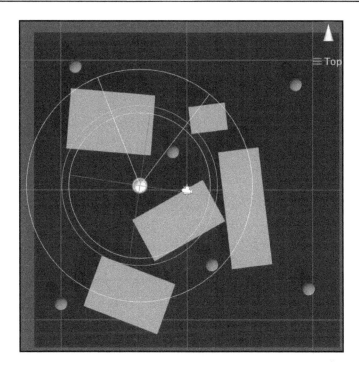

Because we have set the angle value to be at a global angle, we can rotate the character and the view angle will follow the character rotation.

Now let's work on the vision raycast, this part is responsible for detecting what exists in the direction that our character is looking at. Once again, we are going to edit our FieldOfView script that we created for our character:

```
public float viewRadius;
[Range(0,360)]
public float viewAngle;
public LayerMask targetMask;
public LayerMask obstacleMask;
public List<Transform> visibleTargets = new List<Transform>();
void FindVisibleTargets ()
  {
  visibleTargets.Clear ();
  Collider[] targetInViewRadius =
  Physics.OverlapSphere(transform.position, viewRadius, targetMask);
   for (int i = 0; i < targetsInViewRadius.Length; i++)
    {
    Transform target = targetInViewRadius [i].transform; Vector3
     dirToTarget = (target.position - transform.position).normalized;
    if (Vector3.Angle (transform.forward, dirToTarget) < viewAngle / 2)
```

```
    {
       float dstToTarget = Vector3.Distance (transform.position,
        target.position);
       if (!Physics.Raycast(transform.position,
        dirToTarget, dstToTarget, obstacleMask))
           {
             visibleTargets.Add (target);
           }
     }
  }
 public Vector3 DirFromAngle(float angleInDegrees, bool angleIsGlobal) {
  if(!angleIsGlobal)
     {
        angleInDegrees += transform.eulerAngles.y;
     }
   return new Vector3(Mathf.Sin(angleInDegrees * Mathf.Deg2Rad), 0,
      Mathf.Cos(angleInDegrees * Mathf.Deg2Rad));
 }
```

What we have done here, is add the `Physics` information into our script, detecting only the objects that can be found inside of the character `View Angle`. To check if something is in sight of our character, we use a `Raycast` to check if any object with the layer `obstacleMask` is detected. Now let's create an `IEnumerator` function to implement a small delay for our character detecting new obstacles:

```
public float viewRadius; [Range(0,360)]
public float viewAngle; public LayerMask targetMask;
public LayerMask obstacleMask;
[HideInInspector] public List<Transform> visibleTargets = new
List<Transform>();
void Start ()
     {
        StartCoroutine("FindTargetsWithDelay", .2f);
     }
IEnumerator FindTargetsWithDelay(float delay)
{
while (true) {
 yield return new WaitForSeconds (delay);
 FindVisibleTargets ();
 }
}
void FindVisibleTargets ()
 {
 visibleTargets.Clear ();
 Collider[] targetInViewRadius
 =Physics.OverlapSphere(transform.position,viewRadius, targetMask);
```

```
for (int i = 0; i < targetsInViewRadius.Length; i++)
{
 Transform target = targetInViewRadius [i].transform; Vector3 dirToTarget =
(target.position - transform.position).normalized;
 if (Vector3.Angle (transform.forward, dirToTarget) < viewAngle / 2) {
float dstToTarget = Vector3.Distance (transform.position, target.position);
 if (!Physics.Raycast(transform.position, dirToTarget, dstToTarget,
     obstacleMask))
 {
  visibleTargets.Add (target);
 }
 }
 }
 public Vector3 DirFromAngle(float angleInDegrees, bool angleIsGlobal)
{
if(!angleIsGlobal)
 {
 angleInDegrees += transform.eulerAngles.y;
 }
 return new Vector3(Mathf.Sin(angleInDegrees * Mathf.Deg2Rad), 0,
 Mathf.Cos(angleInDegrees * Mathf.Deg2Rad)); }
```

Now that, we have created an `IEnumerator`, the character has a small reaction time that in this case is set to `.2f` to find targets inside of his vision zone. In order to test this we need to make some new modifications inside of our `FieldOfViewEditor` script. So let's open it and add a few new lines of code:

```
using UnityEngine;
using System.Collections;
using UnityEditor;

[CustomEditor (typeof (FieldOfView))]
public class FieldOfViewEditor : Editor{

void OnSceneGUI(){
FieldOfView fow = (FieldOfView)target;
Handles.color = color.white; Handles.DrawWireArc
(fow.transform.position, Vector3.up,
Vector3.forward, 360, fow.viewRadius); Vector3 viewAngleA =
fow.DirFromAngle(-fow.viewAngle/2, false);

Handles.DrawLine(fow.transform.position, fow.transform.position +
viewAngleA * fow.viewRadius);
Handles.DrawLine(fow.transform.position,fow.transform.position +
viewAngleB * fow.viewRadius); Handles.color = Color.red;
Foreach (Transform visibleTarget in fow.visibleTargets)
{
Handles.DrawLine(fow.transform.position, visibleTarget.position);
```

```
    }
  }
}
```

With the new modifications on the code, we should be able to see when the character has detected an obstacle and when that obstacle get out of his vision zone.

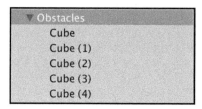

To test this out we first need to select all the obstacles that we have inside of our game:

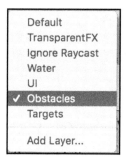

Then assign them the **Obstacles** layer:

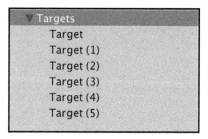

We also need to select all of the **Targets** inside of the game:

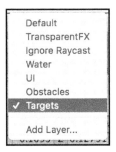

We then assign them the **Targets** layer. This step is very important so that our **Raycast** can identify what is inside of the character field of view. Now, let's click on the character object and define which layer represents the **Targets** and which layer represents the **Obstacles**:

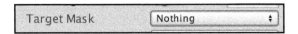

We go to the **Layer Mask** option that can be found in the **Field Of View** script options:

And we choose the **Targets** layer:

Then we go to the **Obstacles** option:

And we choose the **Obstacles** layer.

With this part done we can finally test the exercise to see what happens when the character finds a target.

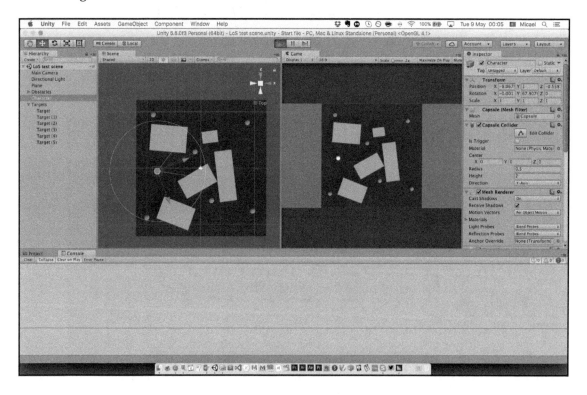

When playing the exercise, we can see that a red line appears connecting the character and the target, when a target gets inside of the vision zone. This represents that our character has spotted an enemy for example.

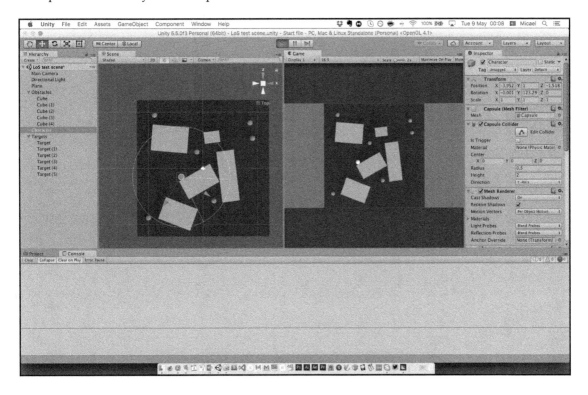

But, when we move our character and we have an obstacle in front of a target, even if the target is inside the vision zone, the character cannot detect him because there is an object in front of him blocking his view. This is why we need to assign the **Obstacle** layer to every object that might block the character vision, that way he won't have any X-Ray vision.

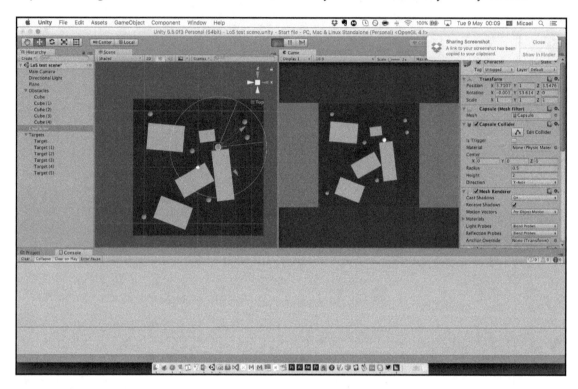

We can also point our character to two targets that both of them will connect to, this means that our character is also able to detect more than one target at the same time, which is very useful to define better strategies and tactics.

Realistic field of view effect

Now that we have the vision detection working, we can move on to the next step and add a realistic field of view effect. This will allow the character to have peripheral vision, making what is seen on the sides less detailed and what is seen in the front more detailed. It is a simulation of our real human vision, where we tend to focus more on what is in front of us and if we need to check something that is on the sides, we need to turn into that direction in order to have a better look.

Let's start by opening our `FieldOfView` script. Then we add a new float variable called `meshResolution`:

```
public float viewRadius; [Range(0,360)]
public float viewAngle; public LayerMask targetMask; public LayerMask
obstacleMask; [HideInInspector] public List<Transform> visibleTargets = new
List<Transform>(); public float meshResolution;
```

Now, we need to create a new method and we are going to call it `DrawFieldOfView`. Inside of this method, we will define the amount of `Raycast` lines that our field of view will have. Also we will define the angle of each line that will be drawn:

```
void DrawFieldOfView() {
 int stepCount = Mathf.RoundToInt(viewAngle * meshResolution);
 float stepAngleSize = viewAngle / stepCount;
 for (int i = 0; i <= stepCount; i++) {
 float angle = transform.eulerAngles.y - viewAngle / 2 + stepAngleSize *
i;Debug.DrawLine (transform.position, transform.position + DirFromAngle
(angle, true) * viewRadius, Color.red);
 }
 }
```

After creating this new method, we simply need to call it from the update:

```
void LateUpdate() {
DrawFieldOfView ();
 }
```

At this point, we can open the game editor and test it to visualize what we have created:

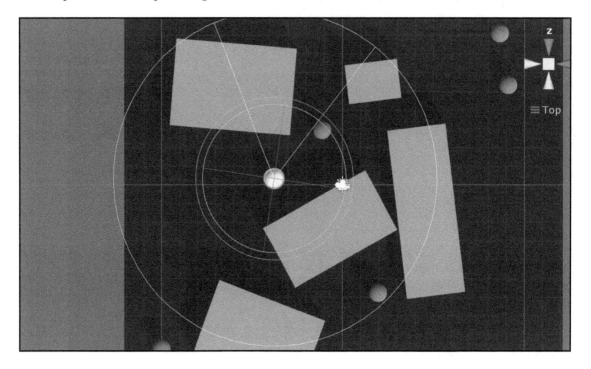

Right away when we press play to test our script, we won't see any difference between the old version and the new one. This is normal because we need to increase the **Mesh Resolution** of our character.

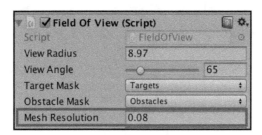

As we can see in the preceding screenshot, we need to add a value in the **Mesh Resolution** variable in order to see the desirable results.

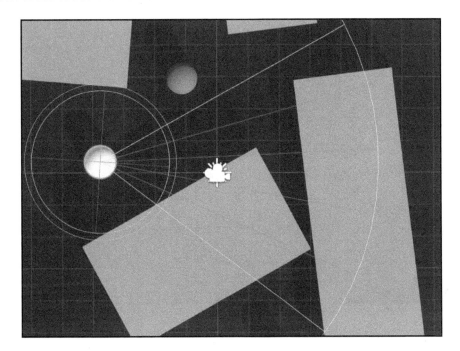

Adding **0.08** into the **Mesh Resolution** variable, we can notice already that on the game editor window, a few red lines appear and that's exactly what we wanted.

If we keep increasing the value, more lines will be added, meaning that more detailed the vision will be, which is exemplified in the following screenshot:

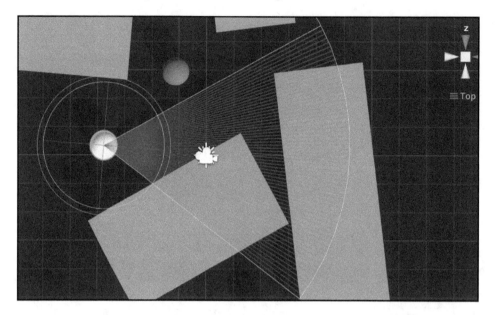

But, we need to remember that increasing this value also increases the device CPU usage and we need to take this into consideration, especially if we are going to have multiple characters at once on the screen.

Now let's get back to our script and add a collision detection for each line, allowing our character to receive information from multiple lines at once. We start by creating a new method in which we will store all the information regarding the raycasts that will be created:

```
public struct ViewCastInfo {
public bool hit;
public Vector3 point;
public float dst;
public float angle;

public ViewCastInfo(bool _hit, Vector3 _point, float _dst, float
_angle) {
hit = _hit;
point = _point;
dst = _dst;
angle = _angle;
} }
```

Once this new method is created we can go back to our `DrawFieldOfView()` method and start adding the raycasts that will detect the collisions for each line:

```
void DrawFieldOfView() {
int stepCount = Mathf.RoundToInt(viewAngle * meshResolution);
float stepAngleSize = viewAngle / stepCount;
List<Vector3> viewPoints = new List<Vector3>();
for (int i = 0; i <= stepCount; i++)
{
 float angle = transform.eulerAngles.y - viewAngle / 2 + stepAngleSize
 * i;
 ViewCastInfo newViewCast = ViewCast(angle);
 Debug.DrawLine(transform.position, transform.position +
 DirFromAngle(angle, true) *
 viewRadius, Color.red);
 viewPoints.Add(newViewCast.point);
}
}
```

To understand the next steps, let's see how a mesh is generated from a script:

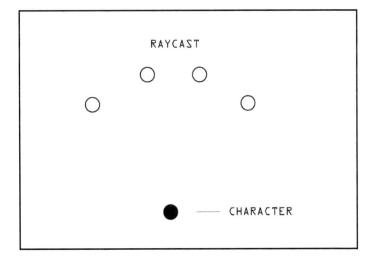

In the preceding diagram, we can see one dark circle that represents the character and four with circles, representing the raycast finish position.

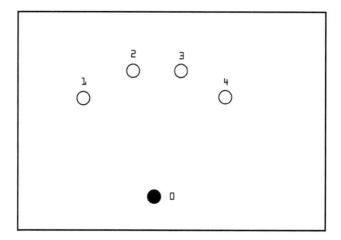

Each vertices has a value assigned to them, the first vertex that starts from the character, is the number zero, then it goes on a clockwise sense with the next vertex starting on the left and continuing counting to the right side.

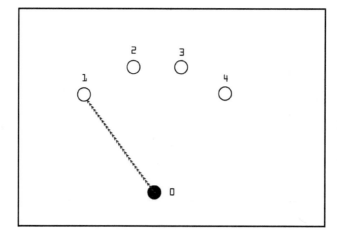

The vertex zero connects to the vertex **1**.

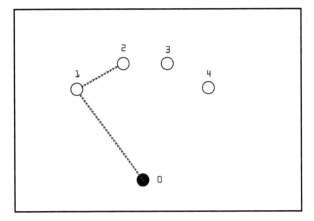

Then vertex one connects to vertex **2**.

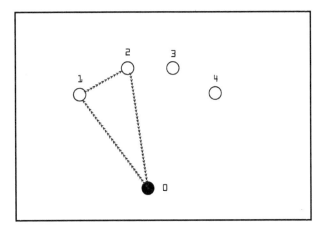

And then vertex two connects back to vertex **0**, creating a triangle mesh.

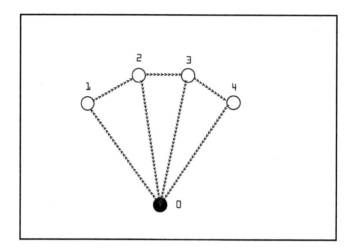

Once the first triangle mesh is created, it continues to the next one, starting from *0 > 2 > 3 > 0* and the second triangle is also created. And finally the last one, *0 > 3 > 4 > 0*. Now, we want to transcribe this information into our code, so in this case the array of the field of view is:

```
[0,1,2,0,2,3,0,3,4]
```

The total number of vertices on this example is five:

```
v = 5
```

The total number of triangles created is three:

```
t = 3
```

So the number of triangles is:

```
t = v-2
```

That means that the length of our array will be:

```
(v-2)*3
```

Now let's get back to our script and add the information that we have solved here:

```
void DrawFieldOfView() {
int stepCount = Mathf.RoundToInt(viewAngle * meshResolution);
float stepAngleSize = viewAngle / stepCount;
 List<Vector3> viewPoints = new List<Vector3> ();
 ViewCastInfo oldViewCast = new ViewCastInfo ();
```

```
for (int i = 0; i <= stepCount; i++) {
float angle = transform.eulerAngles.y - viewAngle / 2 + stepAngleSize * i;
 ViewCastInfo newViewCast = ViewCast (angle);
 Debug.DrawLine(transform.position, transform.position +
DirFromAngle(angle, true) * viewRadius, Color.red);
 viewPoints.Add (newViewCast.point);
 }

int vertexCount = viewPoints.Count + 1;
 Vector3[] vertices = new Vector3[vertexCount];
int[] triangles = newint[(vertexCount-2) * 3];

 vertices [0] = Vector3.zero;
for (int i = 0; i < vertexCount - 1; i++) {
 vertices [i + 1] = viewPoints [i];

if (i < vertexCount - 2) {
 triangles [i * 3] = 0;
 triangles [i * 3 + 1] = i + 1;
 triangles [i * 3 + 2] = i + 2;
 }
 } }
```

Now, let's go to the top of our script and add two new variables, public MeshFilter viewMeshFilter and Mesh viewMesh:

```
publicfloat viewRadius;
 [Range(0,360)]
publicfloat viewAngle;

public LayerMask targetMask;
public LayerMask obstacleMask;

 [HideInInspector]
public List<Transform> visibleTargets = new List<Transform>();

publicfloat meshResolution;

public MeshFilter viewMeshFilter;
 Mesh viewMesh;
```

Next, we need to call those variables into our start method:

```
void Start() {
viewMesh = new Mesh ();
viewMesh.name = "View Mesh";
viewMeshFilter.mesh = viewMesh;
```

```
StartCoroutine ("FindTargetsWithDelay", .2f);
}
```

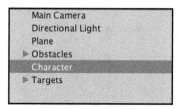

The next step is to select our **Character** object inside the game editor:

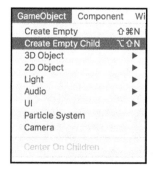

Go to the **GameObejct** section and select **Create Empty Child**:

Rename the object to **View Visualization**.

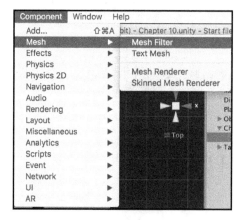

With the same object selected, we go to: **Component | Mesh | Mesh Filter**, to add a mesh filter to our object.

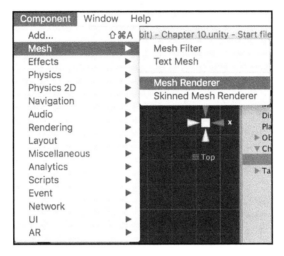

Then we need to do the same for the **Mesh Renderer, Component | Mesh | Mesh Renderer**.

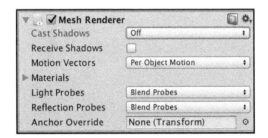

We can turn off the **Cast Shadows** and **Receive Shadows**.

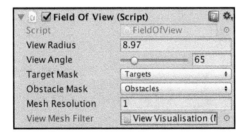

Finally, we add the object that we just created into our script variable **View Mesh Filter** and change the **Mesh Resolution** to any desirable value, in this case we have chosen **1**.

Now, we can return to our script and add edit once again the `DrawFieldOfView` method:

```
void DrawFieldOfView () {
int stepCount = Mathf.RoundToInt (viewAngle * meshResolution);
float stepAngleSize = viewAngle / stepCount;
 List<Vector3> viewPoints = new List<Vector3> ();
 ViewCastInfo oldViewCast = new ViewCastInfo ();
for (int i = 0; i <= stepCount; i++) {
float angle = transform.eulerAngles.y - viewAngle / 2 + stepAngleSize * i;
 ViewCastInfo newViewCast = ViewCast (angle);
 viewPoints.Add (newViewCast.point);
 }

int vertexCount = viewPoints.Count + 1;
 Vector3[] vertices = new Vector3[vertexCount];
int[] triangles = newint[(vertexCount-2) * 3];

 vertices [0] = Vector3.zero;
for (int i = 0; i < vertexCount - 1; i++) {
 vertices [i + 1] = viewPoints [i];

if (i < vertexCount - 2) {
 triangles [i * 3] = 0;
 triangles [i * 3 + 1] = i + 1;
 triangles [i * 3 + 2] = i + 2;
 }
 }

 viewMesh.Clear ();

 viewMesh.vertices = vertices;
 viewMesh.triangles = triangles;
 viewMesh.RecalculateNormals ();
 }
```

Let's test the game, to see what we have done here:

When we play the game, we will notice the mesh being rendered on the game and that's our objective so far.

 Remember to remove the `Debug.DrawLine` line of code, otherwise the mesh won't show on the game editor.

In order to optimize the visualization, we need to change the `viewPoints` from global to local space points. To do this we are going to use `InverseTransformPoint`:

```
void DrawFieldOfView() {
int stepCount = Mathf.RoundToInt(viewAngle * meshResolution);
float stepAngleSize = viewAngle / stepCount;
 List<Vector3> viewPoints = new List<Vector3> ();
 ViewCastInfo oldViewCast = new ViewCastInfo ();
for (int i = 0; i <= stepCount; i++) {
float angle = transform.eulerAngles.y - viewAngle / 2 + stepAngleSize * i;
 ViewCastInfo newViewCast = ViewCast (angle);
 viewPoints.Add (newViewCast.point);
 }

int vertexCount = viewPoints.Count + 1;
```

```
 Vector3[] vertices = new Vector3[vertexCount];
int[] triangles = newint[(vertexCount-2) * 3];

 vertices [0] = Vector3.zero;
for (int i = 0; i < vertexCount - 1; i++) {
 vertices [i + 1] = transform.InverseTransformPoint(viewPoints [i]) +
Vector3.forward * maskCutawayDst;

if (i < vertexCount - 2) {
 triangles [i * 3] = 0;
 triangles [i * 3 + 1] = i + 1;
 triangles [i * 3 + 2] = i + 2;
 }
 }

 viewMesh.Clear ();

 viewMesh.vertices = vertices;
 viewMesh.triangles = triangles;
 viewMesh.RecalculateNormals (); }
```

Now, if we test it again it will be more accurate.

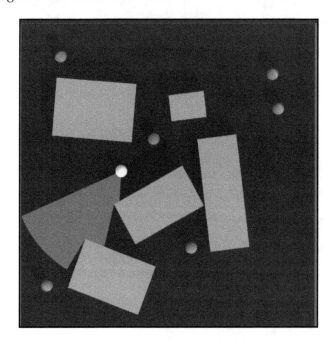

It looks good already, but we can still improve it by changing from `Update` to `LateUpdate`:

```
void LateUpdate() {
DrawFieldOfView ();
}
```

Doing this the movement of our mesh will be smoother.

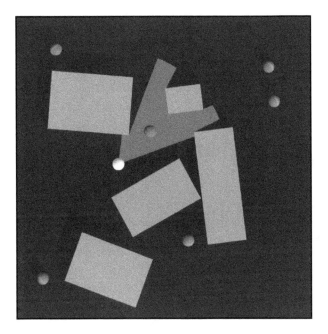

With this part of the script updated, we conclude our example, completing a realistic field of view system into our character.

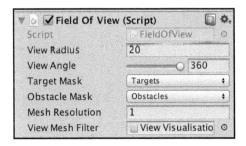

All we need is to change the values in order to fit the results that we are looking for, making our character more or less aware of his surroundings.

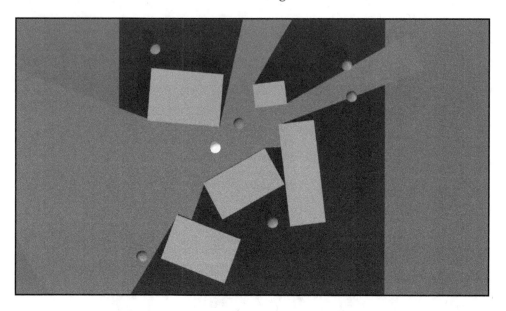

For example, if we set the `View Angle` value to `360`, that makes our character completely aware of what is happening around and if we decrease the value, we will reach a more realistic vision, just like it's used in a *Metal Gear Solid* game.

At this point we are able to pick a stealth game and copy their most iconic features such as realistic vision and audio awareness. We have learned the foundations and now we can start from there and develop our own game.

Summary

In this chapter, we unveiled how stealth games work and how we can recreate that same system so we can use it in our games. We went from a simple approach to a complex one, allowing us to decide what fits better in the game that we are creating, if it relies heavily on stealth or if we simply need a basic system to make our character detect the player by vision or audio awareness. The features that we have learned in this chapter can also be expanded and used in practically any example that we have created before, amplifying the collision detection, the pathfinding, the decisions, animations, and many more features, turning them from functional to realistic.

The way we create games is constantly updating, every game published brings a new or different method to create something, which is only possible if we are willing to experiment and blend everything we know, adjusting our knowledge to achieve the results we want to even if they look extremely complicated. Sometimes it is just a matter of exploring basic concepts and expanding them, turning a simple idea into a complex system.

Index

2

2D animation
  sprites 89, 90, 92
  versus 3D animation 89

3

3D animation
  bone structure 92

A

advanced environment interactions
  about 82
  adaption to unstable terrain 84, 85
  ray cast, used for evaluating decisions 86
advanced pathfinding
  versus simple pathfinding 179, 181
advanced vision detection 292, 294, 296, 297,
  299, 300, 302, 304, 306, 307, 309, 311, 313,
  314
AGGRESSIVE state 25, 26, 27
AI drivers 180
animation state machines 93, 94, 96, 99, 100,
  101, 103, 105, 107, 108, 110, 112, 115
Artificial Intelligence (AI) 8
Assassin's Creed game 214, 215
automated finite-state machines (AFSMs)
  about 38
  chances, calculating 41, 42
  planning 38, 39, 40
awareness
  about 276
  vision awareness 276

B

basic environment interactions
  about 62

environment objects, moving 63, 64, 65, 66, 68,
  70, 73
environment, breaking down by area 79, 81
obstructive environment objects 73, 74, 75, 76,
  78
basic vision detection 279, 281, 283, 284, 287,
  288, 290
bone structure, 3D animation 92

C

collision avoidance 267, 268, 269, 270, 271, 273
crowd collision
  avoiding 243, 245
crowd interactions
  about 213
  communication (attention zones) 225, 226, 227,
  228
  communication (talking to AI characters) 229,
  230, 232
  group fight 220, 222, 223, 224
  planning 220
  team sports 232, 233, 234, 235, 237, 238, 240

D

DEFENSIVE state 22, 23, 25
dynamic game AI balancing 56, 57

E

Enemy AI
  in video games 8, 9

F

FIFA/Pro evolution soccer game 218, 219
finite state machine (FSM) 9

W